LANGUAGE AND LITERACY SERIES

Dorothy S. Strickland, FOUNDING EDITOR
Donna E. Alvermann and María Paula Ghiso, SERIES EDITORS
ADVISORY BOARD: Richard Allington, Kathryn Au, Bernice Cullinan, Colette Daiute,
Anne Haas Dyson, Carole Edelsky, Mary Juzwik, Susan Lytle, Django Paris, Timothy Shanahan

Educating African Immigrant Youth:
Schooling and Civic Engagement in K–12 Schools
VAUGHN W. M. WATSON, MICHELLE G. KNIGHT-MANUEL, & PATRIANN SMITH, EDS.

Pose, Wobble, Flow: A Liberatory Approach to
Literacy Learning in All Classrooms, 2nd Ed.
ANTERO GARCIA & CINDY O'DONNELL-ALLEN

Teaching Climate Change to Children: Literacy
Pedagogy That Cultivates Sustainable Futures
REBECCA WOODARD & KRISTINE M. SCHUTZ

Widening the Lens: Integrating Multiple
Approaches to Support Adolescent Literacy
DEBORAH VRIEND VAN DUINEN & ERICA R. HAMILTON

Connecting Equity, Literacy, and Language:
Pathways Toward Advocacy-Focused Teaching
ALTHIER M. LAZAR, KAITLIN K. MORAN, &
SHOSHANNA EDWARDS-ALEXANDER

Writing Instruction for Success in College
and in the Workplace
CHARLES A. MACARTHUR & ZOI A. PHILIPPAKOS

Black Immigrant Literacies: Intersections of Race,
Language, and Culture in the Classroom
PATRIANN SMITH

Teens Choosing to Read: Fostering Social,
Emotional, and Intellectual Growth Through Books
GAY IVEY & PETER JOHNSTON

Critical Encounters in Secondary English:
Teaching Literary Theory to Adolescents,
4th Ed.
DEBORAH APPLEMAN

Reading With Purpose: Selecting and Using
Children's Literature for Inquiry and Engagement
ERIKA THULIN DAWES, KATIE EGAN CUNNINGHAM,
GRACE ENRIQUEZ, & MARY ANN CAPPIELLO

Core Practices for Teaching Multilingual Students:
Humanizing Pedagogies for Equity
MEGAN MADIGAN PEERCY, JOHANNA M. TIGERT, &
DAISY E. FREDRICKS

Bringing Sports Culture to the English Classroom:
An Interest-Driven Approach to Literacy
Instruction
LUKE RODESILER

Culturally Sustaining Literacy Pedagogies:
Honoring Students' Heritages, Literacies, and
Languages
SUSAN CHAMBERS CANTRELL, DORIS WALKER-DALHOUSE,
& ALTHIER M. LAZAR, EDS.

Curating a Literacy Life:
Student-Centered Learning With Digital Media
WILLIAM KIST

Understanding the Transnational Lives and
Literacies of Immigrant Children
JUNGMIN KWON

The Administration and Supervision of Literacy
Programs, 6th Ed.
SHELLEY B. WEPNER & DIANA J. QUATROCHE, EDS.

Writing the School House Blues: Literacy, Equity,
and Belonging in a Child's Early Schooling
ANNE HAAS DYSON

Playing With Language: Improving Elementary
Reading Through Metalinguistic Awareness
MARCY ZIPKE

Restorative Literacies:
Creating a Community of Care in Schools
DEBORAH L. WOLTER

Compose Our World: Project-Based Learning in
Secondary English Language Arts
ALISON G. BOARDMAN, ANTERO GARCIA, BRIDGET
DALTON, & JOSEPH L. POLMAN

Digitally Supported Disciplinary Literacy for
Diverse K–5 Classrooms
JAMIE COLWELL, AMY HUTCHISON,
& LINDSAY WOODWARD

The Reading Turn-Around with Emergent
Bilinguals: A Five-Part Framework for Powerful
Teaching and Learning (Grades K–6)
AMANDA CLAUDIA WAGER, LANE W. CLARKE,
& GRACE ENRIQUEZ

Race, Justice, and Activism in Literacy Instruction
VALERIE KINLOCH, TANJA BURKHARD,
& CARLOTTA PENN, EDS.

Letting Go of Literary Whiteness:
Antiracist Literature Instruction for White Students
CARLIN BORSHEIM-BLACK
& SOPHIA TATIANA SARIGIANIDES

The Vulnerable Heart of Literacy:
Centering Trauma as Powerful Pedagogy
ELIZABETH DUTRO

Amplifying the Curriculum: Designing Quality
Learning Opportunities for English Learners
AÍDA WALQUI & GEORGE C. BUNCH, EDS.

Arts Integration in Diverse K–5 Classrooms:
Cultivating Literacy Skills and Conceptual
Understanding
LIANE BROUILLETTE

Translanguaging for Emergent Bilinguals: Inclusive
Teaching in the Linguistically Diverse Classroom
DANLING FU, XENIA HADJIOANNOU, & XIAODI ZHOU

Before Words: Wordless Picture Books and the
Development of Reading in Young Children
JUDITH T. LYSAKER

Seeing the Spectrum: Teaching English Language
Arts to Adolescents with Autism
ROBERT ROZEMA

A Think-Aloud Approach to Writing Assessment:
Analyzing Process and Product with Adolescent
Writers
SARAH W. BECK

"We've Been Doing It Your Way Long Enough":
Choo~
JANI

T0377737

For volumes in the NCRLL Collection (edited by JoBeth Allen a
Bookshelf Series (edited by Celia Genishi and Donna E. Alvern
visit www.tcpress.com

Language and Literacy Series, *continued*

Summer Reading, 2nd Ed.
RICHARD L. ALLINGTON & ANNE McGILL-FRANZEN, EDS.

Educating for Empathy
NICOLE MIRRA

Preparing English Learners for College and Career
MARÍA SANTOS ET AL.

Reading the Rainbow
CAITLIN L. RYAN & JILL M. HERMANN-WILMARTH

Educating Emergent Bilinguals, 2nd Ed.
OFELIA GARCÍA & JO ANNE KLEIFGEN

Social Justice Literacies in the English Classroom
ASHLEY S. BOYD

Remixing Multiliteracies
FRANK SERAFINI & ELISABETH GEE, EDS.

Culturally Sustaining Pedagogies
DJANGO PARIS & H. SAMY ALIM, EDS.

Choice and Agency in the Writing Workshop
FRED L. HAMEL

Assessing Writing, Teaching Writers
MARY ANN SMITH & SHERRY SEALE SWAIN

The Teacher-Writer
CHRISTINE M. DAWSON

Every Young Child a Reader
SHARAN A. GIBSON & BARBARA MOSS

"You Gotta BE the Book," 3rd Ed.
JEFFREY D. WILHELM

Personal Narrative, Revised
BRONWYN CLARE LAMAY

Inclusive Literacy Teachings
LORI HELMAN ET AL.

The Vocabulary Book, 2nd Ed.
MICHAEL F. GRAVES

Reading, Writing, and Talk
MARIANA SOUTO-MANNING & JESSICA MARTELL

Go Be a Writer!
CANDACE R. KUBY & TARA GUTSHALL RUCKER

Partnering with Immigrant Communities
GERALD CAMPANO ET AL.

Teaching Outside the Box but Inside the Standards
BOB FECHO ET AL., EDS.

Literacy Leadership in Changing Schools
SHELLEY B. WEPNER ET AL.

Literacy Theory as Practice
LARA J. HANDSFIELD

Literacy and History in Action
THOMAS M. McCANN ET AL.

Newsworthy
ED MADISON

Engaging Writers with Multigenre Research Projects
NANCY MACK

Teaching Transnational Youth
ALLISON SKERRETT

Uncommonly Good Ideas
SANDRA MURPHY & MARY ANN SMITH

The One-on-One Reading and Writing Conference
JENNIFER BERNE & SOPHIE C. DEGENER

Transforming Talk into Text
THOMAS M. McCANN

Educating Literacy Teachers Online
LANE W. CLARKE & SUSAN WATTS-TAFFEE

WHAM! Teaching with Graphic Novels Across the Curriculum
WILLIAM G. BROZO ET AL.

Critical Literacy in the Early Childhood Classroom
CANDACE R. KUBY

Inspiring Dialogue
MARY M. JUZWIK ET AL.

Reading the Visual
FRANK SERAFINI

ReWRITING the Basics
ANNE HAAS DYSON

Writing Instruction That Works
ARTHUR N. APPLEBEE ET AL.

Literacy Playshop
KAREN E. WOHLWEND

Critical Media Pedagogy
ERNEST MORRELL ET AL.

A Search Past Silence
DAVID E. KIRKLAND

The ELL Writer
CHRISTINA ORTMEIER-HOOPER

Reading in a Participatory Culture
HENRY JENKINS ET AL., EDS.

Teaching Vocabulary to English Language Learners
MICHAEL F. GRAVES ET AL.

Bridging Literacy and Equity
ALTHIER M. LAZAR ET AL.

Reading Time
CATHERINE COMPTON-LILLY

Interrupting Hate
MOLLIE V. BLACKBURN

Playing Their Way into Literacies
KAREN E. WOHLWEND

Teaching Literacy for Love and Wisdom
JEFFREY D. WILHELM & BRUCE NOVAK

Urban Literacies
VALERIE KINLOCH, ED.

Bedtime Stories and Book Reports
CATHERINE COMPTON-LILLY & STUART GREENE, EDS.

Envisioning Knowledge
JUDITH A. LANGER

Envisioning Literature, 2nd Ed.
JUDITH A. LANGER

Artifactual Literacies
KATE PAHL & JENNIFER ROWSELL

Change Is Gonna Come
PATRICIA A. EDWARDS ET AL.

Harlem on Our Minds
VALERIE KINLOCH

Children, Language, and Literacy
CELIA GENISHI & ANNE HAAS DYSON

Children's Language
JUDITH WELLS LINDFORS

Storytime
LAWRENCE R. SIPE

Educating African Immigrant Youth

Schooling and Civic Engagement in K–12 Schools

Edited by
Vaughn W. M. Watson
Michelle G. Knight-Manuel
Patriann Smith

Foreword by Awad Ibrahim

TEACHERS COLLEGE PRESS
TEACHERS COLLEGE | COLUMBIA UNIVERSITY
NEW YORK AND LONDON

Published by Teachers College Press,® 1234 Amsterdam Avenue, New York, NY 10027

Copyright © 2024 by Teachers College, Columbia University

Front cover illustration by Nadia Bormotova / iStock by Getty Images.

All rights reserved. No part of this publication may be reproduced or transmitted in any form or by any means, electronic or mechanical, including photocopy, or any information storage and retrieval system, without permission from the publisher. For reprint permission and other subsidiary rights requests, please contact Teachers College Press, Rights Dept.: tcpressrights@tc.columbia.edu

Excerpts in Chapters 1 and 13 from V. W. Watson and M. G. Knight-Manuel, "Humanizing the Black Immigrant Body: Envisioning Diaspora Literacies of Youth and Young Adults from West African countries," *Teachers College Record,* 122(13), pp. 1–28, copyright © 2017 by SAGE. Reprinted by Permission of SAGE Publications.

Excerpts in Chapter 1 from V. W. Watson, and M. G. Knight-Manuel, "Challenging Popularized Narratives of Immigrant Youth from West Africa: Examining Social Processes of Navigating Identities and Engaging Civically," *Review of Research in Education, 41*(1), pp. 279–310, copyright © 2017 by SAGE. Reprinted by Permission of SAGE Publications.

Library of Congress Cataloging-in-Publication Data

Names: Watson, Vaughn W. M., editor. | Knight-Manuel, Michelle (Michelle
  G.), editor. | Smith, Patriann, 1982– editor.
Title: Educating African immigrant youth : schooling and civic engagement
  in K–12 schools / edited by Vaughn W.M. Watson, Michelle G.
  Knight-Manuel, and Patriann Smith.
Description: New York, NY : Teachers College Press, 2024. | Series:
  Language and literacy series | Includes bibliographical references and index.
Identifiers: LCCN 2024005573 (print) | LCCN 2024005574 (ebook) | ISBN
  9780807769805 (paperback) | ISBN 9780807769812 (hardcover) | ISBN
  9780807782446 (epub)
Subjects: LCSH: African students—United States. | Africans—
  Education—United States. | Immigrant children—Education—
  United States. | Transformative learning—United States. |
  Culturally relevant pedagogy—United States.
Classification: LCC LC2771 .E256 2024 (print) | LCC LC2771 (ebook) |
  DDC 371.826/912096—dc23/eng/20240318
LC record available at https://lccn.loc.gov/2024005573
LC ebook record available at https://lccn.loc.gov/2024005574

ISBN 978-0-8077-6980-5 (paper)
ISBN 978-0-8077-6981-2 (hardcover)
ISBN 978-0-8077-8244-6 (ebook)

Printed on acid-free paper
Manufactured in the United States of America

Contents

Foreword   *Awad Ibrahim*   **vii**

1. **Introduction**   **1**
   Vaughn W. M. Watson, Michelle G. Knight-Manuel, and Patriann Smith

PART I: SCHOOLING AND CLASSROOM PERSPECTIVES AND CONTEXTS
Sandra Boateng and Vaughn W. M. Watson

2. **Toward a Reckoning and Affirmation of Black African Immigrant Youth in U.S. P–12 Schools**   **21**
   Omiunota Nelly Ukpokodu

3. **Africanfuturism and Critical Mathematics Education: Envisioning a Liberatory Future for Sub-Saharan African Immigrants**   **43**
   Oyemolade (Molade) Osibodu and Nyimasata Damba Danjo

4. **African Lives Matter Too: Affirming African Heritage Students' Experience in the History Classroom**   **54**
   Irteza Anwara Mohyuddin

5. **A Narrative Inquiry Into Experiences of Black Women in Undergraduate STEM Disciplines in Ontario**   **68**
   James Alan Oloo and Priscila Dias Corrêa

PART II: PARTICIPATORY AND COMMUNAL APPROACHES TO LEARNING AND CIVIC ENGAGEMENT
Michelle G. Knight-Manuel and Dorothy Khamala

6. **Always Remember What's Behind You So You Can Reach What's in Front of You: The Transnational Civic Engagement of a West African High School Student**   **87**
   Patrick Keegan

Contents

7. **An Affect-Centered Analysis of Congolese Immigrant Parent Perspectives on Past-Present-Future Learning in School and at Home** 99

    Liv T. Dávila and Susan A. Ogwal

8. **Imaging and Imagining Activism: Exploring Embodied and Digital Learning Through Filmmaking With African Immigrant Girls During the Pandemic** 110

    Maryann J. Dreas-Shaikha, OreOluwa Badaki, and Jasmine L. Blanks Jones

9. **Social Cohesion, Belonging, and Anti-Blackness: African Immigrant Youth's Civic Exploration in a Culturally Relevant-Sustaining, After-School Club** 129

    Michelle G. Knight-Manuel, Natacha Robert, and Sibel Akin-Sabuncu

PART III: LITERACIES, LANGUAGES, AND LEARNING: TOWARD EMERGING PRACTICES AND APPROACHES

   Patriann Smith

10. **Unboxing Black Immigrant Youth's Heritage Resources** 147

    David Bwire Wandera

11. **Opening Space to Participate—One Nigerian Girl's Use of Visual Arts to Navigate School-Based Linguistic Discrimination** 161

    Lakeya Afolalu

12. **Theorizing Rightful Literary Presence and Participatory Curriculum Design With African Immigrant Youth** 173

    Joel E. Berends, Vaughn W. M. Watson, and Dinamic Kubengana

13. **Conclusion** 191

    Vaughn W. M. Watson, Michelle G. Knight-Manuel, and Patriann Smith

References 197

Index 228

About the Editors and Contributors 241

Foreword

Once in a blue moon, poetry is turned into strong poetry and the autobiographical is turned into a cartography, a fertile ground for rigorous research and well-informed theorizing (Ibrahim, 2020). Here, the *métissage* among identity, language, culture, and race must be the north star, a guide for anyone who is interested in conducting research with African immigrants and refugees in the United States, Canada, and globally. Put together by a group of committed and social justice–informed scholars, *Educating African Immigrant Youth: Schooling and Civic Engagement in K–12 Schools* is, in essence, about how to bring forth the full humanity of African immigrant and refugee youth who find themselves in North American schools, an outline of a cartography that allows possibilities of vibrant schooling and civic lives for these young people. This is all happening, the authors in this edited volume argue, at a time when not only this population is hardly understood and researched, but the Black body (i.e., the umbrella under which these young people find themselves) is under assault.

Though tangently addressed, *Educating African Immigrant Youth* makes a distinction between immigrants and refugees and, given the dearth of studies on this exponentially growing population, proposes different research methodologies that touch on disciplines and subjects as diverse as mathematics, civic education, language, higher education, STEM, teacher education, and comparative education, among others.

One of the major contributions that turns this volume into strong poetry and an exceptional contribution is its proposal of four complementary approaches for teaching and learning of African immigrant and refugee youth. These four approaches should not only be read closely, but also deserve subsequent publication on their own. The editors came to these four approaches from the bottom-up, that is, as conclusions that emerged from their reading of the chapters.

The first approach is influenced by critical race theory and proposes "emboldening tellings of diaspora narratives." Here, there is a need to carve courageous and radical spaces that humanize, where students are able to spell their own names and tell their own stories. Building on this, the second approach calls for a critical pedagogy that navigates the complexity of what it means to teach and learn within a decolonial space that brings into

vii

existence radical hope. This decolonial space will not be created, the third approach argues, unless we enact "social civic literacies to extend complex identities." To explain, it is worth keeping in mind that African immigrant and refugee youth have little to no understanding of what it means to be Black in North America; I refer here to the daily grind of and encounter with Blackness. Indeed, as I have argued elsewhere, there are no Blacks in Africa; once they arrive in North America, they enter the process of becoming Black (Ibrahim, 2020). To account for these complex identity formation processes, the fourth and final approach does not just affirm but accentuates these identities as living beings embedded in knowledges, histories, languages, and cultural practices. Situated in living spaces, these beings and cultural practices are ever more complex, shifting, and changing.

With these four approaches, *Educating African Immigrant Youth* finds itself in a league of its own in its focus on the schooling of African immigrant and refugee youth. First, it affirms and honors their humanity as beings and identities entwined in histories, cultures, and languages. Second, the varied backgrounds of the contributing authors (including early and senior scholars, continental Africans, from many institutions in the United States and Canada) contribute to a painting that is as faithful to reality as humanly possible. Third, the chapters draw on and contribute to an expansive range of theoretical lenses, epistemologies, and ontologies that makes this volume a significant contribution in the fields of teaching, learning, and culturally sustaining pedagogy, among others. Finally, keeping the rhizomatic nature of continental African youth (Ibrahim, 2020) alive—with full subjectivity, desire, and history, and ever more heterogeneous and complicated—is not only something to celebrate, but a treat that I hope the gentle reader will appreciate. To say more is to spoil the beauty of this strong poetry, a major and urgently needed contribution to a continental, African-centered research.

—Awad Ibrahim

REFERENCE

Ibrahim, A. (2020). *Black immigrants in North America: Essays on race, immigration, identity, language, Hip-Hop, pedagogy, and the politics of becoming Black*. Myers Education Press.

CHAPTER 1

Introduction

*Vaughn W. M. Watson, Michelle G.
Knight-Manuel, and Patriann Smith*

Nine days before Marvel's *Black Panther*, the then second-highest grossing opening film of all time (Sims, 2018), opened across the United States to strong reviews and box-office records, Àsìkò, a Nigerian photographer living and working in London, composed what *Essence* magazine called a reimagining of the movie's promotional poster. This (re)envisioning of a popularized narrative, authored by an African immigrant, featured four Black children posed as lead characters T'Challa, W'Kabi, Shuri, and Nakia (Danielle, 2018). Àsìkò, posting this rendering to Instagram, shared how he understood its urgency: "As a kid who read comics Black Panther was one of the very few black superheroes I came across. For a child it is a beautiful thing to see yourself represented in a positive light in pop culture. What is also great is that it's a hero steeped in culture and heritage" (Danielle, 2018, paras. 4–5; see also Àsìkò Fine Art Photography, 2018).

Such a holistic rendering of Black African immigrant youth within and across varied schooling and civic spaces is long past due—a rendering that we as coeditors offer in this book, *Educating African Immigrant Youth: Schooling and Civic Engagement in K–12 Schools*. The need for this envisioning is particularly crucial at a time when the Black African immigrant community stands "among the fastest-growing immigrant populations in the United States," accelerated by immigration, resettlement, and asylum programs since 1990 (Capps et al., 2011, p. 2; see also Lorenzi & Batalova, 2022). Given historicized and contemporary contexts of migration, and the ongoing work of reframing popularized deficit narratives of African immigrant youth and communities, *Educating African Immigrant Youth* addresses a critical need. We present a resource detailing practices, frameworks, and methodologies that can be applied to strengthen how educators, researchers, and teacher educators can improve educational practices and trajectories, rendering visible the interplay of the diverse racial, ethnic, gendered, cultural, linguistic, religious, and transnational identities African

1

immigrant youth enact in their schooling practices. In doing so, we envision roles for youth as dynamic participants and contributors transnationally to schools, communities, and destination and home countries.

CONTEXTUALIZING CONTEMPORARY CONTEXTS OF MIGRATION

Contemporary migration of Black African communities to the United States shapes, and continues to be shaped by, the "new African Diaspora," a community "born in Africa, and who are recent immigrants to the United States" (Falola & Oyebade, 2017, p. 1). As Falola and Oyebade observed, "For the vast majority of these immigrants, America has become a permanent place of abode, which has made the community increasingly visible in many facets of social and economic life" (p. 1; see also Gordon, 1998). Propelled by independence movements in African countries in the 1950s, and increasing migration across six subsequent decades (Gordon, 1998; Zong & Batalova, 2014), the number of African immigrants to the United States increased from 35,000 in 1960 to 130,000 by 1980 (McCabe, 2011 a&b). Thereafter, from 1980 through 2013, the African immigrant community from countries south of the Sahara further expanded to 1.5 million.

Just about midway through this burgeoning growth, Arthur published *Invisible Sojourners: African Immigrant Diaspora in the United States* (2000), a significant contribution to scholarship involving African immigrant communities across social science disciplines. Since Arthur's foundational text, the African immigrant community in the United States has continued to experience considerable growth. For example, approximately half of immigrants from African countries have arrived since 2000; significantly, from 2000 to 2009, the number of Black African immigrants in the United States increased 92% (Capps et al., 2011). A burgeoning African immigrant public in the United States underscores the necessity for *Educating African Immigrant Youth*, a robust text prioritizing the interplay of schooling and civic lives and learning with novel, emerging, and established narratives of African immigrant youth.

African immigrant youth have long demonstrated varied intersectional identities in diverse schooling practices (see, e.g., Awokoya, 2012; Dei, 2012; Hailu & Simmons, 2022b; Kumi-Yeboah, 2018; Ndemanu & Jordan, 2018). Moreover, African immigrant youth enacting complex, embodied practices across the range of schooling contexts, and at the interplay of language, literacy, and civic learning and action-taking, complicate urgent questions of which students may engage civically in schools and communities, and how they may do so (Avoseh, 2011; Chareka & Sears, 2006; Knight & Watson, 2014; Kumi-Yeboah & Smith, 2016; Watson & Knight-Manuel, 2017).

Introduction

Thus, transformative teaching and research to support schooling and civic engagement experiences for African immigrant students increasingly will depend on enacting generative teaching approaches, research frameworks, and methodologies. Such teaching and research assert African immigrant youth as contributors with and amid a kaleidoscope of peers, families, educators, and elders, across the continuum of creative, artistic, embodied practices of authors, playwrights, musicians, and artists of the African diaspora who have long authored and told narratives that affirm, extend, and historicize the strengths of Black African immigrant communities (Boutte et al., 2017; V. A. Clark, 2009; Lozenski & Smith, 2012; Watson & Knight-Manuel, 2020; Wiley, 2005). Moreover, such teaching and research hold possibilities for preparing and assisting teachers, teacher educators, researchers, and community educators to identify key schooling and civic engagement practices associated with students' varied intersectional identities, and to take up approaches and learning contexts that affirm and extend the identified practices (Avoseh, 2001; Banks, 2008; Ladson-Billings, 2004; C. D. Lee, 2008).

These possibilities have become even more inviting with the overall growth of the racial and ethnic diversity of the United States since 2010, punctuating a shifting population "much more multiracial and more diverse" than previously measured (Jensen et al., 2021, para. 8). Underscoring this shift, the Pew Research Center reported that one of 10 Black people who live in the United States are members of immigrant communities (Tamir & Anderson, 2022). Moreover, the U.S. Census Bureau projected that "the Black immigrant population" in the United States will "outpace the U.S.-born Black population . . . by 90% between 2020 and 2060, while the U.S.-born population is expected to grow 29% over the same time span" (Tamir & Anderson, 2022, para. 4). Projections followed the United Nations Population Division report that as "the global population [rises] to more than 9.7 billion by 2050" from 7.3 billion currently, "more than half of the gains . . . will come from Africa" (Ferris, 2015, para. 4).

Underscoring such trends, a community-engaged organization working with African immigrant families in Minneapolis drew 200 people to the first Little Africa Festival in 2014. By 2018, the festival had grown to more than 5,000 attendees. In 2019, festival organizers expanded for the first time to 2 days, and introduced the idea of an African parade, the first of its kind in Minnesota. On a Saturday in August, the parade featured community members wearing clothing extending cultural identities walking to a performance stage in Hamline Park that featured musicians from the Congo, Ethiopia, and Nigeria (Gustavo, 2019). A festival organizer remarked to a newspaper reporter, "We are going to African-dance in the streets of the Capitol city" (para. 7).

Amid increasing migration from Africa to the United States (S. Roberts, 2005), education research literature only recently has begun to unapologetically address complex contexts of anti-Blackness confronting African immigrant communities, and Black people and communities in general, as well as how Blackness transforms educational experiences (American Psychological Association, 2021; Dumas & ross, 2016; Kendi, 2023; P. Smith, 2023a; Walls, 2021). Simultaneously, scholars increasingly challenge and (re)frame how African immigrant youth are viewed in polarizing ways in dominant public discourses such as popular-media narratives (Adichie, 2009; Agyepong, 2017; Alaazi et al., 2020; Imoagene, 2015; Watson & Knight-Manuel, 2017).

For instance, in three successive years, 2014, 2015, and 2016, immigrant youth from Ghana and Nigeria, attending high schools in Long Island, New York, were accepted to all eight Ivy League schools. Admittance offers to the youth, Kwasi Enin, Harold Ekeh, and Augusta Uwamanzu Nna, call attention to narratives of educational attainment in stark contrast to news headlines describing immigrant communities in polarizing ways—as "threats to be feared, isolated, assaulted, and banned from the United States"—even as they reinforce stereotypical narratives about African immigrants as a new model minority (Watson & Knight-Manuel, 2017, p. 280; see also Cooper, 2015; W. Lee, 2016; Ukpokodu, 2018; Zong & Batalova, 2014). We recall, for example, newspaper reports referencing increasingly prominent crossings of individuals from Mexico to the United States. One headline declared, "African migrants are becoming a new face of the U.S. border crisis" (Feinberg & Petrie, 2019), obscuring the humanity of the more than 700 people from Angola and the Democratic Republic of Congo taken into custody by U.S. Border Patrol authorities between October 2018 and June 2019 (Fernandez, 2019). Many had traveled by air from home countries in Central Africa to Central America, then over land, through borderlands; some then journeyed, by bus or train, joining relatives in cities including San Antonio, TX, and Portland, ME—to then encounter that "officials in both cities have had to reassure the public that fears of an Ebola outbreak were unfounded" (para. 3).

The audience whom we engage with in presenting *Educating African Immigrant Youth* includes the range of educators, teacher educators, and researchers concerned with using insights we present to inform curriculum design, teaching practices, and research across topics including immigration studies, Black history, ethnic studies, comparative and international education studies, urban education, and African diaspora studies; methods courses in secondary English, literacy and language, social studies, and mathematics; and contexts of education, youth studies, and reflective practice courses for pre- and inservice teachers and professional development. As coeditors, we situate this text as an urgent opportunity for scholars in the

Introduction

United States and globally who work with African immigrant communities to engage in new conversations and collaborations.

SITUATING THREE WAVES OF EXISTING SCHOLARSHIP

Importantly, in the time since Arthur published *Invisible Sojourners* in 2000—in which he contextualized African immigrant communities in the United States navigating relational roles and cultural identities across contexts of families, communities, and work lives—three waves of social science and education research have detailed teaching, teacher education, and research approaches with African immigrant youth and young adults in the United States and globally. *Educating African Immigrant Youth* marks the vital next step in nearly a quarter-century of work that increasingly has rendered visible Black African immigrant youths' and communities' varied and diverse schooling and civic engagement experiences.

The first wave of this work largely coincided with research published between approximately 2000 and 2010; the second wave, 2010 to 2017; and the third wave, 2017 to the present. This scholarship stands in meaningful narrative contrast to "the violence of separability evoked in the popularized narrative of Black immigrant bodies called to 'go back' to home countries" (Watson & Knight-Manuel, 2020, para. 6; see also Agyepong, 2013, 2018; Ukpokodu & Otiato Ojiambo, 2017), functioning as a pathway to visibility of the full range of experiences that undergird what it means to be African and immigrant.

First Wave (Approximately 2000 to 2010)

In the first wave, research literature largely "documented [the migration] experiences of recent African immigrants" (Takyi, 2002, p. 32). Social science scholars in disciplines such as social work called for researchers and practitioners to attend to the complexity of African immigrant communities' acculturation and transition to the United States (e.g., Kamya, 2005). For example, Takougang (2003) detailed emerging patterns of migration for African immigrant communities that increasingly sought permanent residence in the United States rather than returning to their home countries. In education research, Ibrahim's (1999, 2005, 2008) influential scholarship examined interplays of learning and identity for Black, French-speaking immigrant and refugee African youth in Ontario, Canada, across contexts including hip-hop culture. Traoré (2004) studied how recently arrived African immigrant youth, instructed in curriculum steeped in colonialism, encountered "negative relationships with African American students" (p. 349; see also Traoré & Lukens, 2006). King (2006) conceptualized nuanced meanings of diaspora literacy as "reading the 'word and the world' for the benefit of humanity through various cultural signs in the lived experiences of Africa's people here and there in the world" (p. 345). Research additionally examined social and cultural experiences of African immigrant families in U.S. contexts (Obiakor & Afolayan, 2007); place-based contexts of immigrant migration (Wilson & Habecker, 2008); and approaches and outlooks for career trajectories for African immigrant communities in school settings, including secondary (Mims et al., 2009) and higher education (Stebleton, 2007). Research situated African immigrant youth and young adults generationally, and considered the interplay of identities and various contexts such as religious affiliation (Bigelow, 2008; M. K. Clark, 2008).

As Watson and Knight-Manuel (2017) chronicled, "An established and increasing body of literature investigate[d] experiences of teaching and learning of immigrant youth in the United States" (p. 287; see also, e.g., S. Lee, 2001; Ríos-Rojas, 2011; Valenzuela, 1999). Yet African immigrant youth and young adults remained a less-examined community in education research literature.

Second Wave (Approximately 2010 to 2017)

A second wave of research contextualizing African immigrant youth and young adults in the United States and schooling contexts coincided with a time, 2010 to 2017, when the burgeoning African immigrant population was "significantly outpacing the 12 percent growth rate for the overall foreign-born population during that same period" (Echeverria-Estrada & Batalova, 2019, para. 1). This social science and education research began to address how, in U.S. contexts, African immigrant youth experienced schooling amid diversity (Harushimana & Awokoya, 2011); Nigerian immigrant youth navigated identities across social networks (Balogun, 2011); and immigrant youth and young adults from Nigeria negotiated identities with families, peers, and school communities (Awokoya, 2012).

Ukpokodu and Ukpokodu (2012) explored African-born teacher educators and Africanist scholars' lived experiences and research perspectives on Africa and the United States; authors in Ikpeze et al.'s (2013) volume examined perspectives and experiences of African-born educators, students, and administrators, and the interplay of race, culture, and language, across K–12 schooling contexts in North America (e.g. , Agyepong, 2013). Ibrahim (2013, 2014, 2017, 2019) extended significant work across the interplay of race, immigration, meanings of identity, and contexts of hip-hop. And King and Swartz (2016) conceptualized a model in which highly effective educators "identify and implement those cultural concepts, culturally informed principles, and African-informed pedagogies that support the continuation of freedom defined as knowledge, consciousness, agency, and self-determination" (p. xi).

Introduction 7

Researchers additionally analyzed work experiences of college students from Black African immigrant communities (Stebleton, 2012); discussed the interplay of race and schooling for African immigrant students (Imoagene, 2015; K.J.A. Thomas, 2012); contextualized politics and meanings affiliated with belonging as named by transnational African students in U.S. high schools (Smalls, 2014); and theorized transnational feminist praxis stances (Okpalaoka & Dillard, 2012). Ukpokodu and Otiato Ojiambo (2017), in *Erasing Invisibility, Inequity and Social Injustice of Africans in the Diaspora and the Continent,* examined social and cultural experiences of African immigrant individuals and communities across a range of U.S. contexts, including schools (see also Ukpokodu, 2017). As Watson and Knight-Manuel (2017) wrote, research detailed schooling experiences of immigrant youth in the United States from countries including the Congo (Dávila, 2015), Eretria (Stebleton, 2012), Ethiopia (Mims et al., 2009; Stebleton, 2007), Somalia (Dryden-Peterson, 2010; Oropeza et al., 2010; Watkinson & Hersi, 2014), and Uganda (Muwanguzi & Musambira, 2012). For example, authors discussed how Somali youth experienced the interplay of cultural and religious experiences (Basford, 2010); Ethiopian immigrant high school students engaged transnational experiences (Hersi, 2012); and African immigrant students navigated academic and social spaces of schooling (Njue & Retish, 2010; Park, 2013), specifically Somali Bantu refugee youth (Roy & Roxas, 2011).

Reflective of the presence of African migrant communities in the global African diaspora, as Watson and Knight-Manuel (2017) detailed, research increasingly reported on immigrant youth from African countries across global contexts, including migrant youth to Canada (e.g., Ibrahim, 2013, 2014, 2017) from Sierra Leone and Liberia (Usman, 2012); Ghana, Kenya, Nigeria, Liberia, Ethiopia, Rwanda, Somalia, and Sudan (Dlamini & Anucha, 2009); Togo, Madagascar, the Congo, Burundi, and Rwanda (Masinda et al., 2014), and unspecified African countries (Chareka & Sears, 2006).

Research also focused on immigrant youth in France from countries in North Africa (Beaman, 2012) and in Australia from Ethiopia (Bitew & Ferguson, 2010) and Sudan (Hatoss, 2012). This literature is significant in identifying social processes of immigrant youth navigating experiences of schooling, constructing relationships, and engaging civically since the early 2000s. Moreover, scholars increasingly are examining strengths and assets in teaching and research with immigrant youth from West African countries, while noting challenges and possibilities with which youth grapple.

Knight-Manuel, Watson, and colleagues, since 2011, published a range of research findings examining the interplay of African immigrant youths' and young adults' civic learning and action across educational contexts. This scholarship has rendered visible African immigrant youths' and young adults' long-present experiences of transnational civic engagement (Knight, 2011, 2013); (re)framed narratives of African immigrant women's civic leadership (Knight et al., 2012); and complicated and extended approaches to culturally relevant pedagogies to affirm indigenous knowledges of African immigrant communities (Allen et al., 2012).

This work additionally theorized African immigrant youths' and young adults' *participatory communal* civic engagement within and across schools, families, and internships (Knight & Watson, 2014); conceptualized the interplay of civic learning and an enacted cosmopolitan stance-taking with African immigrant youth and young adults (Jaffee et al., 2014); and examined their negotiations of social–civic literacies and participatory new media technologies (Watson et al., 2014). Knight-Manuel and coauthors considered the interplay of structure and agency of West African immigrant communities (Knight et al., 2015); imagined potentials for humanizing pedagogies with African immigrant girls (C. C. Lee et al., 2016); and named evolving positionalities in culturally sensitive research involving African immigrant communities (Roegman et al., 2016).

Toward the latter years of this second wave of research, a comprehensive review of education research literature on immigrant youth from West African countries in the United States highlighted social processes of navigating identities and engaging civically across heritage practices and indigenous knowledges (Watson & Knight-Manuel, 2017). Specifically, the authors' interdisciplinary framework engaged a *Sankofan approach* to analyze peer-reviewed, empirical literature published between 2000 and 2016 on how immigrant students from West African countries navigated complex identities and engaged civically across multiple educational and social contexts.

The intentionality of a Sankofan lens spoke to how the authors moved purposefully from Eurocentric paradigms toward "ways of knowing grounded in making connections" (Flowers, 2003, p. 40) with past, present, and future changing heritage practices and knowledges of Black African immigrant youth (see Literacy Futurisms Collective-in-the-Making, 2021). As Watson and Knight-Manuel (2017) explained, a Sankofan approach, influenced by several orientations toward African consciousness (Temple, 2010), examines the legacy of cultural and linguistic heritage practices such as language use, and resistance with respect to Eurocentric worldviews of Africa, people of Africa, and immigrant youth from West African countries. Further, a Sankofan approach affords opportunities to disrupt polarizing public discourses and challenge inequitable teaching and learning opportunities for African immigrant youth.

Third Wave (Approximately 2017 to Present)

The urging of a Sankofan approach in teaching and research with African immigrant youth coincided with restrictive migration policies, including two presidential executive orders in 2017 banning travel to the United

Introduction

States from multiple majority-Muslim countries, and historically stringent refugee admittance policies. Additionally, during a period when the United Nations High Commissioner for Refugees noted that in 2018 upwards of 70 million people were displaced globally, including a substantial 6 million from countries in Africa south of the Sahara, policy implemented under the Trump administration by the U.S. Bureau of Population, Refugees, and Migration substantially reduced the number of refugees annually admitted to the United States (Blizzard & Batalova, 2019). Cutting the admittance cap from 110,000 to 50,000 refugees in fiscal year 2017, to 30,000 in 2019, and, in 2021, the "historic low" of 15,000 resulted in the lowest refugee admittance in the United States since 1980 (Blizzard & Batalova, 2019; Hansler & Alvarez, 2021, para. 1; Watson et al., 2022). The 15,000-admittance ceiling was raised by the Biden administration, first to 62,500 in fiscal year 2021, then 125,000 in 2022, and 125,000 in 2023. Yet the actual number as of 2023 continued to lag, as refugee admittances had not kept pace with increases in the annual admissions cap (P. Alvarez, 2022; Watson et al., 2022).

In the current third wave of research involving African immigrant youth and young adults in the United States and schooling contexts, a range of authors have situated their inquiries in the braiding of historically strident migration policies and persistent popularized narratives that label immigrant and refugee youth as threats to be feared, separated from peers and families, and banned from the United States, and simultaneously obscure the challenges and possibilities of educational attainment with which African immigrant youth grapple (e.g., Agyepong, 2017; Nsangou & Dundes, 2018).

For example, Ukpokodu (2018) engaged a multiple methodological analysis approach to examine academic and social discourses that positioned African immigrant students as a "new model minority" (p. 60), a limiting label that "creates a significant obstacle to understanding the needs" of African immigrant students in schools (p. 65). Ukpokodu's impactful scholarship called for "culturally responsive and globally competent" teaching and teacher education, and increased research on African immigrant students across the range of K–12 schooling contexts (p. 60; see also Ukpokodu, 2013). Illustrative of work in this current third wave, Watson and Knight-Manuel (2020) examined empirical findings of their previous and recent research, rendering visible African immigrant youths' and young adults' participatory communal civic learning and action-taking, nuancing the lived experiences beyond imposed preconditions of polarity. The authors asserted "humanizing the Black immigrant body" as a generative theoretical and conceptual lens to pointedly theorize and teach with African indigeneity and diaspora approaches that affirm immigrant youths' fluid past-present-future learning practices and stances. Such framing builds with African indigeneity and African feminist scholars (Chilisa & Ntseane, 2014; Dei, 2017; Dillard & Neal, 2020) to assert vital frames toward anticolonial and decolonial Black solidarity, emphasizing the converging of ontology, axiology, and epistemology borne along a history of legitimizing Blackness and Africanness (Asante, 1987, 1988; Carroll, 2014; Dei, 2017; Du Bois, 2008 / 1903; Watson & Knight-Manuel, 2020).

Guided by such lenses that envision a humanizing of the Black immigrant body, authors have thus pointedly addressed Blackness and complicated contexts of anti-Blackness confronting African immigrants in the United States and globally (Walls, 2021). For example, Patriann Smith (2020c) edited a themed issue of *Teachers College Record* that importantly focused on "clarifying the role of race in the literacies of Black immigrant youth" (p. 1; see, e.g., Bauer & Sánchez, 2020; Braden, 2020; Bryan, 2020; Hotchkins & Smith, 2020; Kiramba & Oloo, 2020; McLean, 2020; Nalubega-Booker & Willis, 2020; Skerrett & Omogun, 2020; P. Smith, 2020c; Warrican, 2020; Watson & Knight-Manuel, 2020). This volume, together with a themed issue of *African and Black Diaspora: An International Journal* examining various experiences of second-generation African immigrants in the United States, edited by Kebede (2019), reflects scholarship since 2017 that has advanced understandings, many of them centering racialization, across a range of research perspectives learned from research with African immigrant youth communities.

Such research has examined culturally responsive teaching approaches with African immigrant youth (Ndemanu & Jordan, 2018); the preparation of teachers of diverse students using historical and theoretical stances (Liu & Ball, 2019); teacher expectations of Somali Bantu youth (Tran & Birman, 2019); processes of race, ethnic, and gender identity formation of Black African girls as demonstrated in documentary film (Hailu & Simmons, 2022b); experiences of African immigrant students' learning and care across schools and home amid contexts of anti-Blackness (Walls, 2021); cultural and linguistic approaches, such as navigating the interplay of culture, language, and identity with African immigrant youth (Kiramba, Kumi-Yeboah, & Mawuli Sallar, 2020; Kiramba et al., 2021; Kiramba & Oloo, 2019); and African immigrant youths' lived educational experiences (Parslow, 2023), including explorations of lived experiences of African refugee youths in public schools in the U.S. Midwest impacted by systemic racism (Bakar, 2023).

This scholarship additionally has addressed transnational civic learning and participation (Dávila, 2021); discourses and perspectives of civic belonging of Central African immigrant youth (Dávila & Doukmak, 2022); and new perspectives toward affective civic engagement and action-taking with West African migrant youth (Keegan, 2019, 2023). Authors explored emerging narratives of West African immigrant youths' academic achievement and success (Kumi-Yeboah et al., 2020; Kumi-Yeboah & Smith, 2017); strategies for academic engagement used by educators in K–12 schools in the United States with recent African immigrant students from countries

Introduction

south of the Sahara (Nkemka, 2022); and how adolescent Ghanaian immigrant girls negotiate contexts of peers, schools, and family as they achieve academic success (Kiramba, Onyewuenyi, et al., 2020).

Moreover, authors analyzed West African Muslim youth navigating intersectional identities in a U.S. charter school (Binte-Farid, 2022); explored narratives of critical mathematics with African immigrant young adults (Osibodu & Cosby, 2018); (re)envisioned humanizing research approaches and schooling contexts with African immigrant girls (Kiramba, Kumi-Yeboah & Mawuli Sallar, 2020; C. C. Lee, 2020; Simmons, 2021b); examined educational experiences in U.S. schools of Black Kenyan immigrant students given dis/abilities labels (Nabwire, 2021); and enacted an ethics of care with African immigrant students and students' educators across the COVID-19 pandemic (Tesfa & Lowenhaupt, 2023). Scholars conceptualized frameworks in writing and rhetorics at the interplay of shared African history and ancestry of Black people, African worldview, and rhetorical traditions extending across Black communities' communicative practices (Browdy & Milu, 2022; Milu, 2021). Authors additionally studied African immigrant youth and gaming futures (Bayeck, 2020); aspirations and achievement (Kumi-Yeboah et al., 2017); the interplay of aspiration, identity, and languaging (Adenekan, 2021), including with Somali Bantu refugee youth (Tran & Birman, 2019); African immigrant youth belonging, claiming space, and enacting a photostory project (Schmidt, 2021, 2022); narratives of visibility with African students in U.S. contexts (Agyepong, 2017); a pedagogy of love in (re)framing popular media narratives of African immigrant communities (Watson et al., 2022); African epistemologies, and methodological approaches with Kenyan youth (Kiramba, 2018); Wandera, 2016, 2020; Wandera & Farr, 2018); and how African American teachers sustain identities of an African immigrant student using Afrocentric praxis (Braden et al., 2022; Johnson et al., 2018).

TOWARD NEW PERSPECTIVES: CONCEPTUALIZING THE *FRAMEWORK FOR EDUCATING AFRICAN IMMIGRANT YOUTH*

This robust third wave of scholarship, bolstered by the two foregoing waves, has ushered forward and opened new possibilities for examining perspectives of educating African immigrant youth, schooling, and civic engagement in the African diaspora. Toward envisaging such new perspectives, in this text, we build with and extend the literature across these three waves to conceptualize a purposeful, generative cross-disciplinary framework that comprehensively addresses the scope and heterogeneity of African immigrant youth and their schooling and civic engagement experiences. This *Framework for Educating African Immigrant Youth* involves four complementary approaches (see Figure 1.1).

Figure 1.1. *Framework for Educating African Immigrant Youth*: **Four Approaches**

1. Emboldening tellings of diaspora narratives
2. Navigating pasts, presence, and futures of literacy, language, teaching, and learning
3. Envisioning and enacting social civic literacies and learning to extend complex identities
4. Affirming and extending cultural, heritage, and embodied knowledges, languages, and practices

Each of the four approaches involves two interrelated features.

1. Emboldening tellings of diaspora narratives involves (a) countering and (b) (re)presenting deficit narratives, and humanizing the Black immigrant body.
2. Navigating pasts, presence, and futures of literacy, language, teaching, and learning involves (a) extending past-present-future learning with and across peers, families, elders, and educators, and (b) informing connectedness and valuing youth as contributors across classrooms and communities.
3. Envisioning and enacting social civic literacies and learning to extend complex identities involves (a) mediating transglobal geographies, migrations, and physical and digital contexts, and (b) demonstrating participatory communal, lived civic learning and action-taking beyond one-time activities.
4. Affirming and extending cultural, heritage, and embodied knowledges, languages, and practices involves (a) developing nuanced understandings of the heterogeneity of Blackness, and (b) drawing on already-present literacies, languaging, and cultural, artistic materials/artifacts and onto-epistemologies (ways of being and knowing) in designing frameworks and methodologies.

Authors in *Educating African Immigrant Youth* address the contours of the four approaches and interrelated features in conversation with pressing questions, suggestions, and recommendations for teachers, researchers, and teacher educators (see Figure 1.2).

We situate the four approaches as embedded in the ongoing, necessary work of teachers and researchers navigating their own shifting identities and positionalities in relation to their work with African immigrant youth (e.g., C. C. Lee, 2020; Mentor & Sealey-Ruiz, 2021; Peshkin, 1988; Roegman et al., 2016) (see Figure 1.3).

Reflective of the scope and heterogeneity of Black African immigrant youth and their schooling and civic engagement experiences, authors in *Educating African Immigrant Youth* build on and extend a range of existing

Figure 1.2. Framework for Educating African Immigrant Youth: Four Approaches and Interrelated Features

Approach:	Interrelated Features of Approach:	Addressed in:
1. Emboldening tellings of diaspora narratives	• Countering and (re)presenting deficit narratives • Humanizing the Black African immigrant body	• Ukpokodu, Chapter 2 • Anwara Mohyuddin, Chapter 4 • Oloo & Dias Corrêa, Chapter 5 • Keegan, Chapter 6 • Dreas-Shaikha, Badaki, and Blanks Jones, Chapter 8 • Afolalu, Chapter 11 • Berends, Watson, & Kubengana, Chapter 12
2. Navigating pasts, presence, and futures of literacy, language, teaching, and learning	• Extending past-present-future learning with and across peers, families, elders, and educators • Informing connectedness and valuing youth as contributors across classrooms and communities	• Ukpokodu, Chapter 2 • Osibodu & Damba Danjo, Chapter 3 • Anwara Mohyuddin, Chapter 4 • Dávila & Ogwal, Chapter 7 • Berends, Watson, & Kubangena, Chapter 12
3. Envisioning and enacting social civic literacies and learning to extend complex identities	• Mediating transglobal geographies, migrations, and physical and digital contexts • Demonstrating participatory communal, lived civic learning and action-taking beyond one-time activities	• Ukpokodu, Chapter 2 • Keegan, Chapter 6 • Dreas-Shaikha, Badaki, and Blanks Jones, Chapter 8 • Knight-Manuel, Robert, & Akin-Sabuncu, Chapter 9 • Afolalu, Chapter 11
4. Affirming and extending cultural, heritage, and embodied knowledges, languages, and practices	• Developing nuanced understandings of the heterogeneity of Blackness • Drawing on already-present literacies, languaging, and cultural, artistic materials/artifacts and onto-epistemologies (ways of being and knowing) in designing frameworks and methodologies	• Ukpokodu, Chapter 2 • Osibodu & Damba Danjo, Chapter 3 • Dávila & Ogwal, Chapter 7 • Dreas-Shaikha, Badaki, and Blanks Jones, Chapter 8 • Wandera, Chapter 10 • Berends, Watson, & Kubengana, Chapter 12

Figure 1.3. *Framework for Educating African Immigrant Youth*

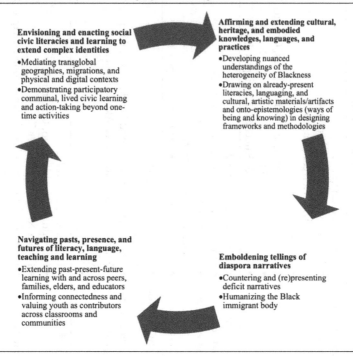

and emerging theoretical frameworks. For example, authors draw on theoretical lenses grounded in African epistemologies and ontologies, including Africanfuturism, diaspora studies, and a Sankofan approach. Authors additionally draw on and extend anti-Blackness and postcolonial lenses; decolonizing approaches; raciolinguistically and culturally relevant-sustaining frameworks; language and literacy as a social practice; community cultural wealth; transnationalism; theater as social action; problem-posing education; transformative and asset-based processes and practices; various forms of capital (e.g., social, cultural, linguistic, navigational, familial); and additive schooling lenses. Engagement with such lenses provokes a stance-taking toward justice, urgently so, as counterpoint to polarizing public discourses that traverse popularized media narratives of brokenness and damage. In doing so, there is a call to address how education often falls short of illuminating the lived realities and heterogeneous experiences of Black immigrants, and migrations and navigations of Black bodies within and across social and transnational geographies and translingual contexts.

Chapter authors engage a range of methodological approaches to render visible an array of Black African immigrant youths' schooling and civic

Introduction 15

experiences extending youths' identities, including narrative portraiture, decolonizing approaches to methodology, qualitative case study, critical participatory visual research methodology, narrative inquiry, ethnography, qualitative interview-based study, and counterstorying. Illustrative of the breadth and depth of disciplinary perspectives that educators and researchers engage with African immigrant youth, authors write within and across a range of schooling contexts: literacy and language education; civics teaching, learning, and action-taking; social studies education; mathematics education; higher education; university and community partnerships; teacher education; urban education; comparative and international education; health education; and after-school initiatives, including filmmaking.

Furthermore, chapter authors address the four approaches and interrelated features of the *Framework for Educating African Immigrant Youth* across three thematic areas. Each of the thematic areas is introduced with a brief overview that provides further details of each chapter. Then, each chapter proceeds with authors elucidating the thematic area. Importantly, authors distinctively include Black African scholars, early-career, and senior scholars from a range of institutions in the United States and Canada.

Part I: "Schooling and Classroom Perspectives and Contexts" is introduced by Sandra Boateng and Vaughn W. M. Watson.

- Omiunota Nelly Ukpokodu writes Chapter 2, "Toward a Reckoning and Affirmation of Black African Immigrant Youth in U.S. P–12 Schools."
- Oyemolade (Molade) Osibodu and Nyimasata Damba Danjo author Chapter 3, "Africanfuturism and Critical Mathematics Education: Envisioning a Liberatory Future for Sub-Saharan African Immigrants."
- Irteza Anwara Mohyuddin writes Chapter 4, "African Lives Matter Too: Affirming African Heritage Students' Experience in the History Classroom."
- James Alan Oloo and Priscila Dias Corrêa write Chapter 5, "A Narrative Inquiry Into Experiences of Black Women in Undergraduate STEM Disciplines in Ontario."

Part II: "Participatory and Communal Approaches to Learning and Civic Engagement" is introduced by Michelle Knight-Manuel and Dorothy Khamala.

- Patrick Keegan authors Chapter 6, "Always Remember What's Behind You So You Can Reach What's in Front of You: The Transnational Civic Engagement of a West African High School Student."

- Liv T. Dávila and Susan A. Okwal write Chapter 7, "An Affect-Centered Analysis of Congolese Immigrant Parent Perspectives on Past-Present-Future Learning in School and at Home."
- Maryann J. Dreas-Shaikha, OreOluwa Badaki, and Jasmine L. Blanks Jones author Chapter 8, "Imaging and Imagining Activism: Exploring Embodied and Digital Learning Through Filmmaking With African Immigrant Girls During the Pandemic."
- Michelle Knight-Manuel, Natacha Robert, and Sibel Akin-Sabuncu write Chapter 9, "Social Cohesion, Belonging, and Anti-Blackness: African Immigrant Youth's Civic Exploration in a Culturally Relevant-Sustaining, After-School Club."

Part III: "Literacies, Languages, and Learning: Toward Emerging Practices and Approaches" is introduced by Patriann Smith.

- David Bwire Wandera writes Chapter 10, "Unboxing Black Immigrant Youth's Heritage Resources."
- Lakeya Afolalu authors Chapter 11, "Opening Space to Participate: One Nigerian Girl's Use of Visual Arts to Navigate School-Based Linguistic Discrimination."
- Joel E. Berends, Vaughn W. M. Watson, and Dinamic Kubengana write Chapter 12, "Theorizing Rightful Literary Presence and Participatory Curriculum Design With African Immigrant Youth."

In the concluding Chapter 13, Vaughn W. M. Watson, Michelle G. Knight-Manuel, and Patriann Smith envision productive possibilities for the *Framework for Educating African Immigrant Youth*, enacted across the four complementary approaches. We consider future directions for teaching and research with African immigrant youth communities, and frameworks, teaching, and methodological approaches grounded in African epistemologies and ontologies for a range of education and social science fields.

Part I

SCHOOLING AND CLASSROOM PERSPECTIVES AND CONTEXTS

Sandra Boateng and Vaughn W. M. Watson

Authors in Part I contribute urgent narratives to current research literature contextualizing lived schooling experiences of Black African adolescent women and girls navigating STEM disciplinary contexts (e.g., Morton et al., 2019; Sparks, 2023; Woods, 2021) and social studies classrooms (Keegan, 2019; Kiramba et al., 2022; Vickery, 2015) in secondary and higher education settings in the United States and Canada. These narratives highlight the pressing need to recognize and affirm the humanity of Black African immigrant youth across educational contexts (Ukpokodu & Otiato Ojiambo, 2017; Watson & Knight-Manuel, 2020). In doing so, authors engage the ongoing necessary work of rendering visible complex, multifaceted narratives of Black African immigrant youth and young adults (Adichie, 2009; Agyepong, 2017; Imaogene, 2015), and underscore several approaches of the *Framework for Educating African Immigrant Youth* (Chapter 1).

Omiunota Nelly Ukpokodu in Chapter 2 illuminates everyday lived experiences of Black African immigrant youth, advocating for their recognition and acceptance in U.S. P–12 schools. Ukpokodu illustrates educational challenges individuals encounter, while underscoring prevalent silences concerning racial violence aimed at Black African immigrants. Ukpokodu additionally explores transnational identities of African immigrant youth navigating diverse cultural landscapes and making significant contributions to home spaces within and across the African diaspora, often without proper acknowledgment. In dispelling misunderstandings about African immigrant youth and emphasizing their considerable cultural knowledge and underused skills, Ukpokodu proposes recommendations to address racial and educational injustices and violence against Black African immigrant youth across U.S. society and institutions.

Oyemolade Osibodu and Nyimasata Damba Danjo in Chapter 3, and James Alan Oloo and Priscila Dias Corrêa in Chapter 5, illuminate critical African perspectives on teaching, knowing, and doing in challenging mathematics and STEM disciplinary learning too typically viewed through a Western gaze (Chilisa & Ntseane, 2014; Dei, 2000). Osibodu and Damba Danjo, for example, raise ontological and epistemological questions about whose mathematical literacies count, and how African Indigenous knowledge, practices, and lived experiences are affirmed across higher education contexts. The authors draw across a tapestry of personal experiences as African immigrant collegians enrolling in secondary and postsecondary mathematics courses in the United States and Canada, and an engrossing literary analysis of the Africanfuturist novella *Binti* by Nnedi Okorafor (2015) to highlight the necessity of embracing diverse mathematical perspectives.

Oloo and Dias Corrêa embark on a narrative illuminating the experiences of two Black immigrant women studying undergraduate STEM disciplines in Ontario, Canada. The authors delve meaningfully into challenges and opportunities in STEM education involving undergraduate students, with pointed emphasis on amplifying lived schooling experiences of Black immigrant women. Urgently, Oloo and Dias Corrêa engage narratives of two students, Hera and Achieng, through an asset-based lens extending Yosso's (2005) community cultural wealth framework. Hera's and Achieng's diverse strengths contribute significantly to their journeys as Black women undergraduate students navigating narratives of educational experiences in STEM learning that name, and reject, staid deficit perspectives.

Irteza Anwara Mohyuddin, in Chapter 4, shares the schooling narrative of Kabeera, attending 9th grade at Honors Academy. Mohyuddin underscores the heterogeneity of Black African students' experiences and the complex and varying levels of recognition that youths' cultural backgrounds, histories, and lived experiences receive, or how they are rendered less present, in schooling contexts. Mohyuddin examines how public school students and a teacher in an African American History class navigate discourses on race and immigration, hindering how students may engage in and navigate racial spacemaking. Mohyuddin urges educators to consider meaningfully the interconnected diasporic struggles of Black lives worldwide, a core principle of the Black Lives Matter movement.

Across Part I, chapter authors engage questions for educators, teacher educators, and researchers, including: How may you design teaching contexts, practices, and research approaches that build with the range of Black African immigrant youths' and young adults' multifaceted identities? How across such teaching and research approaches may you affirm and extend the heterogeneity of Black African students' already-present literacy, learning, and identities?

CHAPTER 2

Toward a Reckoning and Affirmation of Black African Immigrant Youth in U.S. P–12 Schools

Omiunota Nelly Ukpokodu

Today, African immigrants and refugees and their children have become a visibly minoritized community in U.S. society and multicultural democratic nation-states. Yet, across P–12 schools, they remain invisible, ignored, and poorly served. Most often, even in 2023, schools and educators perceive and treat them as relics of Tarzan and the "forever alien" within. A major contributor of this problem relates to the dearth of scholarship (Ukpokodu, 2013, 2017, 2018), schools' and educators' luxury of ignorance about Africa, African immigrants, and their lived realities in U.S. society and institutions, and media bias and misrepresentation. In schools, African immigrant and transnational youth, many of whom are first, second, or third generationers, are denied their human identities. Engaging and relating with them has often taken an anti–Black African deficit-based approach, adversely impacting their personal development, civic literacy, and successful citizenship attainment. The purpose of this chapter is to expose lived realities of Black African immigrant youth that warrant a clarion call for reckoning for the educational violence and disaffirmation of their humanity in U.S. schools. I engage these questions: (1) Who are Black African immigrant youth? (2) What are their lived societal and educational realities and impact on their attainment of critical civic literacy and successful citizenship? and (3) How do U.S. society and schools need to reckon with racial and educational violence perpetrated against them?

DIASPORIC BLACKS AND COLORISM IN AMERICA

For decades, scholars have referenced the eminent historian W.E.B. Du Bois's groundbreaking seminal work, *The Souls of Black Folk* (2008/1903), in which Du Bois made a profound and prophetic statement that "the problem of the 20th century is the problem of the color line" (p. 13). Specifically,

Du Bois posits that "colorism" creates a reality of "double consciousness" in which one feels and lives the reality of twoness—and in some cases, if you are Black, African, and immigrant, a threeness or fourness that creates the phenomenon of "triple marginality" and "quadruple marginality" consciousness. Unfortunately, and sadly, after many decades, and even with noticeable progress, Du Bois's pronouncement remains and rings true. The problem of the 21st century remains that of the color line. Colorism remains and rears its ugly head in the lives of Black, Indigenous People of Color (BIPOC) as they experience every day racial violence and devaluation of their humanity. Whose lives and humanity matter, not only persists but is endemic and pervasive! This is more so for Black people even as they have called out, fought hard, and resisted centuries of dehumanization and racial violence perpetrated against them. Since 2012, we have seen pervasive, senseless shootings and killings of unarmed Black youths—Trayvon Martin (17), Jordan Davis (17), Kendreck McDade (19), Michael Brown (18), Tamara Rice (12) in 2014, Ahmaud Arbery (25) in February 2020, Breonna Taylor (26) in March 2020, reaching its climax in May 2020 with the dehumanizing, brutal killing of George Floyd, a Black, African American man, by a white police officer. The unconscionable killing of George Floyd, watched by millions of people nationally and globally, generated outrage and ushered in a flurry of clarion calls for the United States to reckon with its history and legacy of racial violence and injustice against Black people/ BIPOC (American Civil Liberties Union, n.d.; Carnegie Endowment for International Peace, 2021; Glaude, 2020). More profoundly, the brutal killing of George Floyd exposed harsh and harrowing lived realities of Black people in America, the so-called "land of the free" and of "inalienable [human] rights." For many, pervasive racial violence raised the question: Do Black Lives Matter? The instant galvanization of a multiracial, multiethnic, and multigenerational coalition, a mass social movement, the largest since the civil rights movement, recording between 15,000,000 and 26,000,000 participants (*The New York Times,* 2020; Silverstein, 2021), is a resounding confirmation that Black lives matter, despite the recent decline in support (Pew Research Center, 2023). Nonetheless, the call for the United States (and the world) to reckon with their histories and legacies of dehumanization, racial violence, gross disparities, inequities, and social injustice has begun and is unrelenting, especially as more Black people, including Tony McDade (38) in May 2020 and Rayshard Brooks (27) in June 2020, among others, continue to be violently shot and killed by law enforcement.

MY POSITIONALITY

To frame this chapter, I draw on my more than 3½ decades of personal and professional experiences and active engagement in organizations committed to diversity, equity, inclusion, and social justice. I am a Black, African immigrant American with more than 4 decades of life and lived realities in the United States. I am also a teacher educator of more than 3 decades in U.S. higher education, with research engagement in multicultural, global, immigrant, transformative, social justice education; race narrative discourse; and critical multicultural citizenship education. More relevant and important, I am a parent of two Black men who, because of their race, skin color, ethnicity, and immigrant origins, are susceptible to the racial violence of the anti-Blackness culture, which keeps me awake each night, as they have been subjected to racialized anti-Black African violence. As a multicultural teacher educator and scholar, I embrace and promote an activist-driven teaching purpose. Over the years, I have engaged in extensive study and publications of the lived realities of Black African immigrants that expose not only the societal anti-Blackness violence, but more important, the educational violence against Black African immigrant children and youth that denies them access to quality and equitable education in U.S. public schools. As a doctoral faculty member in U.S. higher education, I have directed several master's and doctoral theses and dissertations on African immigrant students. I bring these experiences to bear as I unpack and illuminate most importantly the educational lived realities of Black African immigrant youth. Recently, I have been inspired and motivated by the call and movement for racial and justice reckoning for BIPOC and affirmation of Black lives. Although the mass social protest for racial reckoning centers on the criminal justice system and law enforcement, the Black Lives Matter movement has forced the United States and the world to engage in conversations that confront not only the historical legacy of race, racial violence, and social injustice, but more important, what must be done to reform institutions deeply ingrained in racist and anti-Blackness practices. On the backdrop of the call and trend for U.S. society to reckon with its history and legacy of dehumanization and racial violence, I write this chapter for the primary purpose of joining other voices to make a clarion call for U.S. institutions, especially P–12 schools, to reckon with the racial and educational violence against Black African immigrant children and youth.

BLACK AFRICAN IMMIGRANTS AND LIVED REALITIES AND RACIAL VIOLENCE

Historically, education has been a vital institutional tool for socializing individuals and groups into the U.S. democracy. Whether explicitly or implicitly, and unfortunately, the education system has been an institutional tool that has operated and continues to operate as a gatekeeper (Apple, 2004; Goodwin, 2010) to schooling experiences, especially curriculum that calls into question: *What knowledge and whose knowledge is legitimate to be taught and learned? Who gets included and served equitably in the system?* Although forward-thinking educators such as Horace Mann (1848), Carter G. Woodson (1933/1900), Jane Addams (1930), and Nelson Mandela (2003), among others, and political figures, including Benjamin Franklin (1749) and Lyndon B. Johnson (1966), envisioned and advocated for education as the "great equalizer," immigrant students have been documented to experience "subtractive schooling" (Valenzuela, 1999) that strips them of human and cultural identities, thereby obstructing and mitigating their successful academic and personal development. This is particularly true for Black African immigrants, who although heralded as America's "new model minority" (Ukpokodu, 2018), are documented to be struggling personally and academically (Boutte & Bryan, 2021; Ghong et al., 2007; Harushimana & Awokoya, 2011; Kumi-Yeboah & Smith, 2016; Traoré & Lukens, 2006). To critically engage this discourse on Black African immigrant youth (BAIY), it is important to begin by contextualizing Black African immigrants and their lived realities in the United States.

Research shows that Black African immigrants in the United States and other Western nation-states, such as Canada and the United Kingdom, often face the dual characterization of (1) being the most educationally accomplished immigrant group (American Community Survey, 2012; Migration Policy Institute, 2019; Pew Research Center, 2019), and (2) being negatively portrayed as relics of Tarzan and inferiority. In 2018, the president of the United States, Donald Trump, decried African immigrants coming from "shithole" countries. Although representing about 4.5% of the U.S. immigrant population, they constitute a significant contribution to the growing diversity of the overall Black population in the United States. Today, one in five Black people is an immigrant or a child of Black immigrants (Lorenzi & Batalova, 2022; Pew Research Center, 2022). While this is welcome recognition, little is known about their lived experiences in the United States. In the multicultural, multiracial U.S. society, the racial or ethnic designation for people of African ancestry is Black or African American, although the Black racial group is not a monolith. Most often, what is reported that garners national attention is the violence against people identifying as U.S.-born Black or U.S.-born African American (except for the 1999 brutal killing with 41 bullets of Amadou Diallo, age 23, a Black African immigrant). Unbeknownst to many people, Black African immigrants also have been victims of police brutality in the United States and other parts of the world. Yet, their names have been silenced and often are unknown. While this is not an attempt to discount the unconscionable, horrific racial violence perpetuated against U.S.-born Black/African American communities, since their forced and involuntary removal from their motherland, or against other marginalized BIPOC, it is to underscore the invisibility or silencing of racial violence against Black African immigrants (see P. Smith, 2020c, for a discussion of "silencing invisibility"). Many Black African immigrants, whether first, second, or even third generationers, have had violent and fatal encounters with law enforcement. For example, the following is a list of some known Black African immigrants racially victimized by the police (Persaud, 2020):

1999: Unarmed Guinean immigrant student Amadou Diallo, 23 years old, brutally killed in New York, when four police officers fired 41 bullets at him as he stood near his apartment building. The news of the brutal and horrific killing was heard around the world. Like that of George Floyd, the killing sparked an outrage and mass protest.

2003: Burkina Faso immigrant Ousmane Zongo, 43 years old, unarmed, killed in New York by a New York City police officer.

2009: Sudanese immigrant Jonathan Deng, 26 years old, killed by police in Iowa City, IA.

2012: Guinean immigrant Mohamed Bah, 28 years old, shot seven times in his apartment in New York City.

2015: Charley "Africa" Keunang, 46-year-old Cameroonian immigrant, killed by police in Los Angeles, CA.

2015: Sudanese immigrant Deng Manyoun, 35 years old, killed by police in Louisville, KY.

2015: Haitian immigrant David Felix, 24 years old, a homeless, unarmed student, killed by police in New York City.

2016: Ugandan refugee Alfred Olongo, 38 years old, shot and killed by police in California.

2022: Patrick Lyola, 26 years old, a Congolese refugee, killed by police in Michigan.

2023: Nahel Merzouk, 17 years old, killed by police, Paris, France.

Undoubtedly, there may be more Black African immigrants tragically killed by law enforcement but unknown due to issues of legalization, documentation, and support systems. Of the above, only Amadou Diallo's brutal shooting and killing received visible attention. While data show that U.S.-born Black/African American people are 2.5 more times likely than white people to be fatally shot by police (Pew Research Center, 2020), there are no data for Black African immigrants shot and killed by law enforcement. But what is clear is that Black African immigrants encounter the same racial violence, racial profiling, police brutality, and criminalization as U.S.-born Black/African American communities (a dynamic made even more complex when Black African "immigrants," some of whom are second generation, are also U.S.-born). Additionally, they are subjected to discriminatory deportation, as they make up 20% of deportees for criminalization (American Civil Liberties Union, n.d.; Black Alliance for Just Immigration, n.d.; Human Rights First, 2022). United Nations reports indicate that African immigrant children are more likely than other groups to experience criminalization and police harassment and brutality, and that they face disproportionate threats to their safety and well-being (Young Center for Immigrant Children, 2020). What is more tragic, and troubling, is that many Black African immigrant victims of police brutality are refugees who sought to escape violence from their homeland only to encounter brutality and violence in a land they yearned for and viewed as free, peaceful, and safe.

BLACK AFRICAN IMMIGRANT YOUTH

Who are Black African immigrant youth? Often, research and discourses about immigrant youth are engaged without clearly defining or explicating who they are. Broadly, immigrant youth are defined as those under the age of 18 who are either foreign born or U.S. born to immigrant parents/families. Some organizations define "youth" as a child/person between ages 15 and 24 (Global Migration Group, 2014; United Nations, 1989; United Nations Population Fund, 2014; World Health Organization, 2019). The African Union Youth Charter (2006) defines "youth" expansively, as any person between ages 15 and 35 years. Regardless, varied definitions place immigrant youth as falling across generations X, Y (millennial), and Z (Pew Research Center, 2019).

Chronologically and educationally, immigrant youth could be those in their adolescence and functioning as young adults. Therefore, I define Black African immigrant youth as those who are in middle school through high school (grades 6 through 12) in U.S. P–12 schools, are ages 12 through 18, reside in an African immigrant family, were born in any African country or are U.S. born with at least one African immigrant parent/family member, and are attending or have attended U.S. public schools (Ukpokodu, 2017). That is, they can be classified as 1.0 (first generation), born in Africa; 1.5 (first generation), born in Africa but immigrated prior to adolescent years; and 2.0 (second generation), U.S. born, with at least one African parent (Ukpokodu, 2018).

While commonalities exist among BAIY due to African cultural ancestry, there are also stark differences between and among them that must be recognized to serve and service them relevantly and appropriately. John Ogbu (1978), in his illuminating seminal work on cultural ecology theory, classified and designated immigrants as "voluntary" minorities (those who willingly choose to immigrate) and "involuntary" minorities (those forcibly displaced due to conditions beyond their control such as war, religious/political persecution, and violence), commonly known as "refugees." Often left out, though, are "undocumented" immigrants who enter the United States without legal documentation. Most often, schools, educators, and especially classroom teachers and counselors do not differentiate between and among these groups, and perceive or treat them as Black students who are

"African American," thereby failing to consider their transnational cultural backgrounds.

Like their immigrant families, BAIY are culturally, geopolitically linguistically, religiously, socioeconomically, and educationally diverse (see Ukpokodu, 2018). Like their Black African immigrant families, BAIY originate from several African countries, including Nigeria, Egypt, Ghana, Ethiopia, South Africa, Kenya, Liberia, Cameroon, Somalia, Morocco, Cape Verde, and Sierra Leone, with a sizeable number from the Sudan, Eritrea, and Burundi (McCabe, 2011 a&b). Many are refugees, escaping economic, political, religious, and social conflicts (American Community Survey, 2009; Capps et al., 2011). Moreover, BAIY are diasporic Black, African, adolescent, immigrant, transcultural, transnational, and transmigrant, and straddle two or multiple culturally different worlds in their desire to experience the "American dream" (Kumi-Yeboah, 2018). Unfortunately, a growing body of scholarship consistently has shown that their desire and goal to attain the American dream is often difficult, as they encounter anti-Blackness and racial, cultural, and educational institutional violence that robs them of access to the knowledge, skills, values, attitudes, and agency they need to live a successful personal and civic life (Knight et al., 2015; Ukpokodu, 2013, 2018) even when their diasporic communities and institutions claim to welcome them (Covington-Ward, 2017; Ghong et al., 2007; Harushimana & Awokoya, 2011; Kumi-Yeboah & Smith, 2017; Ukpokodu, 2013, 2017, 2018). Although limited, growing scholarship on BAIY shows they endure various and persistent marginalization (microaggressions) that include cultural identity invalidation and disaffirmation, stereotyping, stigmatization, bullying, and physical, linguistic, and curriculum and pedagogical violence (Ukpokodu, 2018) in U.S. schools that are supposed to prepare them to become literate, productive, competent, and contributing members of their families, communities, nation, and the larger world.

BLACK AFRICAN IMMIGRANT YOUTH AND LIVED REALITIES IN U.S. SCHOOLS

Racialized Marginalization. Marginalization is a well-documented experience BAIY face in U.S. schools. Past and current research shows that BAIY experience gross invisibility. Even as they are an increasing presence in U.S. schools, they remain an invisible, minoritized student group who suffer and experience various forms of gross marginalization that include homogenization due to their subsumption into the broader racial category of Black/African American (P. Smith, 2023a). This renders them invisible, overlooked, ignored, neglected, and mis-identified (Ukpokodu, 2018), resulting in their personal and academic needs being unmet (Awokoya, 2009; Ghong et al., 2007; Harushimana, 2011). In school environments and classroom spaces, they experience vulnerability and dehumanizing *microaggressions*—brief and daily verbal, nonverbal, behavioral, demeaning and denigrating messages, and environmental indignities. Sue et al. (2007) identify three forms of microaggression—microassaults (verbal and nonverbal hurtful and hateful attacks), microinsults (communication that conveys rudeness, slights, insensitivity, and humiliation), and microinvalidation (communication and interactions that exclude, negate, and discount one's identity). Research shows that BAIY experience and endure these forms in and outside of school (Awokoya, 2012; Ghong et al., 2007; Harushimana, 2011; Kiramba, Onyewuenyi, et al., 2020; Ukpokodu, 2013, 2017). For example, BAIY experience *microassaults* when they are name-called "Ebola" (Ukpokodu, 2018), "Monkey boy" (Kiramba, Onyewuenyi et al., 2020), "terrorist," and "jungle soldier" (Ukpokodu, 2018), and when peers avoid them, exclude them, and refuse to partner with them in group-learning activities; *microinsults* when they are bullied and encounter subtle snubs, stereotyping, mean-spirited teasing, jokes, rudeness, name mispronunciation and shredding, and linguistic violence (Baker-Bell, 2020), and when their accents are mocked, mimicked, and laughed at by both their peers and their teachers; and *microinvalidation* when they are asked malicious, ridiculous, and hurtful questions—"Did you live on top of trees in Africa?" "Did you wear clothes in Africa?" "When are you going back to Africa for good?"—even when they are legitimate U.S. citizens (Ukpokodu, 2018).

These microaggressions have been documented to create disciplinary problems for BAIY who, in an attempt to resist dehumanizing and violent acts toward themselves, are forced to defend themselves and engage in physical fights with peers, yet get further victimized when subjected to school suspension or even expulsion. Although bullying is a common experience across many schools, reports show that BAIY are subjected to brutal and dehumanizing bullying, in some cases resulting in hospitalization (Colletti, 2014). In one case, a video from a cell phone showed the horrifying experience of a boy, age 13, "kicked, dragged through the snow and stuffed into a tree, then hung from his jacket on a tall wrought-iron fence" as he screamed for his life while his attackers laughed (Hoye & Hayes, 2011). Another significant research finding about BAIY is their experience of alienation, isolation, exclusion, and unbelonging, which makes them feel disconnected from schools and communities. In a recent study I directed, participants shared how peers avoided them, calling them "skunk" (meaning, they smell). One participant even shared how his teacher told him to move away because he smelled, after he went to complain to her about the bullying he was experiencing. The feeling of alienation, lack of belonging, and harrowing bullying has been documented not only to contribute to or exacerbate the school dropout or pushout of BAIY, but also to subject them to vulnerability and susceptibility to terrorist recruitment and radicalization (Taarnby, 2005; United Nations, n.d.). This is particularly so for Black African immigrant

Muslim youth, some of whom are U.S. citizens. The anti-Black African immigrant microaggressions toward BAIY adversely impact their self-concept/esteem and positive identity construction and academic achievement. In my study with African immigrant parents and families (Ukpokodu, 2018), participants painfully recounted the harrowing experiences their BAIY endured in schools and classrooms, and the impact on both the parents and families.

Curriculum Violence. While microaggressive acts are aspects of pervasive structural inequities and systemic oppressive and racialized conditions embedded within educational systems that negatively impact BAIY's schooling and educational experiences, the most egregious injustice and violence they face and endure is educational violence in its manifestation in the curriculum and classroom pedagogy. Ighodaro and Wiggan (2011) call it *curriculum violence*, and Richard Milner (2020) calls it *curriculum punishment*. Woodson (1933) recognized and referred to this violence as school and classroom "lynching." Such racialized curriculum violence is an intentional or unintentional orchestration or manipulation of curricular experiences and intellectual colonialism that causes academic and psychological harm to students, as they are dehumanized, shamed, excluded, ignored, compromised, and disenfranchised in their classroom learning. Research on African immigrant students shows that BAIY encounter and endure curriculum violence and intellectual colonialism that subject them to psychological stress, shame, and academic disengagement (Harushimana & Awokoya, 2011; Kumi-Yeboah & Smith, 2016; Traoré, 2006) and underachievement (Curry-Stevens & Coalition of Communities of Color, 2013; Traoré, 2006; Ukpokodu, 2013, 2017, 2018). These studies report how BAIY painfully contend with and endure negative depictions of Africa and derogatory portrayals of African communities in school curriculum (i.e., textbooks, films, videos, reports) (Awokoya, 2009; Bennett, 1990; Osunde et al., 1996; Ukpokodu, 1996, 2018). BAIY in U.S. middle and high schools are shamed when their countries of origin or ancestral roots are portrayed as primitive, backward, underdeveloped, savage, and covered with jungles, wild animals, and diseases (Traoré & Lukens, 2006; Ukpokodu, 1996, 2018). Textbooks, especially social studies textbooks, continue to depict Africa as the "Dark Continent" that had no civilization until Europeans "discovered" it. In my study (Ukpokodu, 2018), I described how a parent was in deep pain as he shared about his high school son's anguish because of the curriculum violence he encountered in class. Apparently, his son had watched in class, along with his peers, a video that depicted the "Ebola" virus having traveled in a suitcase from Africa to America, with the lyrics:

La La La La Ebola
La La La La . . . Rucka Rucka Ali
Uh! I tell you where its from
Africa that's . . . Where Ebola . . . Come . . . West side

It hidden in a suitcase. Two days later it lands in U.S.A . . . (YouTube, n.d.)

Teaching with such videos, films, and materials can cause emotional discomfort, learning disengagement, and harm. Understandably, BAIY react negatively to unpalatable and negative depictions and portrayals of Africa and Africans, and their self-esteem and self-worth are affected when what they see is a distortion and unreality of who they are. Curriculum violence to which BAIY are exposed and the emotions it evokes often push them to react, and in some cases to engage in physical ways and create dislike for their teachers and what is being taught. One participant in my study put it this way:

> I always felt angry inside even though I did not show it. You know, students would come up to me after class and say, "Hey, Ahmed, you must be glad you are in America. That is a terrible life in Africa!" I was particularly mad at the teachers who only showed the bad part of Africa. It made the class laugh and think that all of Africa is bad, starving, and suffering! (Ukpokodu, 2017 p. 18)

Although racism often is viewed as a salient violence against the "Other," Nieto (2018) believes that *linguicism* is the most dehumanizing violence against individuals and groups. Across the scholarship on Black African immigrants, BAIY are reported to experience daily acts of linguistic bias and dehumanization as they are humiliated because of their accents. Agyepong (2013) describes a harrowing experience of curricular and pedagogical violence she faced as a student in New York public middle and high schools. She recounts public humiliation she experienced in classes where she was told by her teacher that her accent was "really thick and hard to understand . . . and to go to the board and write what she had said" (p. 162).

A significant form of curriculum violence that BAIY encounter is the absence of curricular materials that positively reflect their experience and those of their ancestors. In teacher education classes, I often assign a project to my preservice teachers that requires them to review social studies textbooks used in schools. My preservice teachers were quick to observe how, while there were multiple chapters and substantive content on other continents, especially Europe, there was only one chapter on Africa and even then it provided skeletal information that was grossly decontextualized. One preservice teacher shared: "I am teaching a unit on Africa next semester. There is only one chapter on Africa in the entire textbook. But more frustrating is that the chapter information is skeletal with distorted photos. This is a disservice to my students." BAIY, exposed to dehumanizing Eurocentric curricula, texts, and images that do not reflect them or their history, or present distortion and misrepresentation, are unmotivated to learn and also become disengaged and at risk for developing critical knowledge, skills, and commitments to become successful citizens. As Goodwin (2010) noted, "When they fail to see themselves in the texts and images they study, . . . when they witness the marginalization of their families and communities, they realize quickly . . . that America's greatness is not meant for them" (p. 3112). BAIY encounter reductionist curricular experiences that short-change them and put them at risk for academic failure and failed citizenship (Banks, 2017), as they are denied access to critical, reflective knowledge, skills, attitudes, and values they need for performing on assessments and becoming contributing members of diasporic communities. In my study with African immigrant youth and families, participants shared how they often were shoved into crowded, remedial classes designed for English language learners and students with special needs, where teachers merely provided them a curriculum consisting of coloring items and drawing. In my social studies course in Fall 2023, one teacher confirmed the lack of knowledge and opportunity to develop civic literacy her African immigrant students often demonstrate in her history or government class. The teacher reflected:

> [As we discussed in class yesterday], immigrant students are often denied access to relevant courses because of justifications that they should be placed in remedial courses instead. This is disheartening to hear. Now I think my African immigrant students I work with might have this. When I ask them if they remember certain concepts from previous history courses, they always shake their heads and say they did not. I now realize that students may have been diverted from such courses, an outcome that I am saddened to know about now.

Most egregious is the practice of putting all African immigrant students in one class regardless of their backgrounds, status, grade level, abilities, and needs, what I call *worksheet curriculum* (Ukpokodu, 2016), which does not prepare students for college, career, and civic life (National Council for the Social Studies, n.d.).

RECKONING WITH ANTI-BLACK AFRICAN IMMIGRANT YOUTH VIOLENCE

The literature is clear: To be BAIY in U.S., or any Western nation's schools is to be the "Other"—less than, stigmatized, homogenized, invisible, and ignored. Counternarratives and stories of Black African immigrants show that anti-Black African immigrant violence in American schools is persistent, pervasive, systemic, and endemic. While there exists the wild claim of African immigrant academic *exceptionalism* and BAIY being heralded as America's new "model minority," the truth is that collectively BAIY are not faring well in society and schools. This is not to suggest that some BAIY are not faring well. On the contrary, there are some who are academically excelling, but they are a statistical minority (Ukpokodu, 2018) who also may suffer personal challenges, including identity crisis and failed citizenship. This begs the question: *How do U.S. society and schools need to reckon with systemic anti-Black African immigrant youth racial and academic violence?* Reckoning means to force society and institutions to pay attention to and raise awareness about injustice and oppressive systems. More important, reckoning requires a demand for truth, truth telling, redress, accountability, and reform for social justice and positive change. The systemic anti-Black African immigrant racial and academic violence deserves to be exposed and accounted for, which requires a holistic approach both societally and institutionally.

Societal Reckoning

The societal curriculum is omnipresent and overpowering, and implicitly and explicitly transmits messages that can educate and miseducate. Undoubtably, and unfortunately, the societal curriculum is the most significant perpetrator that fosters anti-Black African immigrant youth's violence. Dumas and ross (2016) explain that anti-Blackness is a social construction that concerns all Black people. I submit that there would be no racial and academic violence against BAIY if it did not start in society. The societal curriculum, dominated by the media, consistently and relentlessly has portrayed and presented negative images and distorted representations of Africa, Africans, and African immigrants, which spill into schools and the curriculum, contributing to curriculum violence that BAIY encounter. In 2023, some African countries have appeared on the watchlist of "bad" countries to avoid, displayed at some airports in Western nations. Africa often is presented as a continent of disaster, catastrophe, and disease infestation, needing a white savior to rescue it, with depictions focused on wildlife. Recently, Howard W. French, an associate professor at Columbia University's Graduate School of Journalism, in an open letter, called out CBS's *60 Minutes* (Ip, 2015) for the persistent and recurring misrepresentation of Africa in the media; French noted that the approach to covering Africa is threefold: "catastrophe, foreign savior, and wild animals." He reminded people in the letter:

> Africa is urbanizing faster than any other part of the world. We get lots of stories about urbanization in China—and we should. We don't get those stories about urbanization in Africa[;] there is no counter-narrative. And the media can fall into a vicious cycle of perpetuating the same tired stories—tragic disaster, foreign saviors, exotic animals. (n.p.)

Given the pervasive stereotyping and stigmatization of Black Africa, even as it has made and continues to make major contributions to the world and is rapidly modernizing, French's call-out of *60 Minutes* and the media in general is refreshing and should serve as a model to society and institutions as a whole. To reckon with the anti-African Blackness, it is important to debunk the pervasive myths or misconceptions.

Africa Is Not a "Dark Continent." The United States and other Western nations must begin their reckoning by debunking old and pervasive myths and misconceptions that cast Africa, and its societies, communities, and people, as frozen in the dark ages (Covington-Ward, 2017; Ukpokodu, 1996; Watson et al., 2022). Africa is not a country but a giant continent, the second largest, with 54 countries, many of which are rapidly developing. Many African countries have large cities, with all the modern conveniences, mobile technologies, and communication tools found elsewhere in the world. People live in houses and not on top of trees. Ali Mazrui (1986a, 1986b), in his documentary and published works, illuminates and reminds us that Africa is the "cradle of [hu]man" and the birthplace of humanity and cultures. The media must unfreeze its negative image of Africa and move beyond exoticism and essentialization of Africa and its people. Contrary to pervasive misconceptions, Black Africa has had a long history of flourishing civilizations, such as those that existed in Nubia, Zimbabwe, Ghana, Mali, and Songhay, with people of great heroism; giant warriors such as Mansa Musa and Keita Sundiata of the Mali empire; the sheroism of the women of Dahomey (now Peoples Republic of Benin) and the Amazon women; and Queen Amina of Kano, among others. Hollywood has recaptured the valor of these great giants (albeit their stereotypes) in recent movies such as *Black Panther, The Warrior King,* and *Woman King.* The often-silenced contributions of Black Africa to world civilizations must become part of the positive dimensions in the mainstream media. Black African literacies—indigenous knowledges, ontological epistemologies, stories and histories, literature, arts, music, songs, dance, philosophy, mathematics, culture—are positive contributions of Black African people and their forward-looking developments and accomplishments. Africa is home to accomplished men and women such as the late Nelson Mandela (Nobel Peace Prize winner and former president of South Africa), the late Desmond Tutu (Nobel Peace Prize winner and South African Archbishop), the late Wangari Maathai (professor and environmental activist and Nobel Peace Prize winner), the late Kofi Annan (U.N. Secretary General), Wole Soyinka (playwright and Nobel Peace Prize winner), and many others.

More significantly, compared with Western democracies and nation-states, African countries have been forward-looking and forward-leading, as they have elected more women presidents (Watkins, 2021), such as Ellen Johnson Sirleaf, president of Liberia (2006–2018), Slyvie Kiningi, acting president of Burundi (February–October 1993), Ivy Matsepe-Cassaburi, acting president of South Africa (September 2005), Rose Francine Rogombe, interim president of Gabon (June 2009–October 2009), Agnes Monique Ohsan Bellepeau, acting president of Mauritius (March–July 2012 and May–June 2015), Joyce Hilda Banda, president of Malawi (April 2012–May 2014), Catherine Samba, acting president of Central African Republic (January 2014–March 2016), Ameenah Gurib-Fakim, president of Mauritius (June 2015–March 2018), Sahle-Work Zewde, president of Ethiopia (October 2018–present), and Samia Suluhu Hassan, president of Tanzania (March 2021–present).

Africans as well as friends of Africa and global activists must join in the effort to debunk myths, misconceptions, and biases about Africa. Howard French's activism and modeling is a step in the right direction. He called out the media for its bias and discriminatory reporting on Africa and about Africa, while also galvanizing a movement by securing hundreds of signatures of diverse individuals from across professions and organizations—journalists, academics, researchers, artists, domestic and global activists, among others—to stand in solidarity in denouncing biased media practices toward Africa. In 2014, Delta Airlines was called out for depicting an African country as a place of all wildlife animals, when it used a photo of a giraffe to represent Ghana after the country was defeated by Team USA in a World Cup match (Kelland & Sanchez, 2018). Although CBS did not take the expected responsibility for redressing its biased reporting on Africa, Delta Airlines apologized and took down the image from its website. Whether individually or collectively, bias against and discriminatory reporting or characterization of Africa must be called out and perpetrators held accountable.

Institutional Reckoning (P–12 Schools)

U.S. institutions, especially P–12 schools, are complicit and culpable in anti-Black African immigrant practices and violence. P–12 schools are major perpetrators of anti-Black African immigrant violence against BAIY through everyday marginalization and invisibility they encounter and endure. How do U.S. schools need to reckon with anti-Black African immigrant youth racial and curriculum violence?

Erase BAIY Invisibility. The most anti-Black African immigrant violence against BAIY is their invisibility. Schools and educators must recognize, first, that BAIY are not U.S.-born African Americans. As research abundantly has shown, BAIY often are subsumed under the racial category of Black/African American. Educators must become aware of this misconception and the harm it causes. Second, BAIY, even as they may share commonalities as Africans, are not a monolith. BAIY carry different immigration statuses, such as permanent residency, naturalized citizenship, and nonimmigrant visa statuses (F-1 student visa and H-B and

J V temporary working visas). Some are also undocumented. These legal and nonlegal statuses have differing, unequal, and consequential impact on BAIY's abilities to navigate and negotiate transmigrant spaces in schools. For example, BAIY who are naturalized citizens and are permanent residents will have better opportunities, benefits, resources, and relative security than those with legal, nonimmigrant visas and the undocumented, who will have limited or no access to resources and necessities for living a quality and dignified human life (Ukpokodu, 2018). Some BAIY enter U.S. K–12 schools with strong support and readiness for their educational aspirations (Awokoya, 2009; Waters, 1994; Zong & Batalova, 2017). Some may have the literacy skills, self-regulatory skills, and academic readiness to engage in U.S. schools. Involuntary BAIY, on the other hand, who often are refugees and asylees, are less likely to be educated and to have the skills to navigate their new society and the education system. Some also may lack literacy and proficiency in their native language, which limits their readiness to engage effectively in academic activities. Research and reports indicate that some BAIY are unaccompanied minors who lack adequate resources to support their personal development and academic pursuits (Rana, 2011). For example, BAIY who are refugees enter U.S. K–12 schools with deep physical and psychological traumas and academic challenges, caused by the horrors of war (genocide, massacre, rapes, nightmares of watching family members killed or tortured, dislocation and separation of families, and disrupted schooling), that other African immigrant students may not have. This is not to suggest that involuntary BAIY do not thrive and succeed academically. There have been success stories of the Sudanese "lost boys" (*60 Minutes, 2013*) who beat the odds. Further, BAIY who are Muslims are more likely to experience tremendous challenges in navigating and negotiating the U.S. school system and culture, which are plagued by xenophobia, Afrophobia, or Islamophobia. While BAIY in general experience microaggressions from peers and educators, this is intensified for Muslim BAIY, who are targets of harassment, bullying, physical assault, and name-calling (Abu-Ras & Abu-Bader, 2008; Aroian, 2012; Council on American Islamic Relations, 2012).

Disrupt Homogenization of BAIY. BAIY are not a monolith. The common practice of putting BAIY together into one class or course, assuming ethnic similarity and needs, is a disservice that needs to be dismantled. Disrupting this practice will necessitate collecting and disaggregating demographic, performance, and achievement data of each subgroup to accurately identify their unique abilities, needs, and challenges. More important, educators must understand the difference between African Americans and BAIY groups. Not all Black students are U.S. born. African Americans and African immigrants may maintain a shared racial identity but are not historically, culturally, and linguistically homogenous.

Myth of Academic Exceptionalism. The myth that African immigrants are now America's "new model American," and that they are academically exceptional, complicates and compounds BAIY's invisibility and denies them needed services and access to quality and equitable educational opportunities. Ukpokodu (2018) debunked this myth of academic exceptionalism based on lack of statistical evidence to support the claim. Schools and educators must be trained to disrupt this falsehood. Ukpokodu (2018) called for P–12 schools to initiate practices of achievement data disaggregation to shed light on the true academic performance attainment and success of African immigrant children and youth.

Debunk BAIY's Perceived Intellectual and Linguistic Inferiority. What an oxymoron! On one hand, African immigrant students' academic exceptionalism is touted, and simultaneously they are stereotyped as intellectually and linguistically inferior. Such stereotyping leads to engaging with BAIY using a deficit-based pedagogical approach. BAIY are viewed as deficient because they do not speak English or have mainstream literacy skills when they enter U.S. schools, or because they speak English with an accent that educators and U.S.-born peers disdain and scorn. Schools and educators must recognize that BAIY are multilingual and speak different languages and dialects, some with strong English language proficiency, which they spoke prior to their immigration. The erroneous perception is that all BAIY are newcomers. While some BAIY are newcomers, many are U.S. born and 1.5 and 2.0 generationers who have had the American experience, including achieving English language proficiency, even though their physical traits and names often cast them as newcomers.

BAIY Are Not Relics of Tarzan and the "Dark Continent." As previously discussed, BAIY are vulnerable and susceptible to the old and persistent stereotypes of Africa as the "Dark Continent." Consequently, African immigrant students suffer microinsults as they are name-called derogatory epithets. Debunking persistent and pervasive views of BAIY as relics of "dark" Africa is crucial for restoring their humanity. BAIY are full human beings and not a reflection or relics of Tarzan, savagery, and darkness. Like other youth of Generation Z, Generation Alpha BAIY are strong, tenacious, aspirational, intelligent, and resilient, and are braving today's world of immense complexity and unprecedented challenges.

Reckoning and Recommendation

This chapter has demonstrated the existence and effects of the anti-Black African culture and violence perpetuated against Black African immigrant youth in U.S. society and its institutions, and ways they must reckon and take responsibility to redress and change the trajectory of BAIY. In the following recommendations for change, I identify what BAIY need and how to meet those needs. I discuss three main areas of need: visibility, belongingness, and safety; affirmation of their humanity, including quality, equitable, and culturally responsive schooling, education, and curriculum; and critical literacies.

Visibility, Belongingness, and Safety. BAIY want and need to be visible, belong, fit in, and be physically and psychologically safe. They want and need to be heard. As one high school Black African immigrant said in an interview: "I am human. I want to be a part of the school community and the American society. I want to be heard, seen, and included and I want to be safe and free from bullying." BAIY need school environments and classroom spaces that integrate them and accept and appreciate their humanity. Given the pervasive microaggressions, prejudicial harassment, alienation and violence, and adversarial relationship with U.S.-born American peers, including African Americans, that they face in and outside schools and classrooms, schools and educators must be intentional in creating programs that foster intergroup relations and collaborative learning engagement. Elsewhere (Ukpokodu, 2013), I opined about the danger of relegating and dehumanizing African immigrant students' self-esteem due to alienation, isolation, constant harassment, and bullying. Schools and teachers must develop and implement programs that foster healthy intergroup and intragroup relations, and respectful and humanizing relationships and interactions. Students must be taught to cultivate cultural competence—cultural and cross-cultural understanding, sensitivity, compassion, perspective-consciousness, empathy, kindness, collaboration, advocacy, and change agency. Gay (2018) pointedly illuminates this idea:

> If we are to avoid intergroup [intragroup] strife and individuals are to live in the highest quality lives possible, we simply must teach students how to relate better to people from different ethnic, racial, cultural, language, and gender backgrounds. These relational competencies must encompass knowing, valuing, doing, caring, and sharing power, resources, and responsibilities. (p. 21)

Affirmation of Their Humanity. Like all other students and persons, BAIY need affirmation of their humanity. They need schools and classroom environments that respect and affirm their humanity. Ukpokodu (2016), in her work on Ubuntu-oriented education, writes that educators must view students as full humans with souls and dreams and desires for self-actualization. She identifies what she names as the four As of a teacher's love. Among these are affirmation, which is the act of embracing, humanizing, and legitimizing, dignifying, and validating a student's humanity. This involves schools and educators disrupting and erasing the invisibility of BAIY in schools and classrooms. Teachers' development of an affirming attitude begins with the rejection of long-held, pervasive cultural and intellectual views of BAIY. A teacher with an affirming attitude will seek to understand BAIY's complicated identities and recognize structural inequalities and inequities that impact negatively on their schooling and learning, and act to disrupt them. Affirming BAIY's humanity must involve accepting and respecting their cultural identities, including their language identities (see *Framework for Educating African Immigrant Youth*, Chapter 1). Research indicates that African immigrant students experience inappropriate grade placement due to their perceived language deficiency (Campbell, 1996; Ukpokodu, 2013). This constitutes inequity and injustice. Students should be tested both in English and in their home languages to ensure appropriate grade-level placement. Using culturally familiar materials such as African story books and scaffolding instructional activities will improve their cognitive and linguistic skills, and support effective learning and performance.

Critical Literacies. More than anything, BAIY need quality and equitable education that empowers them to deal critically and creatively with their present reality and learn how to participate in the transformation of their world (Freire, 1970; United Nations' Universal Declaration of Human Rights, 1948). As a minoritized immigrant group, BAIY need to cultivate critical literacy, defined here as knowledge, skills, commitments, and agency, to become empowered, productive, and contributing citizens for themselves, their families, local and national communities, and the world. Often, literacy is understood as mere reading and decoding what is read. But literacy is the construction of multiple discourses (Gee, 1991) and a foundation for acquiring power, privilege, and identity. More deeply, it relates to one's knowledge, history, thinking, speaking, acting, and conducting in any given space or context, and assisting students to connect to their cultural identities. Simply, BAIY need the cultural literacy—social and cultural capital—and cultural competency and literacies to read the word and the world (Freire, 1978). Banks (2017) writes that immigrants who experience successful citizenship possess critical and reflective civic knowledge, skills, attitudes, values, and agency, while those who experience failed citizenship lack such tools. When BAIY are put in classes or courses designed for remediation (Ukpokodu, 2018), they are denied opportunities for cultivating critical and civic literacy they need as future citizens and leaders. It is ironic that immigrant children and youth who need more, often get less. A significant component of quality and equitable education is a *culturally responsive curriculum*. Adrienne Rich (1994) once wrote:

> When those who have the power to name and to socially construct reality choose not to see you or hear you, whether you are dark-skinned, old, disabled, female, or speak with a different accent or dialect than theirs, when someone with the authority of a teacher, say, describes the world and you are not in it, there is a moment of psychic disequilibrium. (p. 199)

BAIY need curricular experiences culturally responsive to them. Immigrant parents and families have pleaded for curricular experiences respectful and responsive to their children (Ghong et al., 2007; Ukpokodu, 2013, 2018). They need curricular experiences that humanize them and inspire their imagination. Therefore, teachers must create and use balanced and stereotype-free instructional content and materials. Teachers must become intentional and systematic in examining and evaluating instructional materials, especially films and videos used in teaching about Africa, to eliminate stereotypes or negative images that shame and dehumanize BAIY. They should examine instructional resources and materials for *linguistic bias* (content and words describing and disparaging Africa, Africans, and their communities as uncivilized, backward, disease-stricken, poverty-stricken, and inferior), *stereotypes* (portrayals of Africa and Africans in derogatory, inaccurate, and less than or subhuman, inhospitable places—as name-called "shithole" by former U.S. President Donald Trump), *invisibility* (absence of Black Africans in human and world history or categorized in subservient positions), *imbalance* and *unreality* (distortion, misrepresentation, and misinterpretation of events about Africa and its people, such as Africans' lack of civilization and education until the arrival of Europeans as their savior), and *fragmentation* (disconnecting events about Africa and Africans from mainstream history, for example, excluding Africans' participation in major events such as the world wars in which Africans fought as foot soldiers and other capacities, given that the war also was fought in imperial colonies in Africa). When I ask my preservice teachers and teachers in my social studies classes about the role Africans played in world wars, they often draw a blank. Some are even surprised by the question—Africans participated in world wars! Additionally, teachers should engage classes in deconstructing negative and biased content and images found in instructional materials and curriculum. Ukpokodu (2018) writes that images harbored by teachers and students that depict Africa as a backward and "dark" continent, a jungle and a place with starving and emaciated, skeleton-like people, as a disease-ridden place rife with "Ebola" children, must be interrogated, discountenanced, and discontinued. An African immigrant community in Multnomah County in Portland, OR, made this plea:

> Our children need to enter schools where teachers understand their culture and the conditions of their arrival in the USA. All teachers who engage with our children need to understand the history, the challenges and the conditions in which our children encounter their world. Understanding will provide an important link to reducing the invisibility and vulnerability of our children. (Curry-Stevens & Coalition of Communities of Color, 2013, p. 9)

Teachers need training in culturally responsive teaching to assist them in systematically, deliberately, and intentionally integrating African perspectives into curriculum. At the middle and high school levels, and regardless of subject matter, teachers actively and regularly should integrate African perspectives into topics. Unbeknownst to many, Africa has produced leading historians, playwrights, artists, and scientists who have contributed to the stock of human knowledge. African Indigenous Knowledge systems and epistemologies present opportunities for integrating African perspectives into the curricular experiences of BAIY that can boost their self-esteem as well as help peers and teachers to have an alternative and positive view of Africa and African people. Examples, which might be used in English, history, or literature classes, are books by Africa's leading historians and playwrights, such as the late renowned Chinua Achebe who wrote *Things Fall Apart* (1959), depicting the precolonial indigenous cultural life of the Nigerian-Igbo society and the invasion of Europeans; or Ngugi wa Thiong'o, often described as one of the greatest writers in history, and author of *A Grain of Wheat* (1967), which engaged the topics of colonialism, heroism, and a people's struggle for liberation and independence from colonialism through tactics of guerilla warfare known as the Mau Mau Rebellion in East Africa. For 3 decades, I have encountered social science and English language preservice and classroom teachers who have never heard of this book. Yet the school subject standards include themes such as colonialism, imperialism, and revolution, among others. We regularly see promotion of resources for teaching about Latin America, Central America, and Asia, but rarely publications of resources for teaching about Africa. Scholars of Black African immigrant education need to engage in collective activism and galvanize a movement and campaign against the invisibility of Africa, African people, and BAIY. A strong and focused commitment to producing and promoting teaching about Africa and its people, including dispelling and debunking persistent myths, misconceptions and stereotypes, and images, is imperative. There is a need for counternarratives about Africa. This can be disseminated through special issues in prominent national and international journals.

Need for Caring and Conscientious Teachers. Within the past 2 decades, much research has focused on preparing teachers and other educators for culturally responsive practices. Often this means teachers are prepared to work with ethnically diverse urban students—African Americans and Latino Americans—but less prepared to work with "sub-ethnic" populations such as African immigrant students. Teachers and counselors need accurate knowledge about African immigrant youth to address their needs and use relevant pedagogy, instructional materials, and cross-cultural interactions. BAIY need an Ubuntu-oriented education, particularly Ubuntu pedagogy, which humanizes them. "Ubuntu pedagogy is premised on the humanistic principle that students have the innate desire to be curious and to learn naturally when their humanity and dignity are valued and affirmed, and when they have the freedom and space to engage their curiosity, imagination, and intelligence (Ukpokodu, 2016). Teachers and educators must cultivate the ethic of care and extend teaching love to BAIY, who come from families and communities with strong communal orientation and close-knit relationships.

CONCLUSION

Black African immigrant youth are an integral part of the growing population in Western democracies and around the world. In any given nation-state, they will be the future leaders and citizens shaping their nations and the world. Research shows that African immigrants increasingly are entering U.S. societies (Lorenzi & Batalova, 2022; Pew Research Center, 2022). This implies that U.S. society and its institutions must reckon with anti-Black Africanness and commit to accepting BAIY, affirming their humanity, and providing access to quality and equitable education that fosters their critical literacies and agency to achieve successful and effective critical citizenship. They must cultivate (1) cultural literacy that fosters BAIY's cultural wealth, cultural intelligence, and competency; intercultural intelligence and competency; and emotional intelligence and competency; (2) racial literacies that foster development of strong racial and cultural identities and agency to fight for their humanity; (3) historical literacy that supports their development of historical knowledge and political intelligence, and social and moral issues of their diasporic communities; and (4) civic literacy that supports their development of responsible citizenship—and being informed and committed to fundamental values for living in America's multicultural democracy. Otherwise, shortchanging Black African immigrant youth is shortchanging America and the world. Therefore, as an educator in U.S. schools, I ask that you ponder the following questions.

TAKEAWAY QUESTIONS

1. How have I examined, reflected on, and analyzed my knowledge, assumptions, stereotypes, and biases about Black African immigrant youth? What did I know before and what do I now know that will transform my engagement with Black African immigrant youth?
2. How do I disrupt the anti-Blackness culture in the space I work in and my classroom to ensure the humanity and dignity of Black African immigrant youth?
3. As an educator, how do I counter the anti-Black African immigrant violence in my curriculum and pedagogy?

4. How do I take responsibility for promoting and fostering Black African immigrant literacies for responsible and successful citizenship?
5. How has this chapter helped me cultivate critical knowledge, skills, and dispositions for reckoning with anti-Black African racial and social injustice?
6. What has been challenging about this chapter and why?

CHAPTER 3

Africanfuturism and Critical Mathematics Education
Envisioning a Liberatory Future for Sub-Saharan African Immigrants

Oyemolade (Molade) Osibodu and Nyimasata Damba Danjo

In Nnedi Okorafor's Africanfuturist novella *Binti*,[1] we encounter a 16-year-old girl named Binti seeking to advance her study of mathematics at the prestigious Oomza University, located on a distant planet. In *Binti*, there were clear indications that Binti was dark-skinned from a country in Sub-Saharan Africa. While on the ship headed to Oomza University, she was treated differently because of her country of origin and the clay substance called *Otjize* that she applied to her skin and hair. Binti lamented, "I felt like an outsider, I was outside" (Okorafor, 2015, p. 21). We view Binti as a Sub-Saharan African (SSA) immigrant who faced challenges similar to and different from those we faced. Despite challenges she faced being *outside*, Binti's mathematics was depicted as harmonious and fit with her people's ways of knowing. For instance, Binti's hair was braided in mathematical patterns that told the history of her people.

BEING HERE AND THERE: ARE WE SSA IMMIGRANTS, INTERNATIONAL STUDENTS, OR BOTH?

Black immigrants in the United States have come largely from the Caribbean, and more recently from Africa. Yet a dearth of research examines experiences of Sub-Saharan African youth in the context of mathematics education. We begin by grappling with whether we would be considered international

---

1. We use *Binti* when discussing the novella and Binti when discussing the protagonist in the novella.

44 Schooling and Classroom Perspectives and Contexts

students or immigrants. Making the distinction perhaps is rhetorically less relevant to Sub-Saharan African communities in the United States, as both groups tend to be treated similarly, yet the distinction importantly extends our lived experiences. Living life as an immigrant—inclusive of being an international student—is complex as you feel both here and there simultaneously. Although Molade has relocated to Canada, she held a student visa (F1) for the 13 years she spent living in the United States. Nyima also relocated to the United States as an international student and remains one while she pursues her doctoral degree. In our conversations as we drafted this chapter, we spent time in conversation and reflection on this topic.

> *Nyima:* I think this identity changes according to time and
> circumstances surrounding one's career goals. I was given the
> international student identity from the visa interview stage and
> came here with that in mind and never to change it, because I
> was just coming to study and going back to develop where I came
> from. However, the international student identity is not a full
> package identity that allows students or African youths like me
> to swim freely in search of that knowledge and freedom which
> was their anchor in coming here in the first place. For instance,
> as a STEM major in a top U.S. research university like Michigan
> State University, I could not take advantage of so many summer
> research opportunities and internships which many other students
> had access to just because I was an international student. Why was
> it impossible for me to have the same enrichments during a whole
> 4-year study period of my life? This and many other realities as
> an international student, make me want to earn an immigrant
> status, to have a full experience in my career aspirations. So do I
> identify as an immigrant; I'll say yes, in progress, because that's
> my intention in the short term.
>
> *Molade:* When I first moved to the United States, I considered myself
> an international student because it made sense. I was new to
> the United States, I planned to return to Nigeria, and felt more
> Nigerian than anything else. I was also practically on an F1 visa
> which is a nonimmigrant visa. Although I remained on a student
> visa in the subsequent 13 years that followed (with a 5-year
> break when I lived and worked in South Africa), I felt as though
> I was becoming more of an immigrant despite what the stamp
> in my visa reflected. First, my tax filing changed because after
> several years in the United States you are considered a resident
> for tax purposes. Furthermore, after having lived in the United
> States since I was 16 years old, it felt like home. I understood

the culture, I learned to drive there, I opened my first bank account there, I got my first job there—essentially, many "firsts" happened for me there. While I knew my stay was temporary, I felt like I lived in the in-between of identifying as an immigrant and an international student.

As Nyima put it, living life as an immigrant is akin to feeling like "*home is still not quite here*—it is still *there*"—a sentiment Binti grappled with frequently. One reason for this perpetual liminal existence is constant reminders that you do not fully belong in the "here" (Amonyeze, 2017; Bhattacharya, 2018). Nyima shared: "This place [the United States] may never fully become home. It may just be like a passing time for you to get to whatever destination you are trying to look for and get back to where you are known and seen." There is an exhaustion that comes from constantly being Othered and correcting others about disinformation being shared about Africa. Essentially, you are in constant refusal of the distorted "education" that "flattens" the diversity of experiences of African stories (Adichie, 2009). Bhattacharya (2018) elucidates this feeling succinctly, stating, "She is constantly reminded of her Otherness in the new country because she is not really 'from here'; her belongingness is always suspect" (p. 11).

WHOSE MATHEMATICS (LITERACIES) COUNT IN U.S. EDUCATION?

Literacy scholars have shifted from viewing literacy as focused strictly on reading and writing in the dominant language(s) of one's community. Such a shifted view involves broadened embodied practices enacted, for example, by historically marginalized people (Omogun & Skerrett, 2021; Watson & Knight-Manuel, 2020). Similarly, we view mathematics literacies as a "tool for liberation" (Moses & Cobb, 2002, p. 12). This view extends Frankenstein's (2010) conceptualizing of critical mathematics education (CME) as using "mathematical ideas in struggles to make the world better" (p. 248). Essentially, we do not view mathematics as a neutral subject, given interpersonal and structural biases that organize mathematics, such as the enrollment in specific mathematics courses, content embedded in mathematics curriculum, and teaching and learning of mathematics. Together, these factors perpetuate and maintain mathematics as a gatekeeping subject (Martin et al., 2010).

In Osibodu and Cosby (2018), I (Molade) wrote about my cousins, held back a grade when they emigrated to the United States from Nigeria over 2 decades ago because teachers and school administrators did not believe they could perform adequately at grade level. This confounded me then as it does now because this decision was not made because my cousins had failed an entrance test or were unable to cope with the demands of school. This decision was made arbitrarily. Both authors experienced similar enrollment challenges in mathematics courses in our first semester as international students at two different U.S. institutions, in different parts of the United States, over a decade apart.

Molade began her university studies in 2002 in the U.S. South, while Nyima began university studies in the Midwest in 2017. Despite the 15-year gap, we experienced similar distrust in our mathematical abilities. Molade, for instance, was advised by admissions officials to enroll in College Algebra, a course not required for her electrical engineering major. However, Molade was able to advocate for herself in her persistent request to be placed in Calculus 1. Unfortunately, Nyima did not experience the same when placed in a non-credit-bearing (NCBR) mathematics course despite being accepted into the neuroscience program. Scholars have documented the disproportionate number of Black students funneled into such NCBR courses (Attewell et al., 2006; Larnell, 2016). Nyima was placed in courses far below her level in her first semester, causing a ripple effect as she had to take multiple courses over subsequent summers to ensure she graduated in 4 years. In our conversation, we wondered about the distrust in the West African Senior School Certificate Examination (WASSCE) certification we both obtained in our respective countries, referencing the standardized exam taken by final-year secondary school students across Anglophone West Africa to confirm completion of their secondary education. Although we are both wary of external assessments, the WASSCE exam is presented as a more accurate representation of one's abilities in a course than the SAT exam, which has been documented to be problematic (Dixon-Román et al., 2013).

Nyima indicated that her WASSCE mathematics score was good: "I don't know what else was needed to *prove* that I am still okay to qualify for college-level mathematics." Nyima at first believed that she and peers were placed into a year-long NCBR mathematics course because they did not submit an SAT mathematics score. Furthermore, scholars have documented the disproportionate number of Black students funneled into these courses (Attewell et al., 2006; Larnell, 2016). Yet, at Nyima's institution, SAT scores were not required for admission. Moreover, one of Nyima's friends from West Africa provided an SAT score in mathematics but still was required to take the non-credit-bearing course.

Nyima also was told by university admissions authorities to take multiple prerequisites before taking required courses because they were simpler and at *her level*. This resulted in her feeling quite unhappy in her first semester and across the year in university because she was not allowed to take courses pertaining to her major; Nyima felt as though she had no agency in choosing her courses. In a study on postsecondary education experiences of African immigrants in Canada, Shizha and colleagues (2020) found that African immigrants tended to be placed in lower tracks in secondary courses based on race and language, and also because of their country of origin. Based on literature around placements of African immigrants in lower courses and prevalence of African Americans in non-credit-bearing mathematics courses (Larnell, 2016; Shizha et al., 2020), our experiences tell us this Othering is not just anti-African, but particularly anti-Black African.

Molade and Nyima come from countries whose official language is English due to the legacy of British colonization. Yet, university admissions in the United States largely require additional proof of English proficiency. While this entrance requirement did not pose a barrier for Molade, Nyima could not afford the Test of English as a Foreign Language exam fee, causing her to delay her admission by a year despite completing the interview for a prestigious scholarship in English. Moreover, when Molade began doctoral studies in 2015, she was still required to take an additional English test to prove her English proficiency despite previously having obtained two university degrees in the United States. These examples underscore that the one-size-fits-all approach in U.S. higher education has material implications across the interplay of multiple mathematics and literacies engagements and outcomes.

READING *BINTI* THROUGH AN AFRICANFUTURIST LENS

While some might argue that Nigerian American author Dr. Nnedi Okorafor's (2019) writing fits within Afrofuturism, she insists there are nuanced differences between Afrofuturism and Africanfuturism. In a blog post, she shared:

> Africanfuturism is similar to "Afrofuturism" in the way that blacks on the continent and in the Black Diaspora are all connected by blood, spirit, history and future. The difference is that Africanfuturism is specifically and more directly rooted in African culture, history, mythology and point-of-view as it then branches into the Black Diaspora, and it does not privilege or center the West. Africanfuturism is concerned with visions of the future, is interested in technology, leaves the earth, skews optimistic, is centered on and predominantly written by people of African descent (black people) and it is rooted first and foremost in Africa. It's less concerned with "what could have been" and more concerned with "what is and can/will be." It acknowledges, grapples with and carries "what has been."

We thus document Binti's immigrant journey, showing the ways Africanfuturism allowed her mathematics to be a space for healing, harmony, history, and a connection to homeland.

BINTI'S IMMIGRANT JOURNEY: MATHEMATICS AS HARMONY

Binti is about a 16-year-old girl from the Himba peoples, first of her people to gain admission into prestigious Oomza University, far away from home on a distant planet. Nyima's words echo Binti's words, as Binti was described as a dark-skinned immigrant/international student surrounded by mostly the Khoush, a group that discriminated against Himba people, who "looked untouched by the sun," or as Binti stated, those who "looked as if the sun was his or her enemy" (Okorafor, 2015, p. 19). Binti was the only member of the Himba people on the shuttle to Oomza, causing her to feel even more alone. While she was able to build positive relationships with others, she felt the tug of being so far from home. Binti remarked poignantly, "Our ancestral land is life; move away from it and you diminish" (p. 21). More powerfully, she later said, "When I left my home, I died" (p. 75). Binti is indicating that when you emigrate from your homeland, a symbolic death occurs that cannot be ignored. Thus, to alleviate this diminishing, to remain grounded, you hold on to elements of your homeland.

On the 18th day on the shuttle, tentacular beings from another planet, the *Meduse*, attacked the shuttle, killing everyone on board except Binti. Binti was saved because she was holding her *Edan,* an ancient piece of technology she found in her desert homeland 8 years prior. The *Edan*, which had been dormant, became activated upon interaction with the *Meduse* and was the medium through which Binti could communicate with and be protected from the alien-like beings. Binti brought the *Edan* on the ship because it was a connection to her home, and doing so proved to be a wise decision. In the *Edan*, we can deduce mathematical and scientific prowess of the Himba people despite being labeled as *tribal*—a term intended to have derogatory connotations. Binti shared that *tribal* is "what they called humans from ethnic groups too remote and 'uncivilized' to regularly send students to attend Oomza Uni" (p. 93).

A throughline in *Binti* showed how mathematics connected Binti to her home, her history, and harmony. For instance, Binti's hair, braided in "tessallating triangles," told the history of her people (p. 31). Here, we see illustrative connections between mathematics and homeland. Moreover, references to the braided pattern of Binti's hair are a nod to how African Indigenous Knowledges show mathematical depth in ways not valued in Western contexts (Fasheh, 2015). Mathematics in Binti's world is deeply rooted in connections to her home, yet for SSA immigrants like us, access to appropriate mathematics courses and valuing of our prior mathematics knowledges when we emigrated, were difficult and wrought with friction.

Okorafor, with her Africanfuturist framing, was intentional in showing that Binti's mathematical knowledge was recognized and valued. Binti's mathematics showed family connections, as she was born with her mother's mathematical abilities and received oral knowledge passed on from her father. The combination of these made her a "master harmonizer" (Okorafor, 2015, p. 37). Contrary to ways in which mathematics is treated as expressionless, an Africanfuturistic treatment of mathematics as evidenced in *Binti* is mesmerizing, filled with emotion, and used for protection. Binti stated, "When I'd sit in the desert, alone, listening to the wind, I would see and feel numbers the way I did when I was deep in my work in my father's shop. And those numbers added up to the sum of my destiny" (p. 39). We see here that mathematics was a space of comfort connecting Binti to home. Binti's mathematics allowed her to escape her current moment through "treeing." Binti shared:

> We sat in my room . . . and challenged each other to look out at the stars and imagine the most complex equation and then split it in half and then in half again and again. When you do math fractals long enough, you kick yourself into treeing just enough to get lost in the shallows of the mathematical sea. None of us would have made it into the university if we couldn't tree, but it's not easy. We were the best and we pushed each other to get closer to "God." (p. 30)

In this examination of mathematics, Binti literally got *lost* in mathematics exploration to the extent that it felt spiritual. We also are attentive to Okorafor's naming this trance "treeing." Trees are sacred in many SSA communities, seen as a place of gathering, a respite from heat, and a space for cultivating community (Maswabi, 2016). Further underscoring the mathematical proficiency of Binti and her people, they took great pride in their indigenous practices. We learn that Binti rubbed her hair and skin with *Otjize*, made from "a mix of red clay from our land and oils from our local flowers" (Okorafor, 2015, p. 85). Aside from her grounding in the *Otjize*, Binti, while under attack by the *Meduse*, repeatedly proclaimed, "I am Binti Ekeopara Zuzu Dambu Kaipka of Namib" (p. 40) to remind herself of who she was and where she came from (Burger, 2020).

CRITICAL MATHEMATICS EDUCATION: REFLECTIONS FROM A COLLABORATIVE PROJECT

In defining critical mathematics education, Gutstein (2016) noted that "although multiple interpretations exist for these terms, U.S. educators mainly refer to 'mathematics for social justice,' and those in other countries refer to 'critical mathematics,' often with roughly the same meaning" (p. 455). Common across these contexts is the purposeful role of CME in research, teaching, and teacher education in proffering possibilities of mathematics as a tool toward social change (Osibodu, 2021). We understand CME to mean scholarship engaging people, particularly youth, in considering ways to use mathematics to understand and address social (in)justices, often beyond the classroom.

In a prior collaborative endeavor with four SSA immigrant youth in Spring 2019, we investigated the ways mathematics is embedded in traditional African practices. We examined the mathematics involved in the development of traditional boats in The Gambia, as these boats tend to be built by people without the types of formal education upheld as valued in society. We found that these practices tended to be absent from formal school mathematics curriculum. After a series of insightful conversations, we decided to examine CME through a public health lens. We were interested in disrupting the presumption that manufactured (Western) medicine is de facto superior to traditional (local) medicines in Sub-Saharan Africa. We note that the meaning of science in mathematics teaching, teacher education, and research tends to be skewed toward Western epistemologies, failing to capture African spiritualities and practices.

We surveyed a small sample of African youth who indicated their preference for manufactured medicine, given the "precision" of dosages embedded within its development. Yet this *precision* does not account for important roles of mathematical intuition embedded in African Indigenous Knowledges, which emphasize "relational knowing, intuition-reasoning and empathy" (Greene, 2019, p. 95) that have been labeled "myths, superstitions, and non-science" (Boutte et al., 2019, p. 15). We pause here to acknowledge that we were both trained in the sciences and are not anti-science. On the contrary, we are both pro-science *and* pro-African ways of knowing.

At the end of our conversation with SSA immigrant youth, we considered the notion of two different types of mathematics, not placing them in a hierarchical structure, but simply acknowledging them as different. One of the youths, Njo,[2] shared:

> So, but there is nothing like *my math* in that like they [traditional doctors] will not tell me it's this concentration that will cause that to you, but they will tell you if you take more than two spoons of this, it can cause this to you. So that is their own [traditional doctors'] maths. So like the difference in the math is what I'm looking at like how do we put that in today's discussion. I think that is something that we can try to disrupt like they [traditional doctors] have their own maths and pharmaceuticals have their own math but are these maths different? Like they are all looking for the same thing so that you who is taking the medicine knows that is the correct amount for everybody. I think they all have the same ultimate goal but me and every other person right now wants the calibrated mathematics like the figured things, the units and everything.

---

2. All names used from this project are pseudonyms.

Africanfuturism and Critical Mathematics Education

In Njo's statement, we observe connections with Binti's experiences. Specifically, while Binti is a mathematics prodigy, the mixture of the *Otjize*, which we later learned held medicinal characteristics as it healed burnt tentacles of the *Meduse*, was not detailed. When Binti discusses mixing the *Otjize*, she makes no mention of precise measurements. We are told simply of a "a mix of red clay from our land and oils from our local flowers" (Okorafor, 2015, p. 85). Later, after the *Meduse* claimed the remaining *Otjize* Binti brought with her from home, Binti used her intuition to make a mix using unfamiliar ingredients as she took residence at Oomza University. As we have spoken in great detail of Binti's mathematical prowess and the way the *Edan*, her technological tool that transmitted mathematical signals, saved her from death and aided communication with the *Meduse*, Binti insisted that it was her *Otjize* that saved her. This honoring of the red clay from her people, which cannot be explained with precise mathematical measurements, is a necessary and important Africanfuturist framing.

Returning to our collaborative project, similar to Binti's Africanfuturist framing, we discussed additional practices that could not be quantified. For example, Njo shared about the Neem tree, which has multiple medicinal properties such as healing headaches, stomachaches, and toothaches, and treating chicken pox. Another youth, Mendrika, talked about a practice in the farming community in which she was raised. After sowing beans, farmers take a few seconds to sit on the land before leaving; failing to do so, they believed, would cause a meager harvest. Our conversation veered into traditional practices, like Mendrika's, that may seem illogical as to why they produce intended results. Njo considered, "To enumerate it is the question. Like how do you put a number to that?" Thus, we argue that intuition and feeling once more remain important components of African Indigenous Knowledges.

Similar to sentiments expressed among youth, connecting mathematics to social issues means quantifying mathematics in some manner. Intuitive knowledges usually come from traditions often passed down orally; while these oral traditions might not be readily present and valued in Western-centric science, they are still valid in African Indigenous Knowledges (A. A. Abdi, 2002; Avoseh, 2000, 2011; Boutte et al., 2019; Greene, 2019). Mendrika synthesized our thoughts perfectly: "Let's say from outside you may feel like that doesn't make sense at all but actually it does work and that is very interesting." Njo further added that Western religion impacted African Indigenous Knowledges during colonization, a sentiment acknowledged by scholars as well (Mignolo, 2007; Ohuche, 1978; Wynter, 2003). Trevor Noah, in his memoir *Born a Crime* (2016), put this accurately, stating, "If you're African and you pray to your ancestors, you're a primitive" (p. 6).

In our learnings with *Binti*, we acknowledge great value in practices that connect one to the land, to the very soil of one's homeland. As Burger (2020) summarizes:

52 Schooling and Classroom Perspectives and Contexts

> Okorafor uses her science fiction novellas to foreground "real," i.e., histori-
> cally verifiable, African traditions like mathematical braiding techniques and
> more abstract mathematical thought, while subtly praising African educational
> systems as better or at least equal to Western ones, highlighting for example the
> reliability and scientific viability of "oral knowledge" (Okorafor, 2015, p. 37).
> (p. 374)

An Africanfuturist exploration sees value both in the type of mathematics that brings harmony and heals, alongside African Indigenous Knowledges that connect SSA immigrants to their homeland. In other words, we can show our mathematical brilliance, obscured by the Western system of hierarchizing mathematical prowess for both Molade and Nyima, while also allowing space for us to hold on to aspects of our culture that keep us grounded.

THINKING WITH AFRICANFUTURISM: TOWARD A LIBERATORY FUTURE FOR SUB-SAHARAN AFRICAN IMMIGRANTS

Mathematics has always been treated as a subject relegated to the elite—particularly in racialized countries such as the United States. Joseph (1987) said it best: "There is a tendency to perceive mathematical pursuits as confined to an elite, a select few who possess the requisite qualities or gifts denied to the vast majority of humanity" (p. 22).

Africanfuturism demands that we center African culture, African history, and more broadly, African Indigenous Knowledges. Moreover, Africanfuturism allows us to consider a new vision of the future without feeling confined to current realities. This is perfectly embodied in Binti's experience as we see a young girl whose vision of mathematics is contrary to the way mathematics is denied to Sub-Saharan African immigrants. Binti, an immigrant herself on a new planet, drew on mathematics while holding onto many aspects of her home and culture. We drew on the collaborative research project to elevate African Indigenous Knowledges within the context of mathematics to highlight the rich and unexplored mathematical heritage that exists in communities—particularly outside of the West (Fasheh, 2015).

Our chapter connects to two approaches in the *Framework for Educating African Immigrant Youth* (see Figure 1.1 in Chapter 1). The first is *emboldening tellings of diaspora narratives* in our attempt to tell a different diasporic narrative and to show an important way of "humanizing the Black African immigrant body" in mathematics education (Watson & Knight-Manuel, 2020). Furthermore, we are rooted in *affirming cultural, heritage, and embodied knowledges, languages, and practices* through emphasizing the "heterogeneity of Blackness" to affirm the diversity of mathematics literacies inherent in different Black communities to include those of us from Sub-Saharan Africa. An important implication of our chapter is to shed light on discriminatory practices that occur when SSA immigrants attempt to enroll in mathematics courses at both the secondary and postsecondary levels. We hope that through Binti's story, and our own, we have argued sufficiently for the strength and richness in mathematics that SSA immigrants bring with them from their homes. We encourage pre-K–20 mathematics educators to advocate for the Black SSA students they are privileged to teach by helping to place them in the appropriate mathematics courses. We also ask that educators open up space for multiple ways of knowing in mathematics in authentic ways that do not make SSA students feel essentialized and Othered. We envision a mathematical future for SSA immigrants that connects them to their homelands, that heals, and that brings harmony and not dissent.

TAKEAWAY QUESTIONS

1. Our chapter presents different conceptions of mathematics literacies. How do you define mathematics literacies?
2. Our chapter captures real experiences of two African immigrant students in two spatially distinct U.S. universities. How can you better understand and assess mathematics literacies of African immigrant students beyond traditional examination structures?
3. How can you center African immigrants' multiple mathematics literacies in your teaching practices?
4. In this chapter, we drew on a young adult novel to ground our conceptions of mathematics literacies. In what ways can you consider multidisciplinary approaches to mathematics literacies (traditional and nontraditional ways) to bring about harmony for African immigrant youth?

CHAPTER 4

African Lives Matter Too
Affirming African Heritage Students' Experience in the History Classroom

Irteza Anwara Mohyuddin

Kabeera, a second-generation Guinean American student at Honors Academy, a charter school in Southwest Philadelphia, navigated a central question about which understandings of racial spacemaking are considered relevant during a discussion around current events, including Black Lives Matter, in her African American History (AAH) class. On occasion, students have the power to reshape dominant historical classroom discourses, particularly if the teacher is receptive to incorporating alternative narratives within the classroom curriculum (Bredell, 2013; Sanders, 2009). In the case of this AAH class, however, student voice was minimized. The teacher, Mr. Daro, rejected Kabeera's perspective—despite his overall ability to enhance classroom discussion by incorporating many student voices—because he considered Kabeera's point to be deviating from the class discussion. By doing so, Mr. Daro troubles the vision of the AAH class as a positive, affirming Black space for all Black students (Coles & Kingsley, 2021), and limits the forms of racial spacemaking permissible within the classroom. I argue that an African American History class sometimes can serve as a hegemonic space, even as the AAH curriculum historically serves to counter hegemonic, white-centered historical narratives. Even counterhegemonic spaces have dominant discourses that: (1) emphasize narrow racial ideologies and (2) center narrow framings of U.S.-centric Black identity to the exclusion of more African diasporic understandings of Blackness (Allen et al., 2012; Imoagene, 2015; Traoré & Lukens, 2006; Ukpokodu, 1996, 2018). This chapter underscores the heterogeneity of Black student experiences and the varying degrees to which their cultural heritage is recognized within the classroom space (see *Framework for Educating African Immigrant Youth*, Chapter 1).

A WEST AFRICAN NEIGHBORHOOD IN SOUTHWEST PHILADELPHIA

By some estimates, from 2000–2012, the estimated African population tripled in Southwest Philadelphia (Matza & Duchneskien, 2013). Many Sierra Leoneans, Liberians, and Ethiopians reside in Southwest Philadelphia, a section of the city known for at least three African mosques (Hauslohner, 2017). Woodland Avenue serves as the epicenter of the neighborhood known as "Little Africa," with shops, businesses, mosques, and churches lining the streets.

Little Africa is the world that many of my West African students inhabited. The majority of students, 25 of 30, were second-generation, American-born descendants of African immigrant parents from West Africa. While students' parents identified as West African immigrants, most notably by identifying with their country of origin, my focal students at Honors Academy self-identified within the pan-African identity and were proud of having been born in the United States. The majority of African students in the school were of West African origin, from countries such as Guinea, Mali, Côte d'Ivoire, Senegal, and Niger. Their school was a reflection of their neighborhood's demographic composition, an extension of their cultural world.

The feeling of neighborhood familiarity entered the hallways of Honors Academy, located a few blocks from the epicenter of Little Africa. Ms. Westing, a history teacher, for example, observed: "I think these kids are a lot more confident, though, in their culture and in their Blackness than the immigrant students I had in New York . . . here, in Southwest Philly, it's an African city" (interview, April 6, 2020). In addition to African youth, Honors Academy also hosted a significant number of African American and Caribbean youth. Although the school did not collect ethnic data, many teachers estimated that at least a quarter, if not a third, of the student body was composed of children of recently migrated West African parents (second-generation West African youth) and recently migrated youth from West Africa (first-generation West African youth).

AFRICAN AMERICAN HISTORY CLASSROOM

Given the diverse range of Black youth identities represented within the student body of Honors Academy, with West African, African American, and Caribbean students who identified with their communities of origin, the African American History classroom in 9th grade intentionally was designed to promote Black pride. It was part of a longer tradition of Philadelphia's Black residents advocating for teaching Black history within schools. The movement for implementing AAH courses in the Philadelphia public schools emerged from 1967 protests by Black students and community members advocating for, among other demands, Black history courses taught by Black teachers (Bredell, 2013; Sanders, 2009). While a concession by white-controlled city leaders led to limited adoption of an AAH course, only in 2005 did the course become a graduation requirement for all Philadelphia high schoolers (Countryman, 2007). In 2020, critics noted that the course still failed to connect Black history to issues of race and racism today, and advocated for a more critical approach to teaching AAH (R. Toliver, 2014).

The AAH classroom for 9th-grade students in Honors Academy served as a counterhegemonic space in opposition to the dominance of "white history" prevalent in many high school history classes across the United States (Bredell, 2013; Chikkatur, 2012; Sanders, 2009). In a white supremacist society built on the foundation of anti-Blackness, AAH served to refute the denigration of Black culture by empowering Black youth with knowledge of their histories. However, even within this counterhegemonic space, teachers sometimes promoted dominant discourses that prevented alternative forms of racial spacemaking in which students like Kabeera engaged. For example, Mr. Daro emphasized narrow racial ideologies and excluded more diasporic understandings of Black identity (Watson & Knight-Manuel, 2020). My case study thus demonstrated how (1) dominant racial discourses were perpetuated by Mr. Daro, as well as (2) how students were unable to counter these dominant discourses.

CONTEXT OF THE INQUIRY

Stemming from ethnographic fieldwork research conducted between 2019–2021, I followed a dozen 9th- to 12th-grade West African Muslim youth who were members of the Muslim Students Association at Honors, attending their history classes, lunch periods, and after-school Muslim Students Association club. I served as an adult mentor sharing the same faith as students, identifying as a practicing Muslim woman of South Asian origin. I met many parents and families over the course of my fieldwork, and families asked me to help in their children's future studies, which I did by offering advice on college admissions to juniors and seniors.

My relationship with Mr. Daro, the AAH class teacher, was cordial, as we shared a passion for history, and we both genuinely cared about the students. Having worked as an African American history teacher in Philadelphia schools, I found history classrooms to be a familiar space, although in this case I was an ethnographer rather than instructor. I spoke with Mr. Daro about my observations of his classroom and students, observations with which he often agreed. However, Mr. Daro pointed out the limitations of his role as a teacher and suggested that too much was expected of teachers, that is, it is not possible to cover every topic of interest to students within the classroom.

THEORETICAL FRAMEWORK

While this study initially began as an inquiry into Black Muslim youth's practices of Islamic self-making, I came to understand that racial processes were integral to theorizing religious self-making. Islamic communities in the United States operate alongside and work within U.S. racial formations to maintain the logic of white supremacy (S. A. Jackson, 2005; Khabeer, 2016), which trickles down into classroom spaces. I draw from Omi and Winant's (2014) work in defining racial formation as "the sociohistorical process by which racial identities are created, lived out, transformed, and destroyed" (p. 109); and by extension, I define racial self-making as the process by which racial identities are lived out by individuals, and racial spacemaking as the ways in which raced individuals both inhabit and envision the spaces that constitute their racial self-making. Racial self-making and racial spacemaking are influenced by discourses on ethnicity that vary across national and geographic contexts (Clarke & Thomas, 2006; Munasinghe, 1997; Pierre, 2020; Ramos-Zayas, 2012; Rana, 2011; Waters, 1999). These varying national contexts prompt scholars to pay attention to national, regional, and local contexts in which racial formation occurs. In addition to noting how racial and ethnic formations in the U.S. national context shape the experience of heterogeneous U.S. Black Muslim communities, I investigate how religious identities play a role in racial formations. The AAH classroom, in particular, was an important setting in which racial self-making and spacemaking were active processes in which Black Muslim youth in my study engaged.

WHOSE BLACKNESS MATTERS?

Mr. Daro, a white teacher who taught AAH for 4 years at Honors, grew up in Philly and was a knowledgeable history teacher. His willingness to participate in my study stemmed from his desire to evolve as a history teacher more attentive to West African and African American Muslim youth in his classroom. However, as illustrated in the exchange with Kabeera, Mr. Daro's pedagogy appeared to promote what Kabeera perceived as a U.S.-centric focus on Black history and Black politics that did not attend to diasporic understandings of Blackness. Despite his desire to improve his understanding of student diversity within the classroom, Mr. Daro, as the exchange indicates, chose not to engage with pushback from students in his classroom, perhaps due to the limitations of online teaching during a pandemic. While Kabeera transformed the class discussion about Black Lives Matter (BLM), ultimately her attempts at broadening the discussion and posing a different form of racial spacemaking seemed not to be as impactful as she had hoped they would be.

The discussion began on October 27, 2020, a day after the murder by police of Walter Wallace, a young Black man in Philadelphia who family members reported was "suffering a mental health crisis" (Philadelphia Rocked by Fresh Unrest, 2020, para. 2). The police killing, captured on video, prompted great outrage among many Philadelphia residents. While acknowledging the tragedy, Kabeera was dissatisfied that no one also talked about the persecution of Black lives outside of the United States. Although she remained an ardent supporter of BLM, Kabeera was disappointed that none of her classmates or her teacher made space to talk about major events going on in West Africa.

Kabeera had been following protests in Guinea, her parents' home country, with growing alarm. About a week before, on October 22, Kabeera sent me a text: "I'm not really paying attention in class because their protesting in the new[s] right now for guinea. And I might go it depends on my mother. It's in New York, real life, not virtual." Kabeera sent me a picture of a large group of protestors from NYC flying the Guinean flag and holding up a sign that said, "No third term for Alpha Conde." Kabeera explained that the protest is "right now. Well two days ago. Alpha Conde wants to go into his 3rd term." Kabeera was angry that Alpha Conde's government had arrested young protestors who were standing up against election fraud, unemployment, and other issues; some of these postelection clashes also had resulted in death (Reuters Staff, 2018). Given that the Black Lives Matter movement was also a movement against violence toward Black people, Kabeera was upset that her peers in school didn't express that Black lives in Guinea mattered as much as in the United States. Kabeera's attempts at broadening discussions of race, that is, to offer an alternative form of racial spacemaking and to incorporate a more global understanding of the Black struggle, were stymied.

PRACTICES OF RACIAL SELF-MAKING AND SPACEMAKING

An underlying pedagogical question in the following classroom discussion is the extent to which it is the responsibility of history teachers like Mr. Daro to consider within their classrooms perspectives outside of the United States, particularly when a student urges the teacher to engage in such discussions. Mr. Daro was emotionally responsive to students, as he created time during class to discuss the police shooting of Walter Wallace. It was clear from my observations throughout the year that having frank discussions with students was a pedagogical tool for him. However, as Mr. Daro clarified during our semistructured interview, he wanted to focus on U.S.-centric topics without deviating from the topic of African American history.

Racial spacemaking suggests that diverse individuals can claim space to more fully express their racial and ethnic selves. Yet in the classroom

African Lives Matter Too   59

exchange, efforts toward alternative racial self-making and spacemaking are limited to an understanding of Blackness that does not encompass broad meanings of the African diaspora.

The exchange took place during the pandemic; all classes at Honors were taught online and used the Zoom chat function liberally. "Many voices" denotes multiple students speaking out loud. All names are pseudonyms.

1. Mr. Daro: I'm sure you've already been informed of the news from last night. It's very heavy for me, it happened four blocks from my house. I was out protesting last night. I'm not in the best place right now. For those who didn't see the situation like me, this man (Walter Wallace) was, he had a knife, and his mother called the police cause he had mental illness.
2. Kabeera (text to me): Yes, I'm fine. It's sad though. I never would of thought something like would happen in Philly.
3. Gigi: That was a messed up situation.
4. Many voices: What makes it crazier is that he had mental illness. This Whole thing is just crazy. They shot him in front of his mother smh [shake my head]. Literally it, it's not fair. Cops beating people, now I'm watching video.
5. Reem: They start looting again, smh. I feel like the police knew what they were doing when they pulled out their guns. They shot him 15 times, it was totally unnecessary. It's heartbreaking. Officers be taught to shoot to kill smh. People been wanted that law, they don't listen. It's not right, I hate that we live in a world full of evil.
6. Kabeera: None y'all had that same energy when we was talking about what is going on in Africa.
7. Reem: cause we didn't really know as much.
8. Gigi: I def did tho cuz whats going on over there is outta pocket too.
9. Reem: ^
10. Kabeera: people was reposting it, it was even on the shade room [a Black-run news social media site]
11. Aniya: first of all how we gon focus on what's happening here and there and that stuff is depressing
12. Reem: fr
13. Aniya: nobody wants to hear about people dying all day
14. Kabeera: that happen before all of this, this was going on for the past week
15. Aniya: NOBODY WANTS TO HEAR ABOUT PEOPLE DYING EVERY DAY
16. Kabeera: welp that's not an excuse

17. Aniya: you talk about it if it's effecting you & it is. Mental health matters.
18. Kabeera: I am.
19. Gigi: moral of the story is black unfairness is everywhere.
20. Reem: yea, but all we can really do is share the message. We can't fly over their but if something happen where we are of course we are gonna make it more affective towards us.
21. Kabeera: I have been reposting.
22. Aniya: as you should.
23. Kabeera: who saying anything about flying over there? You could have been reposting and educating people around you. Y'all just proving my point.
24. Reem: you making it seem like we not doing nothing tho.
25. Kabeera: Bc y'all are not
26. Aniya: I have been reposting
27. Gigi: I been reposting . . .
28. Reem: what else can we do but to repost
29. Aniya: and signing petitions
30. Reem: and pray
31. Aniya: you don't even know what you talking about, you blaming us for smt we can't control
32. Caiah: it's sad what's going on in America and Africa we just got to be strong and stand tall
33. Kabeera: I do know what I'm talking about.
34. Aniya: we are 15–16, what more could you possibly want us to do? I'm curious.
35. Caiah: I feel like at this point it's nothing we can do
36. Aniya: repost? We did it. Like cmon now. Y'all always try to flip it and make our people hate each other.
37. Kabeera: I'm talking bout we had conversation in class about what's going on here or whatever-and not about what's going on in Africa.
38. Aniya: Chile we I'm not arguing with a bigot-
39. Kabeera: . . . cuz I'm right that's why. But okay
40. Aniya: lol
41. Kabeera: so what . . . you stopped class to talk about this but did not last week to talk about what's going on in Africa. But go off.
42. Reem: We talking about it cause it happened here lol and it affected us in our own ways.
43. Mr. Daro: With so much going on in the world, it depends how you use your energy. If it happens in your backyard, it hits different. That's not our country, it comes down later to us. It doesn't hit as hard, it's not literally in our backyard, even though it's still the same thing. I haven't talked about it because I am talking

about imperialism in Africa tomorrow. We can talk about it, it's
the same theme over and over.

DISCUSSION

The impassioned language used by students reflects their desire to grapple
with what it means to care about Black lives. In response to Walter Wallace's
death in their "backyard," Black students reflected that Black people's ability to claim public space and to live in security in their neighborhoods, that
is, racial spacemaking as a form of racial self-making, is constantly under
threat. When Kabeera asserts that Black people's claim to public space also
includes political events in Africa, her perspective is diminished. The students' debate addresses the essential question of which attempts toward
racial self-making are considered relevant within the AAH classroom.
Ultimately, as affirmed by Mr. Daro, students limit their understanding of
which Black selves and which Black spaces matter by confining their attention to just local events.

Kabeera launches the critique against her classmates by stating: "None
y'all had that same energy when we was talking about what is going on in
Africa." She feels that the students are investing much in the issue of Walter
Wallace while not caring at all about the protests in Africa, specifically
Guinea. Reem, an African American boy, responds that he didn't know
what was going on (line 7), to which Kabeera responds that people were
reposting (line 10) as Reem must have seen on her Instagram post. Gigi, an
African American girl, suggests that she did know what was going on, and
disapproved (line 8; although it is unclear whether Gigi reposted the news
about West Africa on her own Instagram story).

Aniya, an African American girl, addresses people's lack of knowledge
as a main issue but explicitly states that it's too depressing to hear about
people dying every day (lines 13, 15). She focuses on the fact that "mental
health matters" (line 17) and that students cannot pay attention to people
dying all day "here and there" (line 11). Kabeera calls out Aniya for not caring about violence in West Africa and points out that the class easily could
have talked about events in Africa the week before (prior to the Walter
Wallace shooting) (line 14). Kabeera's point is that the two events did not
happen simultaneously; therefore, both should have been given full focus
and attention to reaffirm that all Black lives matter. Racial self-making for
Kabeera underscores the belief that the Black struggle transcends national
boundaries—that racial spacemaking should pay heed to both African and
U.S. struggles. Aniya, however, offers a more bounded form of racial spacemaking. Aniya implies that only issues occurring directly in one's proxi-
mate neighborhood matter. The situation in West Africa is over "there" and
does not affect her (and the additional U.S. residents Kabeera is critiquing).

62 Schooling and Classroom Perspectives and Contexts

Gigi tries to diffuse the situation between Kabeera and Aniya by saying that "Black unfairness is everywhere" (line 19) and that Black people should not fight among one another. Gigi further advocates that injustice against all Black people should be addressed, supporting Kabeera's attempts at broadening boundaries of Black spacemaking.

Yet Gigi's attempt at peacekeeping does not stop the argument between Kabeera and her classmates. Reem asserts to Kabeera that as teenagers, they may be limited in activist efforts; "we can't fly over their but if something happen where we are of course we are gonna make it more affective towards us" (line 20). Reem reiterates Aniya's comment that proximity to events shapes one's ability to respond to and address the problem. Kabeera reminds Aniya: "I have been reposting" (line 21), assuming the moral ground for taking virtual action. Aniya shoots back, "as you should" (line 22), indicating that it makes sense for Kabeera to post about West Africa because Kabeera herself is West African. Aniya implies that reposting doesn't give Kabeera any extra moral legitimacy, since it was almost a matter of duty for her based on her African identity. Kabeera understands the critique directed at her, and shoots back, "who saying anything about flying over there? You could have been reposting and educating people around you. Y'all just proving my point" (line 23). Kabeera doesn't believe that it is *only* her duty to post, and accuses her classmates of not caring about Black people in West Africa. Reem is hurt by Kabeera's accusation: "you making it seem like we not doing nothing tho" (line 24). Kabeera reaffirms her accusation: "y'all are not" (line 25).

At this point, Kabeera's classmates are frustrated at being blamed for being uncaring individuals. They respond to Kabeera that they indeed have reposted, signed petitions, and prayed. Reem asks evocatively: "what else can we do but to repost" (line 28), and Caiah, a young African American girl, agrees: "I feel like at this point it's nothing we can do" (line 35). These comments highlight teenagers' beliefs that they have limited power to affect world change. Aniya takes a more combative tone, counters Kabeera's accusations, and declares: "you don't even know what you talking about, you blaming us for smt we can't control. . . . we are 15–16, what more could you possibly want us to do? I'm curious. . . . repost? We did it. Like cmon now. Y'all always try to flip it and make our people hate each other" (lines 31–36). Aniya is fed up with being told that she does not care about Black lives. Instead, she asks Kabeera why she is blaming mere teenagers for larger geopolitical issues and anti-Black violence over which they have no control. Aniya counters Kabeera's accusation by sharing that she too has shared about the violence in West Africa on Instagram (line 26), which was the only concrete way forward Kabeera had suggested in the first place; Aniya is tired of being portrayed as an uncaring person. Aniya believes that her attempts at advocating for Black lives outside of her local community are limited by her lack of political power. She feels restricted to social media as her only form of political expression.

Aniya hurls a counteraccusation directed at Kabeera: "Y'all always try to flip it and make our people hate each other" (line 36). Aniya, who identifies as African American, clearly views herself as a separate "people" from West Africans, a group that Kabeera represents. Aniya accuses all West Africans with the pronoun "Y'all" and says West Africans are trying to "flip it," that is, turn the blame for negative events back on African Americans, rather than finding a common basis for collective action against anti-Black violence. Aniya believes that there are divisions between African Americans and West Africans, which are exacerbated when Kabeera blames African Americans for being passive. Aniya ends up calling Kabeera a bigot (line 38), and Kabeera restates that she is right and has nothing to apologize for (line 39). In the midst of this tense conversation, Caiah takes on the role of bridge builder: "it's sad what's going on in America and Africa we just got to be strong and stand tall" (line 32). Instead of using pronouns such as "y'all" to hurl accusations, Caiah believes that U.S. and African people are both hurt by anti-Black violence. Caiah understands that Black people's understanding of their racial selves is tied to Black struggle around the world. Even if West Africans and African Americans developed separate historical identities over time, the real solution, in Caiah's opinion, was to be strong and stand tall, that is, to find strength and unity by broadening the geographic scope of which Black struggles counted.

Kabeera is not finished after Aniya's counteraccusations. She makes one last attempt to clarify her point:

> I do know what I'm talking about. . . . I'm talking bout we had conversation in class about what's going on here or whatever-and not about what's going on in Africa. . . . so what . . . you stopped class to talk about this but did not last week to talk about what's going on in Africa. But go off. (lines 33–41)

Kabeera actually is addressing Mr. Daro directly in this explanation. She is upset that even her teacher clearly feels that the death of Walter Wallace is more important. Reem responds, "We talking about it cause it happened here lol and it affected us in our own ways" (line 42), reiterating an earlier point about the importance of proximity in determining which events are important (i.e., understandings of racial spacemaking that do not encompass broad meanings of the African diaspora).

Mr. Daro then attempts to explain his choice to have a deep dive in class for Walter Wallace but not about the events in Africa:

> With so much going on in the world, it depends how you use your energy. If it happens in your backyard, it hits different. That's not our country, it comes

> down later to us. It doesn't hit as hard, it's not literally in our backyard, even though it's still the same thing. I haven't talked about it because I am talking about imperialism in Africa tomorrow. (line 43)

Mr. Daro justifies his choice by sharing that "that's not our country [Guinea], it [the news] comes down later to us." Mr. Daro's explanation suggests that news outlets did not report the events in Guinea as thoroughly as they did events in the United States. His latter explanation, "It doesn't hit as hard, it's not literally in our backyard, even though it's still the same thing," is a more substantive statement. Mr. Daro draws on the mental health argument cited earlier in the conversation by noting that events that happen closer are more important than events far away, even though it's "still the same thing." Mr. Daro recognizes that state-driven, anti-Black violence in the United States is parallel to state-driven violence in West African countries. Still, he refuses Kabeera's attempts at expanding meanings of Blackness discussed in the classroom.

Kabeera texted me, "he [Mr. D] doesn't even care." Her disappointment in how the classroom chat went, was palpable. Why was it so difficult for students, and even the teacher, to understand that Black lives everywhere matter? Kabeera's query reflects Strong's (2018) question: Do Black lives matter until African lives also matter? As Strong explains, working for Black causes is not bound to a nation-state but diasporic. However, in the way that BLM has operated in practice, Black lives in the United States have remained central. Kabeera's anger, expressed through responses to classmates, captures the central dilemma: How can Black lives matter more in one nation-state than another, when the theoretical core of BLM is to value the most persecuted, racialized people in society and is built on a foundation of internationalism (Movement for Black Lives, 2024)?

Which forms of racial spacemaking are deemed appropriate within the history classroom, and what does this key question suggest about the borders and boundaries of Blackness within African American history? Kabeera and a group of students subscribed to the diasporic notion of racial spacemaking, where Black youth engage in racial self-making in global efforts toward Black autonomy. A second group of students and Mr. Daro expressed some understanding toward struggles of Black people elsewhere but reflected racial self-making as better understood through a local lens that does not encompass broad meanings of the African diaspora. The underlying pedagogical question is the extent to which it is the responsibility of history teachers like Mr. Daro to consider perspectives beyond the United States within their classroom, particularly when they have students of international backgrounds in the class. Mr. Daro privileges a view of racial spacemaking that does not account for varied meanings of the African diaspora, suggesting that West African students' efforts at self-making and spacemaking are unimportant.

Mr. Daro failed to respond to student prompts in the chat that explicitly connected Black lives in the United States to Black lives abroad. Gigi states: "moral of the story is Black unfairness is everywhere" (line 19), while Caiah connects the struggles in both countries: "it's sad what's going on in America and Africa we just got to be strong and stand tall" (line 32). Students' comments easily provided a jumping-off point for Mr. Daro to address global Black struggles against racism and violence, particularly in the setting of an AAH class already focused on Black lives. Another point of intervention could have been from Aniya's comment: "Y'all always try to flip it and make our people hate each other" (line 36). Aniya highlights tensions between West Africans and African Americans in Honors Academy. Given that Mr. Daro was aware of such ethnic tensions in the school, and that he watched the argument between Aniya and Kabeera unfold, he could have used Aniya's comment as a learning moment to dispel stereotypes the two groups had of each other.

In an offline discussion about this class discussion, Mr. Daro heard my observations about how West African Muslim youth like Kabeera felt that their African identity was being sidelined. He noted that he could see Kabeera's point, but he reiterated that given limited classroom instruction time, he felt that he had to cover content that was most relevant to the majority of the students in the class. Mr. Daro suggested that while political protests in the diasporic community were of note, Black lives in the United States held greater importance as a topic for most students, and for himself. This response did not reflect Mr. Daro's initial desire to participate in this study, that is, to become more knowledgeable about the Muslim West African and African American students in his class.

Extending the work of scholars who study the marginalization of race in history classrooms and the silencing of students (Godreau, 2015; Holsey, 2008), AAH in this inquiry served not as a space for counterhegemonic interpretations but one in which a hegemonic, ethnocentric curriculum solidified views of racial spacemaking and self-making that do not encompass broad meanings of the African diaspora.

TAKEAWAYS

While it is easy to offer pedagogical interventions as an outside observer, teaching is not an easy task, particularly in moments of heightened emotion. Mr. Daro did an excellent job creating space for students to process emotions after a difficult event like Walter Wallace's murder. However, even while creating space for discussion, Mr. Daro prioritized U.S. concerns over an African diasporic perspective, thereby denying Kabeera's multiple identities as second-generation African as well as a U.S. citizen by birth. Valenzuela (1999) describes this process, devaluing student identities, as reflective of subtractive schooling. Instead, Valenzuela offers the example of teachers at Luperon High School engaging in additive schooling by valuing Dominican students' cultural backgrounds and histories, and incorporating these histories into the classroom. The current case offers a counterexample, and encourages educators, particularly history educators, to broaden the scope of whose history (and whose current conditions) are worth discussing in classroom spaces. Ultimately, how can educators support Black students' efforts toward racial self-making and spacemaking even while dealing with racially stressful moments in the classroom? How can educators affirm cultural heritages and diasporic narratives of African immigrant and second-generation students? What are ways teachers can build on African students' experiences to discuss broad meanings of the African diaspora?

I point to the work of Reisman and colleagues (2020), who offer three ways for history teachers to respond to racially stressful moments: draw on disciplinary history literacy, critical literacy, or racial literary approaches. Reisman and colleagues argue that moments in which racially tense discussions occur constitute a chance for teachers to engage in "discretionary spaces" (D. L. Ball, 2018). Discretionary spaces emerge as "moments in which a teacher must exercise judgment while choosing among a set of discursive options, all of which have implications for student learning and social positioning" (Reisman et al., 2020, p. 323). Each of the three approaches—engaging disciplinary history literacy, critical literacy, or racial literacy—can be employed by a teacher to create such a discretionary space. For example, Mr. Daro could have used a racial literacy interpretive frame to notice racial stress in the classroom, as experienced by himself and his students. Next, Mr. Daro could have adopted a critical literacy interpretive frame, through which he would name the racial claim (that some students suggested that Black experiences in the United States are more valuable than in Africa) and then work to demystify the narrative (the reminder that throughout African American history, Black struggles have been diasporically connected) (Pierre, 2013). Each of these frameworks would have helped Mr. Daro navigate this racially stressful moment in the classroom (see also Price-Dennis & Sealey-Ruiz, 2021).

As teachers, we know students can have the power to reshape dominant historical discourses, particularly if the teacher is receptive to incorporating alternative, emerging, and counternarratives within the classroom curriculum. By connecting everyday student observations to pedagogical content, teachers within history classrooms can embolden positive learning environments that can make all students feel valued.

Cultural heritages and diasporic narratives of African immigrant students can be a valuable resource for teachers to draw on within history classrooms to demonstrate the heterogeneity of Black identities to all their students. By valuing African youth as contributors within classrooms, teachers can indicate their respect for diasporic African narratives to students, families, and communities. For educators to continue in their efforts to counter deficit narratives about Black youth within the white supremacist society in which they operate, embracing the value of African lives is also part of the story.

CHAPTER 5

A Narrative Inquiry Into Experiences of Black Women in Undergraduate STEM Disciplines in Ontario

James Alan Oloo and Priscila Dias Corrêa

Across Canada, more girls than boys increasingly complete high school and proceed to a university. In 2016–2017, women accounted for almost six out of every 10 (57%) full-time enrolled students in undergraduate programs (Whitley & Hollweck, 2020). In addition, evidence shows that "seven of the 10 highest-paid jobs in Canada are STEM [science, technology, engineering, mathematics, and computer sciences]-related" (Coe, 2015, para. 3), and STEM careers are among the fastest-growing professions in Canada and across the Global North. Yet, disparities in enrollment in undergraduate STEM disciplines based on race and gender persist, with a marked underrepresentation of Black women (Corrêa & Oloo, 2022). Indeed, while data on student achievement by race are not readily available in Canada (Whitley & Hollweck, 2020), where such information is available, students' experience is impacted by racial identity (Corrêa & Oloo, 2023). For example, Black and Latino students in Ontario are disproportionately placed in applied, as opposed to academic, high school courses (Corrêa & Oloo, 2022), which in Ontario may not qualify for university admission.

A review of the literature on racialized experiences of Black students indicates two common threads. The first is that race-related experiences of Black female students often are associated with a deficit or personal shortcomings on the part of the individual student (Whitley & Hollweck, 2020). Very seldom are racialized experiences of Black women students linked to societal factors outside the student's control or discriminatory practices in educational systems. The second thread is that most research conducted in Canada tends to focus on inequalities related to gender in the K–12 system, not on gender in postsecondary education (Corrêa & Oloo, 2023).

Experiences of Black undergraduate students in STEM disciplines matter. The Black population in Canada is generally younger than the total population (Statistics Canada, 2020). In 2016, children younger than 15 accounted for 26% of the Black population, and 17% of the total population. An understanding of racialized experiences of Black female students in undergraduate STEM programs is necessary to implement transformative actions that enhance their university experiences. Hence, this study is guided by two broad questions: (1) How do Black female undergraduate students in STEM disciplines describe their racialized experiences? and (2) What resilience strategies do Black female undergraduate students in STEM disciplines employ to successfully navigate learning environments in Ontario universities?

This study helps to expand the space for voices of Black female students in STEM disciplines to be heard, and to address the gap in literature by examining experiences of Black female undergraduate students as told by students themselves.

THEORETICAL FRAMEWORK

This study is grounded in the Community Cultural Wealth (CCW) framework (Yosso, 2005), whose origins can be traced to Critical Race Theory, which provides a critical perspective on how systems, including education, reproduce racial inequalities (Corrêa & Oloo, 2022). CCW includes six distinct but related types of wealth that students, such as those from racialized backgrounds, possess, develop, and draw upon during their studies:

1. aspirational capital, described as the ability to maintain hopes and dreams for the future despite the present real and perceived barriers;
2. familial capital or cultural knowledge nurtured among familia (kin), which carries a sense of community, history, memory, and cultural intuition;
3. linguistic capital, namely, social and intellectual skills that accrue from communication experiences in two or more languages or styles;
4. navigational capital or the ability to maneuver through social institutions such as a university campus;
5. resistance capital, which refers to the skills and knowledge that are nurtured and developed through oppositional behavior that challenges inequality; and
6. social capital or networks of people and community resources (Yosso, 2005, pp. 78–80).

CCW is an asset-based framework previously employed in research with racialized students (Yosso, 2005). In contrast to a deficit-based view, which highlights the challenges that (racialized) students face, asset-based perspectives hold that such students have funds of knowledge and forms of capital they draw on to attain success despite challenges. Much has been written about the ineffectiveness of deficit approaches in understanding human differences. Dinishak (2016), for example, argues that a deficit approach "diminishes people's life chances and even their humanity" and may "impede scientific and philosophical progress in our understanding of the phenomena themselves" (para. 5). Thus, our study contributes to research by disrupting deficit-centered discourse around Black student experiences while amplifying Black student voices and validating their strengths.

METHODOLOGY: HOW WE CAME TO KNOW

This study employed a narrative inquiry methodology (Clandinin, 2013), "an approach to the study of human lives conceived as a way of honoring lived experience as a source of important knowledge and understanding" (p. 42). People make sense of their experiences through stories. Kim (2015) suggests that stories cannot be "isolated or independent from societal influence," and hence "we need to be sensitive to the historical and social layers that the story bears" (p. 132). Such historical and social contexts are captured succinctly by what Yusuf (2020) calls "the paucity of Black students in higher education across Canada" (p. ii). This paucity, Yusuf points out, is manifested by the fact that "Black students who are enrolled in [Canada's postsecondary] institutions [often] experience challenges navigating them" (p. ii). Hence, this study aims to unfold and understand racialized undergraduate experiences in STEM disciplines in Ontario.

RESEARCH DESIGN

This study is part of more extensive research examining racialized mathematical learning experiences of Black undergraduates at Ontario universities enrolled in STEM disciplines within Bachelor of Science programs. In this larger study, participants were recruited through a call shared with student organizations and universities across the province. Data collection involved one-on-one dialogic conversations with participants, audio-recorded and transcribed, shaped by semistructured research questions (for more details about the methods used, please see previous research in Kiramba & Oloo, 2020; Oloo, 2022). In the present study, we examined experiences of two Black female undergraduate students, 18 and 22 years old, chosen as they were the only females among several participants in the aforementioned larger study.

RESEARCHERS' POSITIONALITIES

We enter this research space with varied personal and professional experiences (Knight & Watson, 2014), and a commitment to successful learning outcomes for Black students. The first author is a Black male, former high school mathematics teacher, and currently a professor at a teacher education program. The second author is a mixed-race female, former electrical engineer, former secondary school mathematics teacher, and currently a mathematics education professor. The idea for this study developed from our experiences and conversations with students. Shared identities and backgrounds in mathematics helped build and nurture positive relationships with participants.

PARTICIPANT ACCOUNTS

Hera, 18, was born in Ontario, Canada, to immigrant parents. Her mother is from Kenya, and father from Saint Lucia. Hera's stepfather was born in the United States to Ghanaian parents. Hera's older sibling, parents, and stepfather are all university graduates in STEM-related fields. She completed high school in the United States and currently attends a university in Ontario, pursuing a Bachelor of Science in Chemistry. Hera asserts that "chemistry was an easy choice for me because of my experience in high school. I had an amazing chemistry teacher in grade 11." She chose the university she attends because her father and two aunts graduated from the school: "My dad and aunties said that [the university] was a good environment. I also heard from those attending the university that it was a great place." She grew up in the same city where the university is located.

Achieng, 22, immigrated to Canada from Jamaica with her parents when she was 3. Oldest of three siblings, Achieng attends a Bachelor of Science program in Ontario in Financial Mathematics and Economics. She is in her fifth and final year of studies, having completed high school at a private Christian school. Achieng said, "I have only ever gone to private Christian Schools since kindergarten. My parents liked it that way." For Achieng, the decision to go to university was easy. Her parents expected her to go to university.

The following sections present narrative accounts of both participants grounded on five aspects of their undergraduate experiences: (1) the decision to attend a university, (2) the challenges of being a Black female undergraduate student in STEM, (3) pleasant and unpleasant university experiences, (4) motivation to keep going, and (5) advice to prospective Black students and universities.

Analysis of participant narrative accounts indicates the different capitals Hera and Achieng drew on throughout their racialized experiences.

The Decision to Go to University

The influence of family engagement has been impactful on both Achieng's and Hera's academic journeys, and is evident in their stories. Research shows immigrant parents tend to have high educational aspirations for their children (Kiramba et al., 2021; Roubeni et al., 2015), as Roubeni et al. reflect in a study in which an immigrant parent declares their aspiration for their children's education thus: "If we can't do it, our children will do it one day" (p. 275).

Hera and Achieng pondered that support and encouragement from their families and the goals they set for themselves paved their way to university. Hera credits her parents (familial capital) for encouraging her to attend university.

> My parents were like, "You are going to university to get a degree, and you are going to get a master's because the industry is now very competitive; having a bachelor's degree is not enough. A master's degree will set you apart from everybody else." Ever since I was in high school, my parents always said, "You are going to university. You are getting your degrees." So, I was like, okay, I'll do that.

Hera's aspirational capital was also crucial in getting her ready for university. She recalls how she struggled with mathematics in grade school. However, drawing from aspirational capital, she persevered and improved. "I started doing more math books over the summer, and then I began to grasp the mathematical skills and get better. [Now] at university, [I am] taking four math courses already. Overall, I feel like I am a pretty good student."

Like Hera, Achieng highlighted the importance of family support (familial capital) in successful educational experiences. Such support may come in different forms.

> I was always expected to go to university. Both my parents came to Canada as international students and are both graduates of Ontario universities. My dad went to university in the 1980s, and my mom in the 1990s. While that was a long time ago, my dad always tells me, "If I could do it way back then, without technology and resources and phones and Internet, then you could definitely do it now."

Achieng explains how she learned the process of going to university. She relied on navigational capital and figured out things by herself as she could not access information or any additional support or guidance.

> There was no information at my school or anywhere. I had to figure out how to apply for scholarships. I applied for residence on my own. I taught myself. But

then I also found that I was teaching a lot of my classmates how to apply, and the thing was, I only knew from my limited experience, and I was helping them because we did not have guidance or a career counselor to be able to guide us through that process.

Achieng's ambition to go to university (aspirational capital) kept her motivated, and she did not give up. Achieng had a clear notion of which area she wanted to engage; however, she acknowledges this is not always the case:

I have always loved math. But when I got to high school, my love for math just skyrocketed. I enjoyed every single math class I took in high school, so I said it would be nice to do something related to math at university. I always wanted to pursue higher education, and in grade 12, I applied to a few universities and got admission.

Given my experience, I feel like children do suffer because they are, at a young age, making a huge life [career] decision, and they don't have adequate information and guidance. I noticed that a lot of people from my high school ended [up] quitting university or switching programs multiple times.

Challenges of Being a Black Female Undergraduate Student in STEM

Hera and Achieng talked about challenges they experienced, such as virtual learning, being one of a few Black women in classes, and doubtfulness, and how they benefitted from different capitals to cope with challenges. Hera spoke about her experiences and emphasized that the COVID-19 pandemic was challenging for students and professors. She noted that it was often "difficult to ask questions since everybody is on a Zoom call or a Microsoft Teams call and sometimes you have technical issues and stuff like that." Hera continued:

Because many students, including me, often turned our cameras off, it was harder to know anyone besides their names. I can't say if I was treated differently because of my skin color. But, in general, my experience as a Black student at the university and in my program has been pretty good.

Hera resolved not to hesitate to seek help when needed—an example of her navigational capital. She says, "If I'm struggling with a topic, I would email the professor back-to-back until I understood what was going on. I would attend the office hours whenever necessary." Hera also reaches out to graduate assistants (GAs) when needing assistance or clarification. "I would keep emailing GAs and sending them screenshots of my work and be like, I have done this step, but I am stuck here. Would you be able to help me understand where I went wrong? They usually help me out."

As part of her navigational capital, Hera added that in her first year, she joined two clubs. She met two mentors who spoke about their university careers and experiences, helping her through her own experiences. She voiced how clubs helped relieve her stress in a new world like university. When further unfolding experiences as a Black student, Hera said:

> I haven't had any professors or instructors that look like me. Two of them, I don't know their ethnicity, but all the rest are white. Any time I have to ask them a question, I feel like I need to think about how I ask the question and not act like those stereotypes that they probably already have about Black people. So, I don't want the professors to think, "Oh, she'll probably ask dumb questions." Sometimes I get nervous asking professors questions, and I want them to think that I'm smart and I'm not dumb.

Hera explained that when speaking with a professor, she must be more self-conscious and choose her words well so as not to be misunderstood. When Hera described thinking in the back of her mind before asking a question, it was evident how stereotypes, real or perceived, impact Black female student experiences at university. The navigational capital, and even resistant capital, necessary to endure and respond to stereotype threats is complex and significantly impacts and compromises students' mental health (Oloo, 2022).

Stereotype threats and pervasive stereotypes (Kiramba et al., 2021) can be detrimental to students' racialized experiences when students feel isolated. Hera mentioned that she knows only one other Black student, and the student is in the process of "changing his major from chemistry to forensic science." Hera explains:

> To be honest, I'm kind of used to it. I'm not taken aback by it anymore; I don't want that to be a barrier to me. So, I just try to be the representative for everybody else. But you know, it hit me. When he said he was changing his major, I was like, okay, now I'm really the only one. But that's happened to me before in high school. I was the one Black kid or one out of the two Black students in a classroom. I'm kind of used to it now.

Hera relied on aspirational capital to find strength to cope and keep moving forward despite challenges she may have been experiencing. She mentioned how family helped in this process (familial capital): "My family is very supportive. If I'm feeling discouraged, they encourage me and give me words of wisdom." She also mentioned that she listened to music and danced to relieve stress. Hera's discourse speaks to how she draws upon navigational, resistant, familial, and aspirational capitals for inspiration and to overcome challenges imposed by being the only Black female student in class, and still follows along with her goals. In a different study (Hailu & Simmons, 2022a), two Black females of immigrant backgrounds highlight similar experiences in higher education: "Our immediate family members have impacted our awareness of educational opportunities." They continue, "Recognizing the adversity our parents encountered as they adjusted to American culture has instilled in us a sense of resilience, community and cultural wealth . . . and membership to diasporic communities" (p. 5). That is, the self-efficacy of the two females, together with support and expectations of their families and diasporic capital available to them, were critical not only for their success but also in their "absolute belief in education [which] shaped much of [their] . . . aspirations to do well in school" (p. 7).

Achieng spoke about feelings such as loneliness, self-doubt, and pride. She talked about experiences in both virtual and in-person learning environments, and described a situation where she was one of only four Black people, the greatest number of Black students she had seen in an in-person class. Achieng commented on how all the other students would have big communities while there were only four Black students. This sense of isolation struck her, yet she did not expect to push herself into the other groups. She also mentioned the desire to do unique things that not many Black people do, revealing her resistant capital: "It's important that I am one of the few Black students in this [program], and it's not because I am here due to a favor from someone. No, I deserve to be here. Still, there are times when you feel like, do I really belong here?"

Achieng continued by noting her difficulty reaching out and getting support (navigational capital). She explained that if she faced difficulties in a course, she might not seek professors' help because asking for help could strengthen stereotypes.

> Sometimes you doubt your ability, especially in a difficult course or if you don't do well in this assignment. But then it is hard to go see the professor because I don't want them to think that, you know, reinforce some stereotypes about Black people like maybe we are not smart. Maybe that is just my own insecurities that I am projecting onto them.

Achieng provides a clear example of how common, everyday academic experiences result in undesirable and adverse outcomes, specifically for Black students, due to stereotypes and lack of guidance and assistance. In addition, she describes how her Black appearance interferes with what people think about her academic skills. Achieng believes people question her intelligence based on how she looks and presents herself. For example, she felt a sense of self-doubt in her ability when there was less work assigned to her in group assignments. Achieng described the gender impact on her racialized experiences and how she questioned her ability:

> There is also a gender aspect to it, whether it is clear or not, like differences between a white male and a Black female. They [white males] would chat up

[with] the professors, and they would become buddies. Some professors would come in, and every day they were chatting before class with the same students. And I would be like, maybe I'm not putting myself out there enough. But then I'm like, but what if I put myself there and it won't be received well?

Researchers (Maestripieri, 2021; Yosso, 2005) have written about how overlapping structures of disadvantage (age, class, gender, race, immigration status, etc.) affect racialized persons. Maestripieri refers to such structures as "axis of inequality" (p. 3) and suggests the intersections of structures, rather than structures themselves, are key to understanding experiences of racialized populations.

Aside from navigational capital necessary to handle different situations, Achieng explains how her resistant capital plays a role in these situations. She asserts that people tend to make wrong and hurtful assumptions about her:

I can't change the way I look, and I can't change people's assumptions of me. So, I do feel motivated, but at the same time, for me to get to that place, I have to go through a process of feeling hurt and being in my feelings to get to the other side where I want to prove them wrong.

Achieng explained that she shares acquired navigational capital with younger or new Black students, mentoring them and transforming her own doubtful experiences into positive ones. This supportive attitude speaks to development of Achieng's social and resistant capitals.

Sometimes I imagine that people in the class are looking at me and thinking in their heads, what is she doing here? So, when I meet younger or new Black students, I share my experience with them. I tell them both the good and the bad experiences because I guess they could relate. That could mean spinning it into a positive way. Being the only Black girl in my class means you are doing something great and something that not many people do, and you should take pride in that.

Pleasant and Unpleasant University Experiences

Research shows postsecondary students of immigrant backgrounds tend to perceive university experiences differently from counterparts who do not hold immigrant backgrounds; "foreign-born immigrants' students experience college differently than nonimmigrant students including their perceptions of belonging as well as interactions with educators" (Stebleton et al., 2020, p. 11). Therefore, participants in the present inquiry were asked to share pleasant and unpleasant university learning experiences. Hera described pleasant experiences she had as a Black female student in an undergraduate STEM program, including friendships, supportive professors,

Experiences of Black Women in Undergraduate STEM Disciplines

and graduate assistants. Such experiences exemplify the social capital Hera drew on.

> I've had graduate assistants in the chemistry department who were willing to answer all my questions and be there by my side. There are some chemistry professors that have been very kind and very helpful as well. We just had a "Meet the Professor Night" where professors discussed their research. That was one of the highlights of my second year. There is a professor, Dr. TP, who is doing some cool research. I had previously emailed her regarding my interest in her work. I got her response in which she told me about the forthcoming "Meet the Professor Night." I am glad I attended the event and met Dr. TP. I also got to talk to her students there and looked at other professors' research, asking them questions.

Discussions with Dr. TP and students who work at Dr. TP's lab further increased Hera's interest in chemistry and the possibility of working with Dr. TP. Further, she points out that an opportunity to work within Dr. TP's lab would be "a tribute to women in science and women empowerment." Hera also described what she regarded as unpleasant experiences relating to studies.

> I had a bad experience in a course where it didn't feel like there was enough support for the students to do well. I spoke with a few other students to see how they felt and how they were doing in the course. They were also struggling, and they didn't know what to do to get help. I then reached out to the department head, but I didn't hear anything back. I didn't get a reply, so I kind of felt like I was just basically left to just fend for myself. I was upset because I was really struggling in that course. I wasn't seeing any improvement in my grades or just in general with understanding the material. So, what I ended up doing was going through the list of GAs that we had for physics that just graded our labs, and I messaged all of them asking if they were willing to tutor me. I received one response from a GA, and she helped me. She did about two sessions with me, and that went pretty well.

Hera tried different strategies to get help, drawing from her navigational capital. The first attempt was unsuccessful, but she did not give up. She tried another option until she found the support she needed. Hera's determination enabled her to overcome her difficulties.

Like Hera, Achieng also described positive experiences as a Black female undergraduate student in STEM, and how one specific professor made all the difference in her initial university experience when she decided to reach out to him (navigational capital).

> I was taking this class in my first-semester first year, and I realized that they don't teach you real analysis in high school. I had one friend in the class, and

me and her failed the first midterm because we just didn't know what we were doing. We went to the professor, and he was a really great professor. He took the time to really make sure that we understood, and he was very much available to answer any questions and help you understand. Everything was straightforward. Failing the midterm took a great toll on me. I was coming from high school at the top of my class. So, I felt invalidated. I needed to reaffirm my abilities. That first semester, I called my dad and said, "Take me home, please." After discussions with the professor, things started to get better. My marks improved. It was all the motivation I needed.

Urging us not to "lose sight of the challenges confronting Black women," Freeman (2023) writes, "Black women students confront challenges at each step along the educational continuum and in each higher education type" (p. ii). Despite challenges, Black women pursue higher education and graduate in relatively large numbers in Canada (Brunet & Galarneau, 2022) and the United States (Kiramba & Oloo, 2020).

In another instance, Achieng narrated how she was overwhelmed by the number of courses she was taking. Due to lack of knowledge (navigational capital) about minimum allowable courses she could take every term, and due to family and social circle expectations (familial and social capitals), Achieng was taking the maximum course load.

I was feeling burnt out at the end of the second year because I was taking the maximum course load every single semester, which I didn't know that you didn't have to do that. I learned this from my friend. I was asking her, "how many classes are you taking?" She's like, "I'm in four classes," and I said, "Four?" She's like, "Because I can't handle five." When I was like, "You can just take four?" And she says, "You could take as many as you like." So, instead of taking five classes, I started taking four or three per semester, which prolonged my studies by a year. But I feel like it was so essential because then I didn't have those feelings of being burnt out.

Achieng learned from her friend (social capital) that she could take fewer courses each semester, which helped relieve the stress and pressure she experienced earlier.

Motivation to Keep Going

We asked Hera and Achieng to describe what motivated them to keep going. Hera said:

To be honest, there isn't any other way. I know that getting my Bachelor of Science and grad school after that is the way that I want to go. So, I just want to keep pushing and striving to attain that goal. In addition, my parents are

Experiences of Black Women in Undergraduate STEM Disciplines 79

basically my cheerleaders. I have a good support system. I have an aunty, uncles, and cousins who are doctors or are in the science field. My brother is a civil engineer. My mom is a software engineer. They've been telling me about their experience in university and always saying that "you are going to struggle, but if you just push through and keep going, you are going to reach your goal, and you are going to be okay, even though you seem like you are drowning right now." Being a representation for minorities in the science field is also a motivating factor.

Hera's response indicates how familial and aspirational capitals influence her trajectory. When she mentions being a representation of minoritized communities, her discourse speaks to how she employs resistant capital to challenge inequities.

As Achieng neared the end of her program, she reflected on her journey and described how her familial, social, and aspirational capitals contributed to her decision to complete her program.

One thing that has kept me going is knowing how much my family is spending for me to go to university. I didn't want it to be a waste of their investment. Also, even when some of my friends were talking about the fact that you could be your own boss, you could start your own business, and you didn't have to go to university to be successful, I convinced myself that I'm not really a risk taker, so I felt the safer option is to stay [in school] and finish [the program]. Every semester I finished was [a] semester closer to graduation. I wouldn't say that it was some type of a dying love for my program or the university. Rather, it's mainly the fact that I wanted to finish what I had started. But I also like the financial aspect of getting a good job after graduating.

Achieng also acknowledged the social capital she continues to draw on to enhance her experience.

My closest friend from high school actually ended up coming to the same university as me, so we built a community together. I keep in touch with two other people from my high school. But in terms of family, friends, church members and stuff like that, I do keep in touch with the ones from my hometown as well. They have some impact on my studies through encouragement, just checking on you, and letting you know that they are praying for you and are there should you need anything.

Achieng talked about helpful resilience strategies related to her navigational capital. She explained that she tried to stay motivated by adjusting her mindset, being more positive, and not letting herself be influenced by negative emotions. She figured that to have a successful experience at the university, she had to fully feel and acknowledge her emotions to keep focus and move on. "It is important to stay motivated, even if it means motivating yourself. This meant that I had to adjust my mindset. I think I would let myself feel whatever I needed to feel, and then I would flip it into a positive."

Achieng mentioned the role of her parents in listening to her complaints and giving advice (familial capital). Although it did not seem helpful, she considered it a resilience strategy. She added to it, describing how her feelings about dissatisfaction with school should not reflect ungratefulness toward the support of her family.

> I feel like I suppress my feelings a lot. I felt like I wasn't allowed to complain because there was somebody out there who had it worse than me. I felt like I was not to complain because my parents are paying for university, and [there are] so many [people] who have to take out student loans. I have this big blessing and privilege. And here I am, sitting around complaining. I am ungrateful, and so I would think anytime I have something negative to say about the experience or about how I was feeling. I had to open up and tell people okay, listen, this is not me being ungrateful for my opportunity. But it sucks today, and I feel like I should just live in that for a little bit.

Achieng's comments echo findings by Kiramba et al. (2021) that immigrants tend to regard education as the key to better-paying careers; hence Black "immigrant youth are [often] pressured by their parents to succeed academically" (p. 48). However, care must be taken to ensure the pressure does not harm immigrant students—such as Achieng's need to suppress her feelings in order not to come across as being ungrateful for familial support.

Advice to Prospective Black Students and Universities

Hera had a word of advice for Black students, including those from immigrant backgrounds, who were considering postsecondary education.

> My sister is applying for universities right now. I tell her what I would tell any Black student who is thinking about going to university. I'd be honest and say, yes, it's scary; you are going to feel like you are drowning and not knowing what to do. But there is hope.

Hera had some suggestions for her sister, like reaching out to people, finding groups or organizations that have mentorship programs, finding as many sources as you can including YouTube videos or other resources, contacting graduate assistants if you have questions, and ensuring you get a sound support system.

Hera gave suggestions that universities could consider in their attempts to enhance experiences of undergraduate students, including Black women in STEM disciplines: Engage with students. Seek their views and listen to

Experiences of Black Women in Undergraduate STEM Disciplines 81

their voices. Create a safe space for students to ask questions and receive answers. Other suggestions by Hera include encouraging universities to create an environment for connection between students and professors; offering personalizable and reasonable course syllabi; and providing students with additional resources to help in understanding course content.

Drawing on her own experience as a Black female from an immigrant family, Achieng had advice for Black high school students.

> Go to university, especially a university that is away from your hometown. Maybe at some point, find a way to do a semester abroad. Do not lose contact with your home and your community. The people that show support are actually rooting for you, excited for you, happy for you. They can shower you with affirmation and positivity and stuff, and you need that. Make sure you choose a program that you like.

Achieng had tips for universities: Consider representation by attracting students and faculty members from diverse backgrounds. Provide mentorship programs by pairing first-year students with fourth-year students or alumni. Make it easier for students to reach out to professors and find the support they need. Hera's and Achieng's advice strongly emphasizes the importance of social capital to build on students' navigational capital and thrive at university.

DISCUSSION AND TAKEAWAYS

An estimated 47% of the Black population in Canada is Canadian born, with more than half (53%) of the Black population born outside the country (Statistics Canada, 2023). In Ontario and across Canada, data on Black student experience by immigration status tend to be rare (Corrêa & Oloo, 2023). However, it is clear that the Black population in Canada is diverse, and those of immigrant backgrounds have unique educational experiences. This study examined experiences of two Black female undergraduate students with immigrant backgrounds in STEM disciplines in Ontario. We listened to participants' stories of lived experiences, and what those experiences, as lived and told, meant to them. We regard participants as experts and appreciate opportunities to learn from their experiences. Black students and their allies often have called for better educational opportunities and learning experiences (Corrêa & Oloo, 2022). While Black students' voices are not always heard in a safe and respectful space, Black students are eager and happy to share experiences, be listened to, and be taken seriously. That was the intention of this study. Students' narratives confirm that they appreciated the opportunity to tell stories and found it reassuring and liberating. As Achieng stated, "Thank you so much for what you are doing. I think it's great. Thank you for listening to me. I really didn't think that my experience would help anybody, but I feel like if it helps, then it makes everything worth it. So, thank you so much."

By acknowledging Hera's and Achieng's undergraduate experiences from asset-based perspectives, based on the CCW framework (Yosso, 2005), we see all the capitals they bring into experiences as Black women undergraduate students and how they benefit from these capitals to persevere and progress in their studies. These capitals are crucial to successful and rewarding learning experiences. While this study is not intended as a generalization, the experiences of Achieng and Hera provide a glimpse of what could be challenges and opportunities faced by undergraduate students in STEM programs, especially Black female students and Black immigrant women communities. Such a glimpse, made possible through stories of lived experiences, could motivate professors, staff, students, and university communities in general to ensure that Black students and all other students have a comprehensive, fruitful, and authentic university experience. Indeed, this could start much earlier—in kindergarten through high school—to ensure that all Black students, immigrants or not, at all levels of education, have a voice and successful learning experiences.

By expanding the space for Black students' voices, we employ the first approach of the *Framework for Educating African Immigrant Youth* (Chapter 1), which refers to emboldening tellings of diasporic narratives of educational experiences. African immigrant youth have always had a voice. However, for far too long, those voices have been muted or ignored, while narratives that depict African immigrant experience from deficit perspectives have tended to be louder. Through this chapter, we hope to make a contribution in the effort to disrupt deficit perspectives while amplifying voices of African immigrant youth.

"I will tell you something about stories. . . . They aren't just entertainment. . . . They are all we have . . . to fight off illness and death. You don't have anything if you don't have the stories" (Silko, 1977, p. 2). "It is only the story that can continue beyond the war and the warrior. . . . The story is our escort; without it, we are blind" (Achebe, 1987, p 7). So, listen to the stories of Black students.

TAKEAWAY QUESTIONS

1. How significant is the shift from deficit-based to asset-based perspectives when considering the well-being and academic success of Black female students, immigrants in particular, in predominantly white universities?
2. Immigrant students may have high academic expectations that can create pressure, stress, and anxiety, particularly when navigational

capital is yet to be attained. How can educational institutions support Black female immigrant students in achieving their aspirations in balanced, stress-reduced environments?

3. How do intersecting social identities and dominant narratives and counternarratives around gender, race, immigration status, religious affiliations, and so on, impact Black immigrant women in STEM disciplines?

4. Black women's narratives and experiences hold strength and have an impact. Sharing these narratives and experiences is a necessary action for change. How can educational institutions make Black female students' voices heard, in particular in STEM-related programs?

Part II

PARTICIPATORY AND COMMUNAL APPROACHES TO LEARNING AND CIVIC ENGAGEMENT

*Michelle G. Knight-Manuel and
Dorothy Khamala*

As we think about the *Framework for Educating African Immigrant Youth* (Chapter 1), the chapters in Part II invite readers to first situate themselves within asset-based perspectives of African immigrant youth and the knowledges, literacies, and civic strengths they bring to schooling processes across the educational spectrum. In doing so, authors demonstrate how African immigrant youth and their families counter anti-Black, deficit narratives of Africa and Africans/African immigrants with humanizing narratives of how they read the world. For example, Patrick Keegan in Chapter 6 examines how Kadija, a high school student, counters "discourses of Muslims and African migrants as threatening and dangerous" and humanizes the Black African immigrant body through understandings of intersectional identities and civic actions she engages in as Muslim, female, and African.

Kadija's everyday civic actions across multiple contexts—Senegal, France, and the United States—resonate with Knight-Manuel, Robert, and Akin-Sabuncu in Chapter 9, as the authors render visible how 21 high school youth from West Africa, participating in a culturally relevant-sustaining after-school club, take up participatory communal learning. The learning centered on their civic identities and engagement of inequities they experienced, such as job discrimination in multiracial spaces. African immigrant youth's social civic literacies and actions in Chapters 6 and 7 extend understandings of the heterogeneity of Black African immigrant experiences as youth mediate diasporic migrations in diverse schooling contexts.

Throughout Part II, authors also deconstruct the traditional education system, which is confined to the classroom, in relation to learning in after-school clubs, at home, and via technological platforms. In Chapter 8, Dreas-Shaikha, Badaki, and Blanks Jones illustrate African immigrant girls piecing together film footage on their own time, across kitchens, living rooms, and bedrooms, separated by the pandemic from cocreators. Embodied notions of learning depicted further demonstrate how African immigrant girls, as creators of digital texts, challenge dominant notions of teaching as unilateral by participating as dialogic equals with peers at all levels. This shifts traditional portrayals of them as victims of immigration status, racial identity, socioeconomic status, and literacy levels to creative thinkers advocating for societal reforms.

As a former public middle school and adult education teacher who taught English as a Second Language to students and parents from Africa, Vietnam, Mexico, and Guatemala, Michelle Knight-Manuel was always looking for ways to support parents' presence in our schools and learn with them in cultural community centers. In Chapter 7, Dávila and Ogwal remind her of and draw attention to how African immigrant parents grapple through their own affective experiences with schools where teaching affirms (or not) their cultural and language practices as they navigate past, present, and future lives of their children. The authors leverage their collective parental experiences to activate learning opportunities for their children.

Ultimately, the authors in Part II challenge us to consider: How do we center African immigrant youth's perspectives that are not a counter story in our learning spaces? In what ways can educators become aware of, acknowledge, and leverage literacy and civic engagement strengths of African immigrant youth's everyday civic life and actions? And how does (anti-)Blackness matter in African immigrant youth's everyday civic life and actions?

CHAPTER 6

Always Remember What's Behind You So You Can Reach What's in Front of You

The Transnational Civic Engagement of a West African High School Student

Patrick Keegan

> We let society define us too much. We separate ourselves, we humans, starting with the countries, then with the color. . . . If there were not these boundaries . . . you can see two countries that are so close, it's just a line that separates them, why is that there? (Kadija)

Kadija's query demonstrates her critical awareness of the role boundaries play in separating human beings and challenges the moral and ethical basis upon which nation-states claim territory and regulate belonging. Kadija explains how boundaries have been used to divide humans and cause so much conflict in the world.

Transnational youth like Kadija demonstrate a unique perspective on democratic rights that "emerges from occupying a space between nations, with frames of reference that encompass multiple groups and experiences across borders" (Dyrness & Abu El-Haj, 2019, p. 169). This is particularly so at a time when schooling in the United States is stubbornly rooted in conceptions of citizenship conditioned on national belonging (Dyrness & Abu El-Haj, 2019), despite the increasing number of youth with civic ties extending beyond nation-state boundaries (Dei, 2012; Lukose, 2007). Kadija was acutely aware of African migrants' hyper-visibility as both model minorities attaining high levels of education in the United States, and refugees fleeing famine, war, and poverty (Watson & Knight-Manuel, 2017, Ukpokodu, 2018). Additionally, as a Muslim woman wearing hijab, Kadija was subject to religious discrimination and surveillance in public spaces (Ghaffar-Kucher et al., 2022; Keegan, 2019).

Amid polarizing discourses of Muslims and African migrants as threatening and dangerous (Ghaffar-Kucher et al., 2022; Keegan, 2019; Kiramba, Onyewuenyi et al., 2020), I thus discuss Kadija's everyday civic engagement through theoretical lenses of transnationalism (Glick-Schiller et al., 1992) and diaspora studies (Dei, 2012; Lukose, 2007), illustrating how Kadija's civic engagements illuminated a critical consciousness of home in the African diaspora and an orientation to collective social action.

THE CIVIC ENGAGEMENT OF MIGRANT YOUTH
FROM WEST AFRICAN COUNTRIES

The terminology used to refer to different regions of Africa (e.g., Sub-Saharan Africa) and African nation-state borders is based on boundaries carrying a legacy of colonialism, violence, and conflict (Fanon, 1961). I use the description migrant youth from West African countries to acknowledge the diversity of routes African migrants take to reach the United States, as well as their roots as members of the African diaspora (Watson & Knight-Manuel, 2017). Furthermore, popular representations of Africa in the Western media ignore the ethnic, cultural, religious, and linguistic diversity of the African continent. According to prior research, as a result of racialization in the United States and being singled out as model minorities, some migrant youth from West African countries adopt an African American identity, while others affiliate more closely with ethnic or national identities to resist homogenizing discourses of Africa (Awokoya, 2012).

While there is robust literature on migrant youth education and how to build on migrant youth's transnational funds of knowledge (Bajaj & Bartlett, 2017; Bajaj et al., 2017; Sánchez, 2007), few studies focus specifically on the civic engagements of migrant youth from West African countries (see Dávila, 2021; Kiramba, Kumi-Yeboah & Mawuli Sallar, 2020; Knight, 2011; Knight & Watson, 2014). Research with Palestinian and Guatemalan transnational youth found that occupying a space between nations fostered civic action challenging inequality (Dyrness & Abu El-Haj, 2019). For example, Palestinian youth in Abu El-Haj's (2015) research drew on their transnational ties to demonstrate for peace in Palestine and raised money for children in refugee camps in the Middle East. At another high school, transnational students drew upon their knowledge of conditions of scarcity to research water collection and management strategies in their home countries and in drought-prone areas of the United States (Bajaj et al., 2017).

The diasporic ties and political traditions of youth from West African countries have been found to foster a collective responsibility toward multiple communities of belonging and hybrid civic identities (Knight, 2011).

For example, Kwame, a Ghanaian American student in Knight's (2011) study, "shied away from the necessity of community involvement needing to be competitive and based on self-interest," such as competing for a prize awarded to the student or class contributing the most canned goods to a food drive (p. 1283). Instead, Kwame drew on his civic assets to build community in a letter-writing campaign to a congressman urging him to devote more federal funding to address homelessness and hunger.

African political traditions and conceptions of citizenship also contribute to unique democratic citizenship formations (Avoseh, 2001; Dei, 2012). Avoseh (2001) described "active citizenship in traditional African societies [that] pivots on the basic elements of obligations to the community and interpersonal relationships" (p. 481). Knight and Watson (2014) found that migrant youth from West African countries were civically engaged by meeting social obligations to family. As opposed to single, individualized forms of political action, such as voting or doing community service, youth in their study engaged in "participatory communal citizenship" that took place "across lifetime events and geographic locations" (p. 545). A Ghanaian participant referred to this as "Sankofa"—reaching and giving back to her ancestors and family still living in Ghana.

CONDITIONAL BELONGING OF WEST AFRICAN MUSLIM YOUTH

Migrant youth from West African countries also engage in everyday civic practices while having their right to belong predicated on the notion of being "good Muslims" (Ghaffar-Kucher et al., 2022; Keegan, 2019). Post-9/11 especially, Muslim Americans were viewed as perpetual foreigners and expected to assimilate and publicly support U.S. military interventions in majority-Muslim countries. However, younger generations of Muslim Americans are challenging the terms of conditional belonging by publicly displaying their Muslim identities and joining with people of color to challenge institutional racism (Ghaffar-Kucher et al., 2022).

Migrant youth from West African countries who identify as Muslim may find their religion rendered invisible due to stereotypes of how Muslim bodies look in the United States (Ghaffar-Kucher et al., 2022). Yet women and girls from West African countries who wear the hijab are often more identifiable as Muslim and face greater scrutiny, racism, and religious discrimination. In a national study with Muslim youth, Ghaffar-Kucher et al. found that "anger and disdain directed at women wearing hijab were the most consistent forms of overt racism . . . even from teachers" (p. 1061). Therefore, race, religion, and gender intersect in complex ways to condition belonging and shape civic engagements of migrant youth from West African countries (Watson & Knight-Manuel, 2020).

TRANSNATIONAL SOCIAL FIELDS

Glick-Schiller and colleagues (1992) define transnationalism as "the process by which immigrants build social fields that link together their country of origin and their country of settlement" (p. 1). Levitt and Glick-Schiller (2004) use the concept of "social field" to describe "a set of multiple interlocking networks of social relationships through which ideas, practices, and resources are unequally exchanged, organized and transformed" (p. 1009). The concept of a social field helps explain how migrant youth from West African countries maintain social relationships across national borders. Due to the difficulty of travel to their home countries, many migrant youth from West African countries maintain transnational ties through social media and other communication technologies.

Participating in a transnational social field has led some migrant youth to adopt a dual frame of reference by comparing civic experiences in the United States with those in their home countries. Some transnational youth gain an appreciation for political and social rights that may have been lacking in their host countries. The concept of a dual frame of reference has been used to explain why some migrants persevere and achieve academic success in the face of host country challenges by leveraging educational opportunities previously unavailable to them. At the same time, a dual frame of reference can nurture a critical awareness of the "contradictions of Western democracy" (Dyrness & Abu El-Haj, 2019, p. 169). In their research, Dyrness and Abu El-Haj demonstrated how transnational youth developed a critique of "the failed promise of inclusion and equality in their new state" (i.e., the "American dream") and the ways foreign intervention of their host countries (e.g., U.S. imperialism) contributed to the social/political/economic conditions that precipitated their migration (p. 169).

DIASPORIC NETWORKS

In addition to maintaining ties between home and host countries, migrant youth from West African countries also cultivate membership in the African diaspora. As Ritty Lukose (2007) outlined, the field of diaspora studies contributes to our understandings of transnational youths' cultural worlds. An important aspect of the term *diaspora* is that it "entails dispersal across space, especially dispersal of a population across nation-state borders," as well as "an orientation to a 'homeland' as a significant authoritative source of value, legitimacy, and identity" (p. 409). As Kadija explained, she identifies as being from Senegal, but also Africa, because "when they say African, I feel included because it's my root." In addition, Kadija maintained family and social ties to France. Kadija's intersectional ties to the African diaspora fostered a critical awareness of discrimination of Muslims in the wake of the

2015 Paris terror attack. The two constructs of transnational social fields and diasporic networks are brought together in this chapter to better understand Kadija's civic engagement across multiple national contexts. Kadija's multifaceted political awareness stemmed from frames of reference between home and host countries (i.e., the United States and Senegal), and her membership in the African diaspora.

METHODS AND SOURCES OF DATA

To render visible Kadija's civic engagement, data are drawn from a larger study of migrant youths' civic belonging at a school tailored to the academic and social needs of late-arrival migrant students in New York City (Keegan, 2023). Youth participants were asked to imagine a friend or relative from their home country migrating to the United States, and to take photos of places they thought were important for the newcomer to see in their school, neighborhood, and community (Luttrell, 2020). The visual methodology of the study was designed to position participants as knowledge producers in an effort for educators to work alongside youth and recognize youth's agency in the research process (Luttrell, 2020; Watson & Knight-Manuel, 2020). I then conducted a 45- to 60-minute photo-elicitation interview with each participant to learn about the story they wanted to tell with their photos. I asked each participant to select five photos to share in a focus group with youth in the study. Providing youth with an opportunity to share and discuss their photos with different audiences revealed multiple layers of meaning in the photos (Luttrell, 2020). For example, one focus group composed of Muslim youth centered discussion on one participant's photo of a masjid, and how Muslims are treated in the United States as suspect. While this chapter focuses on a single participant, Kadija, the ways in which she engaged civically have significant implications for how educators can learn from and build on migrant youth's sociopolitical consciousness to benefit democratic citizenship preparation for all students.

Throughout the study, I attended to my own subjectivities (Peshkin, 1988), including how my positionality as a white, European, monolingual English speaker affected what participants chose to share and how they represented themselves to me through their photos. For example, in one interview, a participant asked me whether I believed America was a land of opportunity, before sharing her critique of America's failed promise of equality for all. This exchange made me reflect on whether the youth had been reticent to share experiences of racism and injustice with me. At times, my prior role at their school as a field supervisor for preservice teachers also may have led participants to view me as a teacher. My classroom observations and knowledge of the school's approaches to educating migrant youth helped me establish rapport with participants, by referring to common instructional practices like an insider. However, taking the role of teacher may have reinforced power imbalances between myself and participants. For instance, despite my insistence that there were no right or wrong photos, some youth sought confirmation that their photos had met my expectations, like a school assignment. By reflecting on my own subjectivities throughout the research process, I became more conscious of how my own biases affected what I saw and did not see in the data (Peshkin, 1988).

KADIJA'S CIVIC ENGAGEMENT

As a transnational youth and member of the African diaspora, Kadija's civic engagement reflected a critical consciousness of injustice and an orientation toward collectivist forms of action extending beyond one-time activities. I discuss how Kadija's diasporic ties to Senegal, France, and the United States fostered a critical awareness of home and fueled her resistance to deficit narratives of the African continent and Islam; and how Kadija's transnational ties and her African heritage practices fostered unique forms of civic engagement across time and place, and challenged individualistic notions of citizenship.

CRITICAL CONSCIOUSNESS OF HOME IN THE AFRICAN DIASPORA

> We don't know where home is. I mean everywhere is home, like home is just a place where you feel comfortable . . . where you feel safe. We don't know where home is because most people refer to home as your house. Or your home country. . . . If we describe it that way, not everybody feels good about going home. . . . So it depends. (Kadija, interview, November 6, 2015)

Kadija demonstrated a critical awareness of home as a place that transcended fixed boundaries, like the walls of a house or national borders. Kadija's declaration that "everywhere is home" reflected her feeling of being at home in multiple places simultaneously. During our conversations, Kadija referred to a number of places where she felt comfortable and therefore at home: in neighborhood parks, at school in the care of teachers, in her apartment with her mother and siblings, and at the library surrounded by books. Kadija also called attention to the subjective, transitory nature of home, and that for some, one's home or home country may not be a safe or comfortable place. For example, youth migrating to the United States as refugees or asylum seekers fleeing war or conflict may no longer feel at home in their home countries.

Kadija understood home as a set of relationships and feelings attached to places. She described reading as an activity that made her feel at home. As

Kadija explained, "When I open a book, I feel like I'm home. Because reading is just . . . I don't think there is an adjective to describe this, just good." Kadija took a photo of bookshelves in a library to represent her idea of the perfect closet: "Most girls are like I have nothing to wear, [but] I'm sitting here like I have nothing to read. So, that would be my ideal closet, full of books." By distinguishing herself from "most girls" and preferring a closet full of books to read, Kadija challenged Eurocentric notions of Blackness and female beauty (Watson & Knight-Manuel, 2020). Kadija was especially drawn to reading *Hunger Games* (Collins, 2008) and *Divergent* (Roth, 2011), books with strong female characters:

> I feel like that was the first time I read a book where the woman was the main character that was so strong, like the whole society depended on [Katniss] because she fought the man that was supposed to be powerful and brought him down and I just love that. They inspire me in a way.

Kadija drew inspiration from strong female characters in books that challenge gender norms and demonstrate the civic capacities of Black migrant women to lead. In addition to being an avid reader, Kadija enjoyed writing fiction and poetry. She was mentored through an organization called Girls Write Now (n.d.), whose mission is to "break down barriers of gender, race, age and poverty," amplifying marginalized voices in society through storytelling. Kadija was writing a dystopian short story about a girl who lives in a society in which you cannot see your reflection until you are 16.

Kadija's nuanced understanding of home, safety, and belonging was shaped by her African diasporic ties. In research with transnational youth from Palestine and Guatemala, Dyrness and Abu El-Haj (2019) found that "through participating in and navigating between these multiple groups and contexts, transnational youth develop a critical awareness of disparities and inequalities in material conditions, opportunities, and access to rights between and across their multiple communities" (p. 169). As a member of the African diaspora, Kadija's awareness of differential access to rights was informed by ties to Senegal, the United States, and France. She spoke about the discrimination Muslim women faced in Paris following the 2015 terror attacks, explaining: "Yeah, I watch[ed] it all night. It was crazy. . . . I saw [people] beating all these Muslims and stuff like that. And then some store[s], they don't let the Muslim girls with hijab come inside."

Closely entwined with their critical consciousness of unequal access to rights across multiple communities (e.g., freedom of religion, expression, etc.), members of the African diaspora have "an awareness of how their group(s) are viewed and positioned by dominant groups, and of reductive images of their communities from both sides of the border" (Dyrness & Abu El-Haj, 2019, p. 169). Through ties to Senegal, Paris, and the United States, Kadija became aware of stereotypical images of Islam that were directed

94   Participatory and Communal Approaches to Learning and Civic Engagement

toward her as a Muslim woman living in the United States. According to Kadija, following the terror attacks in Paris:

> All these people were commenting on Twitter, and it got me mad because they were kind of talking to me too . . . they were [saying] that we should demolish all the mosque[s], burn the masjid, kill the Muslims, a lot of really stupid things. . . . When I pass by someone who is calling me a terrorist or something like that, I will not answer because I know it's not true, that's not what I am.

Kadija's statement illustrates how her awareness of the dominant discourse of Muslims as threatening was fueled by her transnational and diasporic ties. Kadija and I met during the 2016 presidential campaign of Donald Trump, who called for increased border security, including a wall on the U.S.-Mexico border, and a total ban on migrants from several Muslim-majority countries. As a form of civic engagement, Kadija countered stereotypes of Islam with her own narrative of Muslims as respectful of all living things, and believing that you should treat others the way you want to be treated.

In addition, Kadija challenged popularized stereotypes of Africa, educating individuals that Africa is a continent, not a country, and explaining the diversity of languages, ethnicities, and cultures found in African countries (Awokoya, 2012; Watson & Knight-Manuel, 2017). Kadija described how she responded to prevalent stereotypes of Africa:

> People thought [Africa] was just a big zoo, this big forest with a lot of animals. [Someone] asked me in 9th grade, did you ever see an elephant? Aren't you African? And I'm like what are you talking about? You don't see an animal until you go to the zoo. They [say] speak African for me, and it's so annoying. I'm just like, it's a continent.

Kadija's diasporic ties to Senegal, France, and the United States gave her a unique perspective on global events, which educators can learn from and build on to benefit democratic citizenship preparation for all students. For example, in 2021, conservative politicians in France introduced legislation to ban women and girls from wearing headscarves during sporting events, sparking the global #HandsOffMyHijab protest. Students could compare such civic responses to Islamophobia across different national contexts, deepening their perspectives on religious freedom and women's autonomy (Diallo, 2021).

Collective Action to Sustain African Diasporic Community Ties

> Some people come here and forget all about themselves. They just want to live the American life, and forget totally about their culture. . . . Always remember where you come from, that's what I would tell them. . . . Always

remember what's behind you so you can reach what is in front of you.
(Kadija, interview, November 2, 2015)

Kadija's advice to youth migrating from West Africa reflected the value she placed on remembering where she came from, not forgetting her cultural roots. Her belief that future action must be rooted in understandings of the past "invoke[d] the West African symbol of the 'Sankofa' bird who is looking around behind to see where he is going" (Dei, 2012 p. 109; see Figure 10.1 and description in Chapter 10, this volume). For members of the African diaspora, the importance of "knowing where [you] are coming from in order to know where [you] are going" can be a means of maintaining cultural ties to home and preserving a collective memory of the past (Dei, 2012, p. 109). Remembering cultural histories included Kadija's maintaining connection and responsibility toward family and community. Kadija's orientation toward collective action mirrors that of migrant groups growing up in transnational social fields (Dyrness & Abu El-Haj, 2019), while being rooted in African political traditions of a collectivist ethos and communal responsibility (Avoseh, 2001; Dei, 2012).

As a symbol of the interrelatedness of past, present, and future, the African philosophy of Sankofa provides a counterpoint to civic engagement rooted in individual success and the myth of meritocracy that predominates in the United States. When I asked Kadija how she remembered where she came from, she referenced her grandparents and an aunt who raised her in Senegal. Kadija made the most of educational opportunities in the United States to honor her mother and grandfather:

> Like taking the example of school, [it] can be really annoying waking up early and I don't really feel like coming. My mom worked really hard for me to be here. And my grandpa, since I was little, he was taking care of me. I don't know if he's going to be living to see me successful but I want him to be like part of me.

Kadija's notion of success was rooted in collective responsibility toward her family and community, not individual effort alone. Kadija carried her grandfather with her and wanted him to be a part of her achievements. As a transnational youth, Kadija was aware of support that was behind her so that she could reach what was in front of her.

Kadija's advice to remember your roots included a civic orientation toward collective action. Dyrness and Abu El-Haj (2019) found that Dominican and Palestinian youth recalled "a communal life where they belonged and where neighbors helped each other out" in their home countries (p. 171). This collectivist ethos "translated into ways of being and acting in their host country," including a "sense of responsibility for their families in precarious conditions across far-flung borders" (p. 171). Kadija expressed similar sentiments, including missing the sense of community she felt in Senegal. Kadija described community life in the Bronx as more focused on individuals than the community: "I'm not saying nobody cares, it's just . . . you care most about yourself. And there [in Senegal] it's really rare that two people don't know each other in a way, or they're not related. And here it's like everybody is a stranger." The African political and philosophical tradition of Sankofa contributed to Kadija's civic engagement in the United States on behalf of family and African diasporic communities.

Kadija's critique of individualism has important implications for how educators can tap into transnational youths' civic consciousness. Teachers could build a community of care in classrooms in which students support one another's learning in a family-like atmosphere, instead of an environment where students compete against one another to succeed. Kadija singled out teachers who not only taught her academic content, but also provided emotional support. In describing one teacher, Kadija said, "She is not like our teacher, she's our friend, when we don't feel good, she doesn't feel good either. And she cares, and she makes us know that she cares, and that means a lot to us." Civic educators can build on the sense of collectivism migrant youth from West African countries bring to school, rather than focus on individual, one-time actions as a form of civic engagement, like voting or competing with peers to donate canned goods to a food drive (Knight, 2011).

DISCUSSION AND IMPLICATIONS

Schools and educators both can learn from and build on the transnational assets that youth like Kadija bring to their preparation as citizens. This study's implications extend exemplary approaches to educating migrant youth, with special consideration of the needs of students from West African countries (Bajaj et al., 2017; Bajaj & Bartlett, 2017). I also align this study's findings with the *Framework for Educating African Immigrant Youth* (Chapter 1) to highlight how teachers can build on transnational funds of knowledge (Sánchez, 2007) migrant youth bring to their learning to critique Western democratic institutions.

Migrant youth from West African countries could leverage their sense of belonging to the African diaspora to take civic action in support of democracy. Similar to Congolese students in Dávila's (2021) study, who were "keenly aware of the powerlessness of citizens in political contexts where democratic ideals and processes are non-existent or fragile at best," Kadija's ties to France as a member of the African diaspora made her aware of Muslim women's transglobal rights struggles (p. 863). Teachers can provide transnational youth with opportunities to leverage their critical consciousness of democratic representation to study histories of imperialism in Africa, and how colonial legacies influence debates about Muslim women's bodies and religious symbols in France and the United States today. Additionally, a curriculum that teaches about relationships between European colonialism in Africa and settler colonialism in the United States engages students from West African countries in learning critical history beyond Eurocentric onto-epistemologies (Dozono, 2020).

Teachers also could build on the collectivist ethos of migrant youth from West African countries to envision and enact social–civic literacies. Rather than focus preparation for democracy on individual one-time political acts, teachers could provide opportunities for students to link civic engagement to caring for their home communities and affirming their heritage practices (e.g., Abu El-Haj, 2015; Bajaj et al., 2017; Keegan, 2019; Knight, 2011; Watson et al., 2014). Teachers and schools could reinforce interconnections between home, schooling, and civic engagement, moving beyond narrow definitions of academic achievement as individual, personal success, and creating family-like spaces in classrooms. For example, in one high school, students were encouraged to tailor school presentations for family members in their home countries by bringing pictures of cousins and grandparents to school (Bajaj et al., 2017). Presenting to family members would help students such as Kadija see their persistence in schooling as a form of civic engagement that stretches across time and place, benefitting African diasporic communities.

Finally, youth from West African countries can be encouraged to participate in political activities transcending national borders and challenging monolithic stereotypes of Africa and Islam across national contexts. Challenging deficit narratives of Muslims and "Africans" is an important opportunity to build on transnational youths' funds of knowledge to engage civically. For refugee or asylum-seeking youth fleeing violence or persecution, civic engagement could be directed toward helping communities they were forced to leave behind. For Kadija, "home" referred not only to a geographic location like the United States or Senegal, but also to places she felt safe and comfortable, as well as relationships fostered through reading and writing. Whether through photography, or other literary and artistic expression, youth from West African countries can promote multifaceted stories of Blackness, including diverse routes migrant youth take to the United States, and foster ties to homeplaces across the African diaspora. Rather than preparing youth as patriotic citizens loyal to a single nation-state, educators can nurture multifaceted affiliations migrant youth from West African countries have to people and places rooted in caring relationships with teachers, friends, and family across the African diaspora.

TAKEAWAY QUESTIONS

1. How will you learn about civic experiences of migrant youth from West African countries in your classroom to be able to integrate

their transnational funds of knowledge and African heritage practices?

2. In what ways can you foster a culture of learning and success based on communal responsibility, and promote an ethic of care in your classroom?

3. How can you build on interconnections between family, schooling, and civic engagement rather than focus on individual, one-time actions as forms of civic engagement?

4. What opportunities will you provide for migrant youth from West African countries to challenge dominant discourses by authoring their own stories of what it means to be African, female, Muslim, citizen, and/or migrant?

CHAPTER 7

An Affect-Centered Analysis of Congolese Immigrant Parent Perspectives on Past-Present-Future Learning in School and at Home

Liv T. Dávila and Susan A. Ogwal

Immigrant parents in the United States historically have faced challenges in connecting with their children's teachers and school leaders, in large part because of real or perceived incongruency between home and school in terms of language, cultural norms, and community funds of knowledge (Moll et al., 2013).

We analyze interviews conducted in 2018–2019 with four immigrant parents from the Democratic Republic of Congo (DRC) who work with or whose children attend or have graduated from K–12 public schools in a small U.S. midwestern city, guided by the following questions: (1) How do Black immigrant parents from the DRC (re)frame deficit narratives of African immigrant children, families, and communities? (2) How do they situate languages, literacy, and racialization in their parenting of school-aged children? (3) How do their knowledge and feelings related to parenting lead to action and affective agency?

A focus on a small group of Black African parents from the DRC allows for unique perspectives on past-present-future learning to support research, pedagogy, and practice engaging immigrant family/indigenous epistemologies to foster humanizing school–family relationships.

IMMIGRATION, RACE, AND PARENTING SCHOOL-AGED CHILDREN

Recent research has examined African immigrant parents' aspirations for their children in U.S. schools (Dryden-Peterson, 2018; Roubeni et al., 2015) and influences of messages conveyed by African immigrant parents to their children that reinforce ethnic pride or harmful stereotypes against African

Americans (Thelamour & Mwangi, 2021). Collectively, studies point to challenges parents experience as they interface with schools and in parenting children in the United States, including language barriers, racism, and xenophobia.

Research also shows a positive correlation between immigrant parents' educational aspirations for their children and children's motivation and achievement in school, and that immigrant children and their parents tap into community cultural and linguistic resources, as means of facilitating positive academic outcomes, that often differ from those used by white middle-class families (S. Alvarez, 2017; Kumi-Yeboah et al., 2017; Tadesse, 2014). However, research on Black African immigrant parents' perspectives on language, literacy, race, and belonging in and outside of educational contexts is scarce (Braden, 2020), and even fewer studies have examined perspectives of Black African immigrant parents from countries where English is not an official language.

THEORIZING AFFECT, LANGUAGE, LITERACY, AND RACE

The recent "affective turn" in social sciences and humanities has ignited new attention to emotions and embodied dimensions of language and literacy teaching and learning (Leander & Ehret, 2019). In our research, we apply Bucholtz et al.'s (2018) definition of affect as "the simultaneously cognitive, perceptual, and emotional experience of embodied encounter with the material world" (p. 3). We are inspired by and extend the work of scholars who have contributed nuanced understandings of intersectionality and affect, critically examining white supremacy and embodiment in literacy events in school (Grinage, 2019). We are also inspired by the groundbreaking work of Watson and Knight-Manuel (2017, 2020) in research on Black immigrant youth's civic learning and on intellectual engagement with anticolonial epistemologies toward the humanization of Black immigrant bodies in educational research.

Like Osibodu and Damba Danjo (Chapter 3) and Wandera (Chapter 10), we integrate into our work non-Western(ized) African analytical frameworks emphasizing heritage resources Congolese parents tap into as they respond to racialization, anti-Blackness, and linguistic marginalization they and their children experience in the United States. Chilisa (2019) and a range of African scholars (e.g., Ikhane & Ukpokolo, 2023) have long written that African epistemology is relational—what scholars now may name as affect oriented—stored in spoken, written, and embodied communication, traditions, myths, and folktales (Afolalu, Chapter 11, this volume; Oloo & Kiramba, 2019; Omolewa et al., 1998; Ngugi wa Thiong'o, 1986). We thus explore Congolese immigrant parents' perspectives on past-present-future learning and affective agency through African relational epistemologies, drawing on words, expressions, and accompanying emotive responses.

THE RESEARCH CONTEXT

This exploratory qualitative study draws on individual, in-depth interviews with four Congolese immigrant parents in a small city in the midwestern region of the United States where immigrants, the majority from Mexico, Central America, China, and the DRC, constituted roughly 12% of the population. Since the early 2000s, when Congolese refugees first arrived in the city through sponsorship from local churches, the overall population of residents born in the DRC has grown significantly and was the fastest growing immigrant community in the city during the time of this study (Ogwal, 2020). Many Congolese immigrant adults are from urban areas in the DRC, where they earned the equivalent of an associate's or bachelor's degree, and held positions in professional fields (e.g., finance, journalism, medicine, education). These adults have experienced largely downward professional mobility in the United States, working in warehouse or manufacturing jobs in surrounding communities (Ogwal, 2020). A significant proportion of the Congolese community is from rural areas in less-industrialized and more conflict-ridden eastern provinces of the DRC.

This study took place in 2018–2019, a period during which the Trump administration placed bans on immigration from Africa, the Middle East, and the Caribbean. Although participants were not asked to comment on the political climate in the United States or the DRC, responses to interview questions may have been influenced by broader international, national, and local racialized discourses around immigration and citizenship. In addition, we approach our analysis with recognition, although it was not raised specifically by participants, that white and Anglo-supremacism serves as a catalyst of tensions between African, Afro-Latinx, and Afro-Caribbean immigrants, on one hand, and African Americans and racially and linguistically minoritized communities, on the other (Okonofua, 2013). We frame participants' comments in light of their children attending multiracial public schools in which they interact with peers, many of whom are also marginalized in school and society on the basis of race, ethnicity, and language backgrounds.

RESEARCH PARTICIPANTS AND PROCEDURES

Four Congolese parent participants (pseudonyms are used throughout) were recruited by the first author to participate in this study (see Figure 7.1).

All four participants graduated from private or parochial high schools, and with the exception of Julie, earned an advanced degree in the DRC. They considered themselves to be middle class and had children currently enrolled in or recently graduated from local public schools. Recruitment occurred through purposeful and snowball sampling; for example, the first author was given Soleil's contact information by a teacher who partook in

Figure 7.1. Participants

Name	Role	Education in the DRC	Years in the United States	Current Occupation
Julie	Mother of two children in elementary school	High school	4	Store clerk
Soleil	Mother of four children in elementary and middle school	College	8	Store owner
Rita	Mother of two college-aged children who attended K–12 in the United States	College	16	School district family liaison
Jacques	Father of one child, an infant not yet in school	College	11	Public school dual-language teacher

her earlier research on Central African high school students (Dávila, 2019, 2021). Soleil owned and managed an African food market in the community. Julie, a cashier at the market, volunteered to participate when she learned of the study from Soleil. Soleil recommended contacting Jacques, who taught in a French–English dual-language immersion program housed in a local elementary school. Jacques introduced the first author to Rita, who worked as a family–school liaison for the school district. In addition to full-time jobs, Soleil hosted a weekly radio show for Congolese immigrants; Jacques founded and served as director of a Congolese community organization; Rita was involved in school- and church-based youth after-school mentoring programs. Each saw themselves as interlocutors for Congolese parents as an entity, reflected in their reported speech in each interview (e.g., "Congolese parents feel that . . . ," "X works the second shift at Y so they cannot be with their children after school").

Data Collection

The first author conducted two 30- to 60-minute audio-recorded interviews with each participant over the course of 1 year. Participants responded to open-ended questions in English and French around educational experiences in the Congo, views on schooling and parenting in the United States, and perceptions of experiences of recently arrived Congolese immigrant parents of school-aged children. Interviews were transcribed, and segments of interviews in French were translated by the first author.

We individually read through transcripts and engaged in a collaborative process of looking for patterns of phenomena and generating themes from the data, background literature, and analytical framework, resulting in the following themes: changing roles and responsibilities; challenges associated with language barriers, education background, racism, and xenophobia; and enacting affective agency in parenting. We recalibrated initial codes by rereading interview transcripts, looking for words illuminating affect in participants' responses to our questions about parent–school dynamics (e.g., fear, pride, shame, or nostalgia). These words and phrases are italicized in interview data included in the findings section for emphasis.

AUTHOR POSITIONALITIES

In harmony with indigenous and decolonial epistemological frameworks, we critically reflected on ourselves as "knower[s], redeemer[s], [and] colonizer[s]" (Chilisa, 2019, p. 220) throughout our research. This necessitated understandings of how our positionalities influenced our approach to the research and relationships with participants, as well as how affect and emotion played out in our interactions with parents. It also encouraged us to contemplate our roles in likely reinforcing Eurocentric, white supremacist paradigms through our research as outsiders inquiring into participants' perspectives. In further reflecting on Grinage's (2019) analysis of how bodily positioning of a focal teacher participant, Mr. Turner, influenced his classroom's affective register, we were inspired to consider how our *selves* are implicated in the "affective entanglement of bodies, ideas, texts, affects, and so forth," as we undertook this research (Dernikos et al., 2020, p. 437).

The first author is a parent of school-aged children, former high school and community college language teacher, and educational researcher at a local university. She was aware of the ways in which her whiteness, linguistic background as a native speaker of English and speaker of French and other European languages, and university connection may have influenced the nature and tone of interviews, and that participants may have sought to render a picture of how they wished to be perceived. She approached the research with affirmative stances toward multilingualism, immigration, and social justice more broadly, which influenced her interaction with participants as well as interpretations of their perspectives.

The second author was a graduate research assistant in education during the time of this study. She is a former child refugee from Uganda with a background in social services and educational research. Having firsthand knowledge as an African woman who spent most of her formative years in U.S. schools, she acknowledged both the biases and emic perspectives she brought to analysis of data due to her insider status within the local African community. Together, we approached the study with respect for and a desire to learn from participants' and each other's worldviews (Mkabela, 2005).

FINDINGS

Findings are presented in three interrelated strands aligning with our intent to explore how Black immigrant parents from the DRC (1) envision roles and responsibilities with regard to their children's education; (2) name challenges experienced; and (3) enact affective agency in parenting.

Envisioning Roles and Responsibilities

Each of the four parents emphasized pressures they and other Congolese immigrant parents feel in helping their children navigate differences between home and school, including loss of their home languages and culture, and frustration over children being socialized into a U.S. education system that simultaneously grants too many freedoms in school and marginalizes them as English learners who are Black and African. Pivoting between nostalgia for the Congolese education system and disdain for children's more casual relationships with teachers in the United States, Jacques shared:

> When I was in school in Congo, I learned that regardless of the teacher's age, I needed to respect them to the same degree as my parents. . . . But when [children] arrive at school here, they find lots of liberty. Teachers [here] can't touch kids, can't hit them, and kids develop behaviors that conflict with Congolese norms. They know that in school they are free, and at home they need to behave.

Soleil's response mirrors that of Jacques:

> We [Congolese adults] have grown up in a [educational] system that corrects [in the DRC]. . . . You cannot respond to an adult "shut up!" or "leave me alone!"

She believed that teachers should establish and maintain an authoritarian ethos in all aspects of schooling to establish orderly classrooms and prevent disobedience in school and at home.

Julie expressed a similar concern:

> The struggle is trying to keep the [African] values. First of all, when it comes to respecting older people, we have that. We have that respect, you know I respect you, older people. But here in America, it's not like that. We [parents] need to teach the kids to keep that.

A related area of concern expressed by participants was peer socialization in school. They all noted that while Congolese parents want their children to develop friendships, they are concerned with possibilities of their children being exposed to alcohol and drugs by their American peers, and that parenting in the United States necessitates a degree of surveillance many Congolese are not accustomed to. Jacques commented:

> The thing is in Congo, we don't have kids who smoke marijuana, drive and drink, and whatever. But here, if parents are not teaching kids to keep [their] values, they might suddenly start smoking weed. That's the struggle that we—as parents, and [our] kids encounter when we come here. Kids are lost between "my dad would do this, my parents would do this, and I want to please my friends."

Jacques emphasized the diversity of parental responses, while acknowledging his worry for children who have little contact with their parents:

> There are parents who let it be. They say it's a generational difference. There are also parents who say, "here it's my house, school is something else." At home they maintain African discipline. But it's hard because many parents work all day, or all night, they come home to eat, clean up, and sleep. They don't have time for their kids. They don't see their kids. That's a danger.

Soleil was more adamant that parents accept responsibility for guiding their children:

> Yeah, Congolese children adapt, but parents also need to do their work. They need to be receptive to how their child is doing in school. . . . Our responsibility . . . parents need to help work out conflicts between kids too. [Parents] have problems too, but we are adults, and this is our responsibility. . . . So I gotta teach [my kids]. I always make sure that "hey, you can't say this, it's not right."

Referring to resources in the Congolese community, Julie noted the importance of the church in supporting Congolese parents and children: "There's a few African churches over here, and French-speaking churches. They teach [kids] how to live in the United States, and how to live in the community, and how to behave themselves. So that's good."

Naming Challenges Experienced

Language and Literacy Barriers. Participants noted that many Congolese parents feel inferior because of language and cultural differences, their race, and limited education in the DRC, in addition to practical barriers, such as lack of time to help children with homework and lack of transportation to, or time for, school visits. When asked to reflect on experiences as a newcomer and immigrant who did not speak English, Soleil shared, while choking up: "I felt like *a zero*, an *illiterate*, someone who had *never* studied . . . so I stayed home." She added, "I think the first challenge that Congolese parents encounter is language barrier because you can't do anything [here]

106   Participatory and Communal Approaches to Learning and Civic Engagement

without [the English] language." From Soleil's perspective, many parents feel helpless because of their perceived inability to communicate directly with teachers without the help of a translator; this often leads them to self-isolate and disengage from daily aspects of their children's schooling.

All participants reflected on how having earned a college degree in the DRC made them more confident than parents who had minimal schooling (e.g., less than a high school degree), even if their credentials were not validated in the United States. Jacques shared:

> A parent who has not studied is going to have trouble supporting their child, even doing homework together. Most [Congolese] parents have not studied, and you see this behavior where parents don't know what they [teachers] want. When I say someone isn't educated, I mean that they didn't go to high school. . . . That's where conflicts start because the parents can't help with their kids' school. In general, they can read and do math, but writing in French or English is hard for them. They feel bad about this.

Adding to this, Jacques engaged in a critique of African values that he feels run counter to American expectations with regard to schooling, including the expectation that parents will or should foster children's literacy development at home:

> In the Congo, we don't have the time or culture to read. Children learn to read in school, but we don't have public libraries like you have here. You need to push kids to read. And then you need to push Congolese parents to come to school. They think it's a pastime. Even when you send home fliers about parent–teacher conferences, parents don't come. I don't think they read them. It's an African illness (C'est la maladie Africaine).

In addition, each participant commented on the value of knowing how to read and write in French, an official language of the DRC, and the language in which children are taught to read and write in school in the DRC. Rita asserted with an air of pride:

> The most valuable language is French. Because [speaking French] means that you went to school [you were well-educated in the DRC]. If you know how to speak good French, you are valuable. Lingala is given to everybody. Everybody speaks Lingala even if you don't know how to write it.

Tangentially, Julie shared the struggles many Congolese parents face with writing: "I still write my sisters back home in French and make sure my French is still good. But here my friends and their kids, they speak French, but writing it . . . no."

Racism and Racialization. Of the four participants, only Rita specifically mentioned race and racism as a barrier to parental involvement, and that many Congolese parents feel unwelcome in their child's school. Rita also mentored a group of middle and high school-aged girls from the DRC who frequently brought up the racism and social exclusion they experienced at school. She shared:

> There are a lot of parents and kids in schools that are frustrated because they feel that people don't want them because they are African. And that part of the globe is poor. When you come to America, people think that you are nothing because you came from Africa . . . I try to raise [kids'] morale and say, "Though you are from this part of the globe that they call dark, you can be somebody here and you can show them then that you have something greater inside of me that you can help with." In this way I help the parents by helping their kids. I tell them, "We came from the dark side of Africa, but we have something greater inside of us."

Rita, who is employed by the school district as a community liaison, has presented on this issue at school district sessions on equity, where she emphasized the importance of "emotional stability of African kids, and kids who are African American—all kids who are Black," in her words.

Enacting Affective Agency in Parenting

Language-related barriers experienced by Congolese students and parents led Soleil, Jacques, and others in the local Congolese immigrant community to advocate for two French–English dual-language immersion programs, which were established in two public elementary schools in the community in 2015 and 2017. Since then, the school district has hired Congolese teachers and interpreters who work with students in school and communicate with Congolese parents. The district also incorporated trilingual communications to students and families in the district (English, Spanish, and French) as a means of fostering stronger home–school ties.

Rita's work as a family–school liaison brings her in close contact with parents with whom she discusses ways in which they can help their children in school. However, the responsibility to educate parents and their children comes at an emotional cost to her; she explained:

> You see, I'm, I'm very emotional. [her eyes becoming teary] I cry easily because I'm emotional. But, certain people, some people when they see me, they say that's a strong woman. I'm not. I pray a lot and I cry a lot . . . I continue to find my voice. I continue to work hard. Because they need me everywhere, everywhere.

DISCUSSION AND IMPLICATIONS

The emotional strain of providing support for the Congolese community is heard and seen through her words and tears. Rita also expresses hope that her work will make a positive difference in the Congolese community.

Taken as a whole, findings shed light on barriers non-English-speaking African immigrant parents may face in navigating roles in relation to their children's schooling in the United States. First, participants' words and expressions demonstrate their affective agency as "the interactional experience of moving and being moved" to take action in support of Congolese children and their parents (Bucholtz et al., 2018, p. 4). An African epistemological frame lends insights into particularities of relationships between parents and children, families and schools, individuals and languages (and raciolinguistic ideologies) they are surrounded by, and past-presence-future of language and literacy, teaching, and learning.

Also evidenced in interviews was the circulation of deficit perspectives within the Congolese community, particularly toward parents who received less than a high school education and had little or no French language oracy or literacy. Although similar to findings of earlier studies (Kumi-Yeboah et al., 2017; Salami et al., 2020), research heretofore has not explored how ideologies related to class differences circulate within specific adult-immigrant groups, and how financial insecurity can affect relationships within African immigrant families and hamper parents' ability to cultivate "African values" in their children.

Second, parents' perspectives on their children's peer socialization in school were similar to those unearthed in Thelamour and Mwangi's (2021) study, although not specifically referring to African American peers. Paradoxically, as Roubeni et al. (2015) conclude in their research, parents' discouragement of socializing and identifying with American peers may result in children further distancing themselves from home languages, culture, and relationships.

Third, the relatively high value participants placed on French and English languages over African languages is also noteworthy and indicative of how oracy and literacy in a colonial language may be deployed by immigrants to assert prestige over other members of their community. This is further complicated by racial and linguistic hierarchies in the United States that privilege Euro-Western languages and epistemologies (Chilisa, 2019) and reinforce and are reinforced by white supremacy.

Finally, that participants were moved by their own experiences and corresponding emotions to work toward building positive relationships between parents and schools, and children and parents, highlights the "affective dimension of agency, and the agentive dimension of affect" (Bucholtz et al., 2018, p. 5). Through perspectives as members of the local Congolese immigrant community, parents (all participants), and school staff (Jacques and Rita), their responses articulate a deep connection between feeling and knowing, and knowing and acting.

In conclusion, we encourage research and pedagogical practice to bring renewed focus to relational and affective dimensions of past-present-future learning in and outside of school that promotes the well-being of Black African immigrant children, their families, and communities. For example, a fundamental point emerging from this study is that to be racialized as an immigrant (child or parent) in the United States is a deeply emotional and embodied experience that cannot be understood through empirical data alone. Our research stresses the importance of legitimizing integrative indigenous knowledge systems and affective experiences of immigrant parents of school-aged children, in both research and teaching.

In tandem with this point, we encourage further scholarly application of indigenous research methodologies framed by relational epistemologies, including participatory research approaches allowing marginalized communities to collectively share knowledges and experiences in order to promote empowerment and change. Finally, in generating affect-oriented understandings of how African immigrant parents negotiate uncertainties, contradictions, and expectations, as well as opportunities associated with all aspects of their children's education, we hope this research compels teachers to continuously disrupt harmful ideologies and engage with and advocate for their students and parents to extend past-present-future learning within and across communities and schools.

TAKEAWAY QUESTIONS

1. How would you describe parent–school engagement that is both affirming and relational? What are potential barriers to and avenues for fostering this kind of relationship?
2. Consider how language background and race factor into African students' and their parents' sense of belonging in school. How might you develop and apply your knowledge of each toward developing positive parent–school engagement?
3. How does affect, emotions, and embodied dimensions of language and literacy teaching and learning bear out in your teaching, and in your relationships with students and parents?

CHAPTER 8

Imaging and Imagining Activism
Exploring Embodied and Digital Learning Through Filmmaking With African Immigrant Girls During the Pandemic

Maryann J. Dreas-Shaikha, OreOluwa Badaki,
and Jasmine L. Blanks Jones

Ramatulai, 16, was sitting calmly, framed in the small box of the Zoom meeting, watching herself act in her own short film being played on the main Zoom screen for visiting viewers. Her head wrapped in a subtly colored scarf and soft eyes smiling, Ramatulai watched footage of herself taking up a very different pose—dominating the whole screen as she towered over another teenage girl, Adama. When Ramatulai filmed the scene, she placed her cell-phone camera at a low angle to capture her domineering stance and haughty sneer, arms akimbo, as she knocked Adama's books out of her hand. Now, as Ramatulai's short film concluded, she reflected, still gently smiling: "It's been difficult for me to take the part of a bully because I never bullied someone before. I just came from Africa . . . and never experienced bullying in America."

Making this short film pushed Ramatulai, a Sierra Leonean girl newly emigrated to Philadelphia, to embody the role of oppressor, a bully in an American school. In a manifestation of the aims of Paulo Freire's *Pedagogy of the Oppressed* (1996) and Augusto Boal's *Theatre of the Oppressed* (1979), Ramatulai observed power relations and internal conflict within the bully, and chose to transform her on-screen character from an oppressor into an ally through empathy and reconciliation. "I'm very sorry for what I've done to you all this while . . . can we be friends now?" she offered, continuing on-screen, now sitting and leaning forward, softly angled in a midshot to convey sincerity to Adama. As a Freirean analysis might suggest, the dialogue and expressed desire for justice reflect a critical transformation in "the world" through performance of "the word" in filmmaking. Crucially, as an African immigrant teenager, Ramatulai's self-directed filmmaking and

110

performance add an exciting new dimension to understandings of Black girls' critical digital literacies, an understudied area of literacy studies (Garcia et al., 2020). We observe and reflect on the embodied knowledge, power dynamics, and hope revealed through short films created by Ramatulai and her peers in collaboration with university students. It is our hope to inspire high schools, universities, and youth programs to similarly aim to nurture young people's creative expression, sense of activism, and civic engagement.

CONTEXT OF THE COURSE

Ramatulai and peers were part of a graduate-level course, Health Messaging in Africa: Public Performance as Community Health Education, offered in Fall 2020 in the Master of Public Health program at the University of Pennsylvania. Six graduate and one undergraduate student enrolled, and five 15- to 17-year-old African immigrant girls joined from the local African Family Health Organization (AFAHO), which advocates for health and well-being of African and Caribbean immigrant communities in Philadelphia. The instructor of record held a Master of Public Policy degree, was a doctoral candidate in Education and Africana Studies at the time of the course, and had nearly a decade of arts education leadership experience with youth in Liberia, West Africa. She cofacilitated the course with two theater artists from Liberia, who shared with students strategies they used to lead a street theater campaign during the Ebola epidemic to reach more than 300,000 people with health awareness messaging (Blanks Jones, 2018). A teaching assistant with experience in youth filmmaking and a youth empowerment program leader from AFAHO completed the instructional team in support of African immigrant girls (see Table 8.1).

The COVID-19 pandemic required a shift from in-person live dramatic performances to entirely virtual classes, rehearsals, and performances. Students planned, wrote, performed, and recorded stories in Zoom video meetings; edited both Zoom footage and individually recorded footage from separate homes; and screened final films for the university community, families, and the general public in a Zoom meeting.

Flexibility was key to ensuring that the transition of the course to Zoom happened smoothly and in a way enabling the competencies to be met for the course while honoring community partner requests. It was expected that students would learn to "work with others to create a vision for fostering collaboration and guiding decision making in local communities" and "create audience-appropriate communications strategies of public health content, both in writing and through oral and embodied presentation" (course syllabus). These competencies required creativity and implementation in a digital environment, in resource reallocation, and in teaching-team expertise. Connecting to the *Framework for Educating African Immigrant Youth*

Table 8.1. Course Participants and Instructors

Organization	Participant	Name	National identity	Gender
AFAHO	Youth from the community	Ramatulai	Sierra Leone	Girl
AFAHO	Youth from the community	Adama	Sierra Leone	Girl
AFAHO	Youth from the community	Martina	Liberia	Girl
AFAHO	Youth from the community	Sky (Sukurat)	Burkina Faso	Girl
AFAHO	Youth from the community	Sara	North Sudan	Girl
AFAHO	Youth from the community	Mercianne	Democratic Republic of Congo	Girl
University of Pennsylvania	Graduate student	six master's students; one undergraduate student	two identified as African	five identified as women
University of Pennsylvania/ Burning Barriers Building Bridges (B4 Youth Theatre)	Instructor	Jasmine (coauthor)	United States	Woman
B4 Youth Theatre	Instructor	Silas	Liberia	Man
B4 Youth Theatre	Instructor	Hannah	Liberia	Woman
AFAHO	Instructor	Yves Marie	Haiti	Woman
University of Pennsylvania	Instructor	Maryann (coauthor)	United States	Woman
University of Pennsylvania	Audience participant	OreOluwa (coauthor)	United States/ Nigeria	Woman

Note: The participants and their films are featured on the course's public website: www
.sites.google.com/view/performance-for-public-health

(Chapter 1), these focus areas prioritized diaspora narratives as students were invited to challenge deficit narratives of the Black African immigrant body in the field of public and community health. In enacting culturally responsive strategies that engaged community audiences, course organizers also engaged civic literacies that facilitated communal and participatory movement building across physical and digital contexts.

Film, as a pedagogical modality, provided a means to reengage the body in a digital class environment that felt largely disembodied, requiring everyone's attention to how bodies were showing up on screens to tell a story. Our class format engaged the body through whole-class games and songs, singing with cameras on, moving and chanting in spite of video and sound lags. Some of the final film products still retain these disjunctions, as students used CapCut, a free, beginner-level video editing app that worked on phones, tablets, and computers—any device they had access to; and youth worked across varying conditions—household background noise, sibling or parent interruptions. Filmmaking was taught as a skill anyone could learn on any device, challenging narratives of technical expertise that often bar individuals who are not professionals and low- or no-budget film creators. This is not to say that filmmaking does not require technical expertise, but rather that giving young people opportunities to learn through care-driven pedagogies supports critical and collaborative learning (Vasudevan & Riina-Ferrie, 2019). Technology, like dialogical theater, is in flux, transparent, and improvised—an unfinished form (Boal, 1979) instead of a rigid, omniscient, perfected form for students' mere passive use.

PARTICIPANTS AND COAUTHOR POSITIONALITY

In our practitioner roles as teaching assistant, instructor of record, and participatory audience member, our positionality and relation to African immigrant girls in the course are important to ethnographic analysis. As adult participants in positions of authority, we hold an awareness that youth civic engagement and activism that we support and study, are rife with tensions across a gerontocratic divide and, as scholars note, often are managed into impotence when adults with positional power enter the picture (Clay & Turner, 2021). Moreover, as a diverse group consisting of two heterogeneous Black-identifying coauthors and a white coauthor, we are conscious of our racial and national identities with respect to African immigrant girls, and how our identities influence our interpretation of their work (Strong & Blanks Jones, 2023). Thus in class discussions and later analysis, we all, and the white coauthor in particular, entered in a position to always learn and listen.

"AFRICANNESS" AND NEW POWER DYNAMICS

The immigration histories of Ramatulai and her peers is essential to understand in contextualizing their local community and K–12 educational experiences. Their immigrant identities show up in course interactions and our analysis, by virtue of the partnership between the African Family

Health Organization and the University of Pennsylvania differently than does the "Africanness," which may or may not include an immigrant identity, for the course's other African participants. This distinction of African immigrant girls is important in understanding the complexity of power dynamics in the course, and how synergies in identity and experiences required all participants to constantly be reflexive in negotiating roles and responsibilities.

Africana scholars such as Paul Gilroy (1993) and TsiTsi Jaji (2014) demonstrate how linkages within the political category of Blackness extend beyond deterministic and essentialist notions of Africa and the diaspora. When teachers take up the labor of centering African cultural heritage (through carefully selected readings, class structure that promotes African leadership, etc.), they engage students in a citizen-centered politics, challenging limited, deterministic conceptualizations of African cultural heritage, particularly as it pertains to immigrant girls in the U.S. context. In other words, when students' cultural heritage is foregrounded pedagogically and politically in the classroom, students can take on important roles and civic identities that are not subsumed under a flattened view of African identity. As we centered the presence and power of intersectional identities in our course, African immigrant girls engaged fully as course participants and, in turn, as powerful actors in the development of civic literacy practices.

For example, guided by the community organizing for playwriting model used in the Liberian nonprofit B4 Youth Theatre, students participate in community organizing strategies, including an issues summit, stakeholder analysis, and power mapping to "locate themselves and other actors and institutions. They then use this information to create characters and write a play that constructs solutions to the problems they have identified" (Blanks Jones, 2018, p. 144). A trained coach facilitates the learning process, but analysis and construction of a performance piece is a collective project of student participants. Thus "citizen-centered politics" (Boyte, 2004, p. 53), whereby everyday politics become the terrain of the people as they learn the arts, such as filmmaking, and skills of citizenship, make assumptions about legitimacy and power of the state, and assert grassroots notions of power to claim space from the state.

CONCEPTUAL FRAMEWORK

The study design enables an engagement with both the critical embodied and digital literacy practices of African immigrant girls. This work is thus informed by Freire's *Pedagogy of the Oppressed* (1996) and work in New and Critical Literacy studies (e.g., Heath, 1983; Scribner & Cole, 1981; Street, 1984) concerned with how power operates based on what gets defined as literacy and who gets to define it—rather than on filling students' minds with "universal" or "neutral" skills removed from social, cultural, and political resonances. Such work conceptualizes literacy as "social practice" beyond positivist, cognitivist, "autonomous" (Street, 1984) conceptions of reading and writing.

Our inquiry is further informed by Boal (1979), who, in *Theatre of the Oppressed*, conceptualized the agentive notion of a "spect-actor." Similar to how Freire challenges the "banking model" teacher–student encounter in traditional classrooms, Boal argues that theater was originally "free people singing in the open air" before "ruling classes took possession of the theater and built their dividing walls" (p. 19). A theater, or poetics, of the oppressed, Boal argues, invites the spectator to "assume the protagonic role"; the spectator "changes the dramatic action, tries out solutions, discusses plans for change—in short, trains himself for real action" (p. 122). In this way, the spectator and the actors become "spect-actors" invited to share power and agency. Therefore, reading, writing, and performing "the word" on stage emerges as a counterhegemonic act of resistance and transformation in "the world," and vice versa.

Literacy scholars have since expanded understandings of the potential for theater and performance to build critical literacies and disrupt systems of oppression (Badaki, 2023; Medina & Campano, 2006; Vasudevan et al., 2010; Whitelaw, 2019). Moreover, like Boal, literacy scholars have amplified the need to understand the body as a locus of activity, attending to ways in which power moves through, with, and in relation to the physical body within learning spaces (Badaki, 2020; Enriquez et al., 2015; Grumet, 1985; Johnson & Vasudeven, 2012; Luke, 1992). As Siegel (2015) writes in Enriquez et al.'s edited volume on literacy and the body, "The absence of the body in literacy scholarship ignores the ways in which literacy pedagogy has schooled the body" (p. 27). Watson and Knight-Manuel (2020) argue for a repositioning of African immigrant literacies that renders visible the ways in which citizenship and identity are coconstructed over time through cultural, historical, and collective meaning-making. They urge educators to "humanize the Black immigrant body," which they argue has been largely ignored and/or exploited within mainstream U.S. education. While there has been work in this arena to understand the literacies of Black girls (Haddix & Price-Dennis, 2013), immigrant students (Campano et al., 2016), as well as African immigrant students (P. Smith, 2020c; Watson & Knight-Manuel, 2017, 2020), there have been fewer concerted efforts to understand how African immigrant girls engage both a "pedagogy" as well as a "poetics" as the ongoing work of unpacking and developing their embodied, literate selves within digital spaces.

We thus designed an engagement with both the critical embodied and digital literacy practices of African immigrant girls. Critical theater-making offers the opportunity for what Boal calls "demachinization," or the process by which one can "break the body free of its self-imposed prison, from removing the social masks affiliated with cultural expectations and partaking in social conditioning for thinking and acting" (2002, p. 29; see also Monea, 2022; Noy Meir & Larcher, 2020). Whereas Black girls' critical literacy encompasses their multiple ways of making meaning from reading and writing their worlds (Price-Dennis, 2016), we focus on understanding how African immigrant girls give meaning to actions within digital spaces, a largely understudied aspect of literacy studies (Garcia et al., 2020).

METHODOLOGY

This study engages ethnographic and practitioner research to "jointly build knowledge by examining artifacts of practice" as well as to "interrogate . . . assumptions, construct new curricula, and engage with others in a search for meaning in their work lives" (Cochran-Smith & Lytle, 2009, p. 54). Such an approach extends a legacy of engaging ethnographic methods in literacy studies (Heath, 1983; Scribner & Cole, 1981; Street, 1984); more recent expansive notions of textual and narrative analysis, drawing from such field as media studies (Kress & Van Leeuwen, 2001; Stornaiuolo & Thomas, 2018; Thomas & Stornaiuolo, 2016); and practitioner or action research methods (e.g., Carr & Kemmis, 1986; Schön, 1995).

All three authors come to this work with practical and pedagogical interest in ethnographic film as a multimodal research art. Therefore, ethnographic vignettes of the films that constitute our data collection are chosen and analyzed through a lens of critical digitality. In ethnographic film, "digitality's bending of time and space recalibrates the dyadic relationship that serves as centerpiece and pivot point for the entire ethnographic encounter" (J. L. Jackson, 2012, p. 495). Our analysis focuses on possibilities of teaching and learning that supersede traditional confinements of academic courses through the "bending of time and space" made most visible in ways the girls pieced together film footage on their own time, from their own kitchens, living rooms, and bedrooms, separated from cocreators by the pandemic. We re-viewed more than 10 hours of recorded content to understand how power shifts both within dynamics of learning environments and the girls' films, and we analyzed camera angles and gestures for how they present bodies as more or less powerful. We ask how the structure of the course led to understandings of position and power that enabled our African immigrant youth community partners to produce, or constrained them from producing, work that arose from their own concerns. We then analyze the films ethnographically with attention to power dynamics prevalent due to or in spite of pedagogical context of the course (Blanks Jones, 2015; Dattatreyan & Marrero-Guillamón, 2019).

Two years after teaching this course, our practitioner inquiry included in-depth discussions with note-taking among ourselves, rewatching course films and class recordings of screening and learning activities (power mapping, stakeholder analysis, issues summit), and analyzing youths' dialogue, movement, and gestures within videos. We did not focus on written text appearing in videos or writing. As course goals centered civic engagement as a driver of improved public health, our selection of video-based evidence was informed by ethnographic filmmaking, foundational analytic constructs around popular education in the work of Freire and Boal, and Black girls' critical literacies.

The interplay between embodied and digital literacies in the course centered multiplicities of human communication and collaboration. Participants played and interacted through the Zoom platform. Facilitating, enacting, and embodying critical dialogue took on different formations than in a physical place-based setting. L. Roberts et al. (2021), engaging a Theatre of the Oppressed approach through Zoom, noted how digital design aspects like being able to switch views from focus individuals to gallery view, use chat during performances, turn cameras on and off, or change one's name on their image, expanded and limited embodied experiences of theater-making. Similarly, African immigrant girls in this study used Zoom and filmmaking to unpack multiple layers of human interactions, finding opportunities to employ critical literacy through "awareness of power relations, recognition of contextual factors, and a focus on action and change" (Garcia et al., 2020, p. 347). Our practitioner and ethnographic analysis aimed to understand how participants understood, challenged, and changed power dynamics that developed during the multilayered creation of these short films.

FINDINGS

All five African immigrant girls leveraged digital technology and used embodied performance to explore and express aspects of their personalities that emerged as critically literate, agentic, and activist. Over Zoom, through filmmaking, and within a pedagogical framework of dialoguing (Freire, 1996) and performing (Boal, 1979) resistance, the girls authored and embodied characters, scripts, and stories that subverted power structures and authorities familiar to them in their own lives, thus practicing social solutions for the real world. Characters the girls created and embodied all undergo critical and brave transformations on-screen: In their film "For Cryin' Out Loud," Martina convinces Sky that COVID-19 is as much a Black Lives Matter (BLM) issue as is police violence, and they brave COVID-19 exposure to join a BLM protest; in "We Need a Break," Sara courageously confronts teachers and the superintendent to ask for longer breaks away from the screen during online schooling; in "Silent Tears," Ramatulai develops the maturity to admit social insecurities and apologize to Adama.

118   Participatory and Communal Approaches to Learning and Civic Engagement

Our study also reveals how the girls' embodied performances humanized the disembodied digital Zoom space and added possibilities to the girls' digital literacy skills. Beyond functional mastery of digital tools, the girls harnessed technology to "practice a form of critical autonomy that allowed them to perform identity work and experiment with different identities"—such as BLM activists and student leaders (e.g., Garcia et al., 2020). Such engagement speaks to ways in which concerted efforts to highlight and understand experiences of African immigrant youth can support them in making "sense of their lives as engaged participatory communal citizens" (Watson & Knight-Manuel, 2020, p. 10). While trying on characters and trying out solutions, the girls reflected on their own image on-screen and the invisibility of Black bodies, voices, and concerns in digital news media (Walsh & Burnett, 2021; Watson & Knight-Manuel, 2020). Several of their creative and critical decisions are captured in the following vignette about one of the three films the girls made.

Vignette 1: Wielding and Critiquing Digital Power

Martina and Sky titled their film "For Cryin' Out Loud" to capture their exasperation and indignation at being deemed invisible and silenced by "those in positions of power." In the film, Martina convinces Sky to join her at a Black Lives Matter march in Philadelphia, despite Sky's fear of contracting COVID-19 in the protest crowds. Martina helps Sky to see how the pandemic, poverty, and police brutality are interrelated public health issues disproportionately affecting their community. They discuss their families' struggles to afford the basics while staying safe from both police and COVID-19 during the lockdown. As the girls slip between on-screen identities and real selves in writing, practicing, and performing this dialogue, they group together Black American and African immigrant communities, suggesting a sense of solidarity wrought out of racism collectively experienced by national, cultural, and linguistic groups across the African diaspora.

After Martina's and Sky's dialogue, the scene cuts to a striking mid-close-up of Sky as she wordlessly communicates to viewers her decision to join Martina at the march. In this prolonged 16-second shot, she slowly and deliberately puts on a black mask with "Black Lives Matter" emblazoned across it in glittering text (see Figure 8.1). As a powerful complement, Sky added the chant "Black Lives Matter" on repeat in her editing timeline to play throughout this decisive moment. Sky positioned her tablet camera center screen, favoring her eyes as they stare straight ahead and say all that her masked mouth does not (yet). Sky's symbolic silencing of her own mouth with the mantra she would later join in shouting, and her editing decision to linger on her face without speaking or moving, show just how

Imaging and Imagining Activism 119

intentionally the girls were applying digital tools and technical skills in "creative resilience" to the silencing and dehumanization of Black bodies by the pandemic, the police, and society (Gallagher et al., 2016; Pangrazio, 2016; Watson & Knight-Manuel, 2020).

At the Black Lives Matter protest, the girls are interviewed by an impassive, uninterested white news reporter (portrayed by a university student) who only half listens. When the reporter asks the girls a question they already answered, Sky responds, "Oh my God, really? Didn't you just hear

Figure 8.1. Sky's 16-Second Shot of Her Brave Transformation in "For Cryin' Out Loud"

what we just said right now?" Martina emphatically repeats their concerns: "Those in positions of power are not hearing us poor people who cannot protect themselves from the police or COVID. They don't understand how it is being poor so the only way we can get through to them is by showing them that our life matters!" Before the reporter briskly wraps up her story, the girls take the opportunity of airtime to chant, "No justice, no peace! No justice, no peace!"

In the reporter scene, the African immigrant girls subtly criticize dominant digital news media's tendency to ignore, underreport, or misrepresent concerns of Black Americans (see Figure 8.2). By expressing outright frustration with the reporter's disengaged attitude and questioning, they show an awareness of how digital news media can "reinforce issues of social class, race and gender" (Pangrazio, 2016, p. 169). At the same time, they use that same biased media platform to explain their concerns, showing deft multiliteracies in navigating various worlds using different registers (Price-Dennis, 2016). As Garcia et al. (2020) found in their study of Black girls' use of technology for activism and agency, Martina's and Sky's "ability to enact a critical digital literacy practice to advocate for social justice and civil rights reflects their understanding of how society is stratified in ways that create disparate and unequal experiences for minoritized populations" (p. 354). By critiquing the "ignorance" of "those in positions of power" toward "us poor people," Martina and Sky upset the assumed authority of elected officials and TV journalists and challenged their holds on truth (Freire, 1996).

Figure 8.2. The Reporter (Top), Martina (Center) and Sky (Bottom) in Their Short Film

Imaging and Imagining Activism   121

Figure 8.2. (*continued*)

Vignette 2: Power Shifts in Front of and Behind the Camera

In another film, we observed how power dynamics off-screen allowed a critical power shift on-screen. In her short film titled "We Need a Break," Sara, as director, screenwriter, and lead actor, wrote of two Black high school students petitioning their mostly white teachers and the district superintendent, Dr. Hite, for longer breaks between online classes during COVID-19.

122 Participatory and Communal Approaches to Learning and Civic Engagement

Sara was clear on what she wanted students to achieve in the film, but her initial filmed footage inadvertently showed the youth wordlessly deferring to authority figures. Unconsciously, she had granted teachers more speaking lines and the superintendent the sole decision-making power as well as the final words and final footage on-screen before the credits rolled. The high school students made few appearances and spoke little as school administrators argued about youth's points and spoke on their behalf.

Incongruities in Sara's script were noticed by the filmmaking teaching assistant and a graduate student collaborator. Since the structure of the course encouraged Freirian dialectical equality between facilitators and participants, and recommended dialogue and community-organizing strategies to work through issues and differences in perspectives, the teaching assistant and graduate student approached Sara with respect and understanding. Together, they reflected on the message this power dynamic would send to youth viewers. Sara then rewrote and rerecorded a scene to give more agency to youth characters (see Figure 8.3).

Scene 4: A Zoom meeting between students, parents, teachers, and the superintendent, Dr. Hite, to discuss the students' proposal for longer breaks between online classes.

Teacher 1: This is not a problem. When I was a student, I had more homework than all of these students. Students should be doing the same work and putting in the same hours at home.

Teacher 2: Calm down, we should be listening to Dr. Hite.

Sara: No, you need to listen to us, the students.

Superintendent: OK everyone, calm down . . . (He proposes a compromise.)

Sara: (Rolls eyes) OK, I think that's a reasonable compromise. I'm willing to accept that proposal.

Boy Student: While it's not exactly everything we asked for, we know it's a step in the right direction.

Scene 5: Later, the two students discuss the meeting with the superintendent.

Sara (on the phone with the Boy Student): The meeting went OK. I felt like these adults didn't listen to what we were saying and they constantly talked over us. And I even had to stop them to tell them not to talk over us. Even though we used our voices, we still didn't get everything we wanted. Next time, we need to work together so we can make online learning work better for everybody. (End of film)

Figure 8.3. A Still of Sara From Her Film "We Need a Break"

As we rewatched these scenes for this study, we remembered and reflected on the human interplay off-camera between the teaching assistant, graduate student, and youth participant. Although the students knew they could do little to change the superintendent's final decision or curb their teachers' intent to control them, Sara's subversive eye roll and proactive planning for "next time" show that her performance eventually became a "rehearsal of revolution" (Boal, 1979, p. 155).

Vignette 3: Humanizing the African Immigrant Girl Body

Studying the physical presence and the framing that the girls adopted was also important to our ethnographic analysis. "Silent Tears," the film described in the opening of this chapter and created by Ramatulai and Adama, allowed us to deeply observe the girls' intentional physicality and digital framing. As we structured this course, we were aware of the tendency for academic spaces like ours to sideline bodies, presence, and perspectives of community "partners," especially those from racialized and low-income backgrounds. In contrast, this course positioned community youth as directors of their own projects and their own bodies. In Boal's (1979) notion of "image theater" (p. 134), the body, and the descriptive interactive positions it can assume, are the most powerful and unambiguous form of communication—clearer than the spoken word.

In Boal's notion of image theater, spect-actors physically position others' bodies on stage until the bodies resemble a discernible image—and consequently a meaning, a message, and an emotion. Physical framing of the body has the power to impact our perception of multiple truths and possibilities for human understanding. When, in "Silent Tears," Adama curls up and crouches against her bed crying, her camera on the floor to capture her from the bottom up, she appears relatable rather than unfamiliar, challenging viewers to humanize instead of exoticize African immigrant girls. When Ramutulai towers over Adama with her camera angled from below to capture her full length in a long shot, she appears powerful and dominant (see Figure 8.4). They are urging African immigrant girls to take up more space

Figure 8.4. Ramatulai (Top) and Adama (Bottom) in Their Film "Silent Tears"

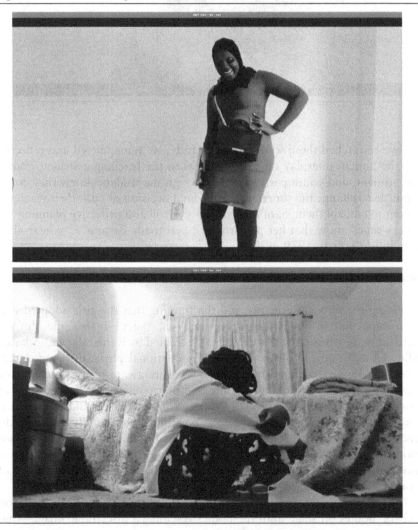

Imaging and Imagining Activism

and enter the conversation; consequently, they also are urging us, their instructors and dialogical equals, to humanize their bodies and acknowledge the daily negotiations they make to render visible their bodies, voices, and ideas (Watson & Knight-Manuel, 2020).

DISCUSSION

Through practitioner and ethnographer lenses, we observed instances of embodied, critical digital literacies in African immigrant girls' filmmaking processes, editing decisions, and performances, and in their final films, the first they had ever made. The instructors' pedagogical approaches positioned African immigrant girls as agentic creators of digital texts, rather than passive users or victims of technology (Garcia et al., 2020), a significant step away from dominant depictions of African immigrant girls and women as victims of immigration status, racial identity, socioeconomic position, and education or literacy "level." These depictions are pervasive within mainstream, positivist, linear definitions of literacy, education, and technology. Connecting back to the *Framework for Educating African Immigrant Youth* (Chapter 1), this course countered deficit narratives of African immigrant girls. As the girls moved deftly between whole-class improvisation games, breakaway discussions with graduate students, and editing workshops with their African Family Health Organization peers, all the while sitting in their home environments, we recall Price-Dennis's (2016) observation that Black girls' (and, we add, African immigrant girls') literacies are "in essence . . . multimodal and embody a critical stance that fosters dexterity across genres, platforms, audiences, and registers" (p. 338), helping the girls navigate multiple worlds in multiple ways, thus lending themselves well to the possibilities offered by multimodal expression in this class, such as embodied performance and digital editing of images and sounds.

A desire to make the world more equitable shone through in performances and films, from Sky's last words to the reporter, "We hope our voices will finally be heard," to Sara's vow to "work together so we can make online learning work better for everybody," to Ramatulai and Adama's ending message, "Together we can stop bullying." With our African immigrant participants, we observed, as Price-Dennis (2016) found with a group of 5th-grade Black girls, that "Black girls' literacies that occur in digital spaces have the potential to be transformative and helpful in constructing a model for being fully human in the world and working to make conditions for others more humane" (p. 340). In their reading of the world, the girls all identified and performed ways to remake it, displaying "creative resilience" to structural inequalities (Gallagher et al., 2016). Like improvised encounters enacted by Gallagher et al.'s youth participants residing in an urban shelter, African immigrant girls' films compel us to view their solutions from a "critical-affective stance" and to recognize empathy, frustration, and hope.

Furthermore, Boal's "legislative theater" method invites spect-actors to join a role-play about a familiar sociopolitical conflict, act out solutions, and then discuss and brainstorm policies or laws that should be advocated for and passed. Our class became a training ground for legislative theater in both the filmmaking and the final screening of the films for viewers. African immigrant girls experimented with how to leverage their research on issues impacting their lives and the lives of peers, and how to serve as advocates for policy change through the arts. The Philadelphia Mayor's Commission on African and Caribbean Affairs attended the film screening and encouraged the girls to write a policy document recommending how the city could engage African youth. While they did not actually write it, their boldness during the screening in giving voice to issues that impact the lives of African youth gave them an audience with powerful actors within local government and demonstrated that African youth should be involved in local policy deliberation spaces.

Finally, both the high school girls and university students gained core course competencies of learning to "work with others to create a vision for fostering collaboration and guiding decision making in local communities" and to "create audience-appropriate communications strategies of public health content, both in writing and through oral and embodied presentation" (course syllabus). In the pursuit of culturally competent strategies to engage community audiences in multidirectional communication, they engaged civic literacies that facilitated communal and participatory movement building that spanned multiple physical and digital contexts.

Lessons learned by the African immigrant girls, university students, and facilitators of this university–community partnership are transferable to high school and university courses, projects, programs, and partnerships. We reflect on three takeaway questions and how our study addresses them.

TAKEAWAY QUESTIONS

1. How can educators and schools meaningfully integrate performance and film to embrace their students' social, political, global, and local concerns?

   We observed that African immigrant girls were eager to perform, film, and (re)present the issues that affect their lives, families, schools, and communities. Their clarity should embolden us, as educators, to embrace students' social justice and cultural concerns, and accept that education (mainstream, alternative, or otherwise) is *never* neutral, apolitical, or removed from the challenges our students, especially our Black and African immigrant students, face outside of school. Moreover, performance, improvisation, and filmmaking can provide a liberating space for youth of color to try on characters and try out solutions, to interrogate and re-create their worlds. In our class, the African immigrant girl students used their bodies, clothes, COVID-19 face masks, cell phones, tablets, and laptops as tools for their "rehearsals of revolutions" (Boal, 1979, p. 155), as they engaged in community organizing strategies, dialogue, and performances, reaching for solutions to social problems near to their hearts.

2. How can educators and schools cultivate learning spaces that acknowledge and encourage African immigrant girls' critical, embodied, digital, and civic literacies?

We call for an expanded understanding of critical digital literacy that is predicated on the agency of African immigrant girls to use their bodies and their digital tools to read, interrogate, and re-create their worlds (Garcia et al., 2020). As highlighted in the *Framework for Educating African Immigrant Youth* (Chapter 1), instructors can support their students in envisioning and enacting social civic literacies and extending their complex identities. It is our hope that educators and practitioners will expand their understanding of literacy and find varied, layered ways to harness Black girls' critical digital literacy, multiliteracies, and multimodal storytelling and performance to support Black and African immigrant girls' knowledge production, truth telling, identity exploration, and confidence building.

3. What new learning possibilities arise for African immigrant girl students when educators and schools reconstruct learning spaces in their favor? And in turn, what can educators and schools learn from African immigrant girl youth when in these reenvisioned learning spaces?

We feel hopeful about educative models, such as those used in our course, that break down traditional structural barriers and power dynamics inherent in formal academic spaces and in technological gadgets. We positioned African immigrant girls as dialectical equals with university students and facilitators, breaking down the "teacher–student contradiction" (Freire, 1996, p. 45), by allowing them to speak first, change the direction of discussions, write their own film scripts, and have the final word. Moreover, we constantly adjusted timings, duration, and topics covered in our filmmaking workshops to suit their needs and their availability, given their other classes and home responsibilities. When class time, space, or resources are limited, we recommend educators wield the class platform and digital tools in favor of Black and African immigrant girl youth by granting them more opportunities to express and explore their ideas, experiences, wonderings, and solutions through multiple literacies.

The intentionality that went into our selection of readings from Africa, setting up the course structure, and identifying coeducators representative of and focused on African immigrant populations effectively foregrounded African immigrant girls' cultural heritage pedagogically and politically in the classroom, without flattening them into a single "African" identify. In conclusion, we reflect on how the African immigrant girls in our university course taught us new dimensions of embodied digital and critical literacies, and performed for their communities hopeful versions of the world, awakening aspects of their personalities still alive today, more than 2 years later. They compelled us to believe more strongly than ever in the creative agency, knowledges, and lived experiences of Black girls and African immigrant girls—for they have much to teach educators, universities, leaders, and the world.

CHAPTER 9

Social Cohesion, Belonging, and Anti-Blackness

African Immigrant Youth's Civic Exploration in a Culturally Relevant-Sustaining, After-School Club

*Michelle G. Knight-Manuel, Natacha Robert,
and Sibel Akin-Sabuncu*

Many African immigrant youth enter the United States during critical periods of identity formation, including civic identity development and enactment. More than half of the 137,618 African immigrants living in New York City as of 2021 relocated from West Africa (Baruch College, 2019). They bring a rich diversity of languages and cultures. However, Immigration and Customs Enforcement deportations, vitriolic anti-immigrant, anti-Muslim sentiment, and a view of African migrant asylum seekers as the new face of crisis at the southern border (Solomon, 2019) highlight tensions African immigrants have been experiencing over the past 10 years. Due to this and "the U.S.'s long history of criminalizing [B]lack and [B]rown youth via race-based policing and media representations" (Koyama & Subramanian, 2014, p. 20), Black African immigrant youth's civic identity and engagement may be formed and emerge in schools and in a society where anti-Black sentiments adversely affect Africans. We use the term *Black African immigrants* to signal the connection between experiences of West African immigrant youth and global anti-Blackness, which is the historical and current marking of Black bodies as Other, nonhuman, and irreconcilable with any sense of social or cultural regard (Dumas & ross, 2016; Grant et al., 2020). Anti-Blackness continues to be prevalent in the broader organization of American society through laws, policies, practices, curricula, and general dysconsciousness in civic everyday life (Dumas & ross, 2016; King, 2015).

Notwithstanding the reasons for immigrating or premigration status, African immigrants in the United States may experience racism not present in home countries (Harushimana & Awokoya, 2011). Furthermore, Mwangi's (2017) review of studies on Black immigrants draws attention to a critique

129

of the "universal Black experience," highlighting overreliance on assimilationist theoretical framings to address Black immigrants' heterogeneous educational and social experiences as they intersect, for example, by country, social status, and religion. Given the growing body of literature attending to African immigrant youths' schooling and civic lives, our purpose is to highlight experiences and perspectives surrounding educational and social injustices, foregrounding Pan-Africanism, sociopolitical awareness, and civic identity/literacy, among twenty-two 1.5- and second-generation youth[1] from West Africa who participated in an after-school African Club for 2 years. Theoretically, we draw on tenets of cultural competence and critical consciousness within culturally relevant-sustaining education and the Sankofan approach to address the following research questions: (1) What experiences did West African immigrant youth discuss in the African Club? and (2) How did they make sense of their civic identities, development, and engagement?

THEORETICAL FRAMEWORK

To understand how African immigrant youth make sense of their experiences in the United States and challenge social injustice, this inquiry draws upon an interdisciplinary framework grounded in culturally relevant and sustaining pedagogies (Ladson-Billings, 2014; Paris & Alim, 2017) affirming cultural, heritage, and embodied knowledges, languages, and practices. Additionally, we engage a Sankofan approach to disrupting inequities affecting immigrant youth from West African countries (Dei, 2012; Watson & Knight-Manuel, 2017) and thus render visible how they navigate pasts, presents, and futures of literacies—reading and understanding civic everyday life.

Culturally relevant education engages three tenets: academic achievement/ student learning, cultural competence, and sociopolitical/critical consciousness (Ladson-Billings, 2009). In this study, we focus on cultural competence, facilitating students' appreciation and celebration of their cultures of origin while gaining knowledge of others, and also sociopolitical consciousness, which encourages the understanding of social inequalities and their causes to disrupt educational injustices influenced by larger historical and sociopolitical contexts. We view sociopolitical consciousness as an awareness of and ability to act against societal inequities disadvantaging students of color. Culturally sustaining education, therefore, calls on teachers to recognize how education received by students is always socially and politically situated, and to be cognizant of roles in facilitating development of students' sociopolitical awareness (Dallavis, 2013; Paris & Alim, 2017). With regard to the population under

---

1. Immigrant youth who are 1.5-generation arrived in the United States after age of 6 and before age 12; second-generation immigrants are born in the United States with at least one parent born outside the United States (Rumbaut & Ima, 1998).

study, Watson and colleagues (2014) have demonstrated that teachers can encourage African immigrant students, through civic learning opportunities, to participate in dialogic consciousness-raising and critical conversations to confront and assess existing social (in)justices. However, in supporting and leveraging critical consciousness of African immigrant students, educators need to broaden conceptualizations and enactments of culturally relevant pedagogy to "move beyond subsuming African immigrants into the demographic category 'Black'" (Allen et al., 2012, p. 13), as there is not a monolithic Black immigrant experience in the United States.

In conjunction with culturally relevant and sustaining pedagogies, we engage the Sankofan approach, referring to the Adinkra pictorial symbol of the Akan culture in Ghana, with a bird looking back as simultaneously its body is positioned to move forward, illustrating how the past illuminates the present and that the search for knowledge should include past experience and wisdom (see Figure 10.1 and description in Chapter 10, this volume). The use of the Sankofan approach in our inquiry engenders interrelated relationships of past, present, and future diasporan practices that attend to historical thinking and preservation of African culture and philosophies (Temple, 2010). Together, culturally relevant and Sankofan approaches extend African onto-epistemologies through understanding African immigrant youths' perspectives of educational and social experiences revealed during participation in the African Club.

AFRICAN IMMIGRANT YOUTHS' CIVIC IDENTITIES

Few educational research studies have focused on civic engagement and identity development of 1.5- and second-generation African youths and their contributions to American civil society and their home countries. This is of critical importance given that much of the literature on civic learning is situated in white, middle-class learning experiences, and emerging scholarship has focused on experiences of Latinx and Asian youth. In a study done by Kumi-Yeboah and Smith (2016) that examined factors promoting awareness and enhancement of critical multicultural citizenship education among Black immigrant youth, it was observed that youth navigated understanding and awareness via class discussions, inquiry-based learning, and cultural, social, and language differences. Youth expressed that "open communication" during class discussions allowed them to reflect on past experiences in democracy and acquire knowledge about citizenship, and helped them develop a deep understanding of how to take action and make viable decisions to solve individual and group problems. Extending these insights, Watson and Knight-Manuel (2017) conducted a review of educational research on social processes of navigating identities and civic engagement impeding West African immigrant youth from accessing equitable and high-quality educational experiences. The review noted that immigrant youth from West African countries demonstrate a complexity of experiences, enacting civic stances related to local knowledges, and complicating an interplay of past, present, and future educational experiences pertaining to immigrant civic life across different teaching and learning settings and within local/global contexts.

To illustrate, Knight (2011) discussed the global lifestyle and civic engagement of one African transnational immigrant youth. The findings note that African immigrant youth think and act based on complex, multiple, shifting civic identities, crossing the borders of community, state, nation, and the world to address social concerns. However, as Kumi-Yeboah and Smith (2016) argue, Black immigrant youth largely experience difficulties with civic engagement in schools, which suggests schools must reform curriculum to incorporate histories and backgrounds of immigrant youth to advance multicultural citizenship education and enhance democratic education for all students. Knight and Watson (2014) and Watson et al. (2014) explored understandings of how 1.5- and second-generation African immigrant youth engaged in civic actions using participatory new media technologies such as the Internet, and social media beyond one-time events, illuminating the potential to (re)conceptualize traditional forms of (in)formal citizenship teaching and learning opportunities across contexts and relationships of peers, families, home, and school communities in the United States, Africa, and globally. They found these learning contexts promoted opportunities for African immigrant youth's participatory communal citizenship by engaging them in critical exploration of social problems, and providing them with learning opportunities that fostered emergent thinking, questioning, and awareness of social injustices faced by them and African Americans in the United States.

CULTURAL/ETHNIC CLUBS

Cultural/ethnic clubs within the schooling context are "third space[s]" (Doucet & Kirkland, 2021) where African immigrant youth contend with transnational identities, feelings of belonging, and vicissitudes of settling into the United States. In particular, cultural/ethnic clubs can provide a space for African immigrant youth to think about, negotiate, and make meaning of experiences and visions of citizenship (Doucet & Kirkland, 2021; Schmidt, 2022). Currently, there is limited literature on African immigrant youth and ethnic/cultural clubs. However, a few studies have detailed experiences of African immigrant youth, and some of the literature on Haitian immigrant youth, and more broadly Black immigrant youth, is useful for understanding African immigrant experiences.

After-school social clubs and sports teams can be places where Black immigrant youth gain civic knowledge and skills for social change

(Kumi-Yeboah et al., 2020; Kumi-Yeboah & Smith, 2016). Studies done by Schmidt (2022) and Doucet and Kirkland (2021) found cultural/ethnic clubs to be significant social spaces where African and Haitian immigrant youth can freely challenge and play with complex ideas about racial identity and cultural and national belonging, and exercise resistance against obstacles and injustices. These important parts of civic identity formation impact and inform youths' civic actions. Within the Sankofa club in Schmidt's (2022) study of African immigrant youth, students interrogated notions of belonging, and it was found that youths' identifications and social navigations were "shaped by transnational flows" (p. 47) with networks that transcended national boundaries. The Sankofa club empowered African immigrant youth and supported ethnic, national, and transnational belonging by "[affirming] their shared experiences being bullied, connecting with family, and respect for elders, which shaped their . . . engagement with people and places" (p. 57). In turn, students in this club resisted negative representations of Africa while contemplating how they are situated in the diaspora.

The study of a Haitian immigrant ethnic club by Doucet and Kirkland (2021) found that the club was not only a space of solace and sanctuary, but a place to "test and exercise resistance against demoralizing forces" (p. 626). Youth were able to discuss and question issues of racism occurring in school and challenge existing power structures designed to undermine them. Similar to Haitians, African immigrant youth have been found to experience discrimination, unwelcoming school environments, and stereotyping as a result of negative media portrayals of their origin country and culture (Kiramba et al., 2021). Research also has shown that African immigrant youth move in and out of multiple identity possibilities, and between different worlds, to determine civic identities and actions in different social contexts and transnational spaces, such as cultural/ethnic clubs, that extend beyond national borders (Awokoya, 2012; Schmidt, 2023). For example, Doucet and Kirkland (2021) found the Haitian club to be a space of "fluidity for Black adolescent development" (p. 628) as youth "shifted . . . through domains of being and becoming . . . [moving] from being African American to Haitian to Black, from citizen to foreigner refugee . . . intersecting and subject to change with respect to space and time" (p. 629). At the college level, African student ethnic clubs/associations have been found to positively influence student identity, to help students cope with isolation and exclusion, and to be a resource for connecting and learning about diverse African students (Onyenekwu, 2017).

RESEARCH METHODOLOGY

To render visible African immigrants' civic identities, development, and engagement, we focus on data drawn from a larger qualitative study of 1.5- and second-generation African immigrant youth who participated in an after-school club (the Africa Club) and their perspectives on educational and social experiences. Specifically, students who participated in an after-school club at a public comprehensive urban high school (Treasure High School) in the Northeast were recruited by an administrator within the school. The purposeful sample (Bogdan & Biklen, 2007) of participants from West African countries reflected a variety of ages, generations, genders, languages, and countries of origin (see Table 9.1).

Positionalities

The authors come to this study with multiple personal and professional experiences and commitments to research centering perspectives of African immigrant youth, viewing participants as creators of knowledge (Boveda & Annamma, 2023; Milner, 2007). As a Black woman, former public school teacher, and teacher educator, Michelle Knight-Manuel builds upon prior experiences of how African immigrant youth negotiated multiple, intersecting, and intersectional identities and their marginalization in society, especially in educational spaces. Natacha Robert is a doctoral student in the field of curriculum and teaching. As an Ayitian immigrant, her experiences as a student and an educator contribute to understandings of how Black immigrant youth come to form racial and civic transnational identities within the United States. Sibel Akin-Sabuncu is a teacher educator in Turkey whose background and experiences with immigrant/refugee students in Turkey and the United States supported different interpretations of the data both as an insider/coauthor and an outsider/visiting scholar in the U.S. context. Together, the authors' collective backgrounds are critically important in their research for and with African immigrant youth.

Data Sources

The data in this chapter come from a larger study conducted over 2 years. We conducted observations of 15 weekly 2-hour sessions during the Africa Club. Fieldnotes and memos were written after each meeting (Emerson et al., 2011). During group discussions, we offered prompts developed from the ongoing research (Chilisa, 2019). These involved, for example, how youth see themselves reflected in various communities such as in the United States, Africa, and the African diaspora. Working in small groups (three to five students), participants conducted Youth Participatory Action Research (YPAR) projects to investigate conditions in their schools and/or communities that they identified as being unjust (Cammarota & Fine, 2008).

Data Analysis. Informal and formal data analysis is ongoing and iterative. Informal data analysis occurred when the authors discussed the data in research team meetings (Wasser & Bresler, 1996). Formal data analysis occurred primarily with the data from participant observations,

Table 9.1. Participant Demographic Chart

Name	M/F	Age	Year(s) Participated	Country of Parental Origin	Language(s)	Generation	YPAR Project
Kofi	M	15	2017–2019	Ghana	Twi, English	2	1
Kwame	M	17	2017–2019	Ghana	Twi, English	2	2
Kojo	M	17	2017–2019	Ghana	Twi, English, Spanish, French	1.5	1
Abiodun	M	16	2017–2019	Nigeria	English	2	2
Adjua	F	15	2017–2019	Ghana	Twi, English	2	1
Abeo	M	16	2017–2019	Nigeria	English	1.5	5
Abaeze	M	17	2017–2019	Nigeria	English	1.5	5
Amadou	M	16	2017–2019	Guinea Conakry	Fulani, Arabic, English	1.5	4
Ihuoma	F	14	2017–2019	Nigeria	English	1.5	1
Chetachi	M	15	2017–2019	Nigeria	English	2	5
Edosio	M	18	2017–2019	Nigeria	English	1.5	3
Abena	F	15	2018–2019	Ghana	Twi, English	1.5	N/A
Ifechi	M	16	2018–2019	Nigeria	English, Igbo	1.5	3
Lebechi	F	15	2018–2019	Nigeria	English	1.5	3
Kobby	M	14	2018–2019	Ghana	Twi, English	2	3
Emmanuel	M	16	2018–2019	Togo	English, Hausa, Ewe, French	2	2
Bintou	F	16	2018–2019	Mali	English, French	2	2
Bakary	M	16	2018–2019	Gambia	Sonnke, English	2	4
Komi	M	16	2018–2019	Togo	English, Ewe	2	2
Yacouba	M	17	2018–2019	Burkina Faso	French, English, and Mossi	1.5	N/A
Abal	F	17	2018–2019	Ghana	Twi, English	1.5	5
Stacy	F	17	2018–2019	Ghana	Twi, English	2	4

group discussions, and YPAR projects by multiple authors. We coded the data according to concepts from the literature on culturally relevant education, such as race, racism, discrimination, inequality, Pan-Africanism, and a Sankofan approach focusing on African immigrant youths' transnational heritage practices and indigenous knowledges. To establish the trustworthiness of the research, we utilized in-depth data collection, prolonged engagement at the site and with the data, and data source triangulation.

FINDINGS

Before presenting our findings, we provide a depiction of activities African immigrant youth participated in as members of the Africa Club. Across the 2 years, youth participated in varied activities, such as a fieldtrip to Broadway, walking tours of their neighborhood, visually mapping their belonging in varied communities, viewing videos, engaging in discussions about their views on and stereotypes about Africa, and creating YPAR projects. We focus on two themes: (1) Pan-Africanism and a sense of belonging and (2) navigating racial awareness, anti-Blackness, and economic realities of a societal curriculum.

PAN-AFRICANISM AND A SENSE OF BELONGING

The Africa Club was found to be a Pan-African space that facilitated the development of African immigrant youth's sociopolitical consciousness and cultural competence. The club was a space where African immigrant and African American youth from different countries expanded on and fortified their cultural competence by engaging in dialogue, interacting, and building relationships contributing to their cultural/ethnic civic learning and identity formation. The club also served as a space where African immigrant youth built upon their sociopolitical awareness as they engaged in discussions promoting social cohesion.

The Africa Club provided space for students to negotiate civic identities by seeing their interrelatedness even though they came from different African countries and the diaspora. For many African immigrant youths, being in the club provided a sense of social acceptance that made them feel safe, welcome, and like a family. One student in the club stated, "I didn't know that many African people . . . but then after I came here, I started socializing with more people and [I] got to know people better and I am happy to have a new family." The Africa Club also functioned as a space where many youths learned about their heritage and those of peers for the first time.

Social Cohesion, Belonging, and Anti-Blackness 137

> I left Ghana when I was like 5. . . .
>
> I've never been back. Being in this Africa Club has almost been like . . . reconnecting with my roots . . . some people go back to their country because they wanna reconnect to it. This has been like my kind of version of that and I really enjoyed it. (Year 1, Session 15)

Doucet and Kirkland (2021) mention that for many students, ethnic clubs are the first opportunity immigrant youth have to explore their heritage and/or ethnic-racial identities (see *Framework for Educating African Immigrant Youth*, Chapter 1, and Chapter 4). When African immigrant youth gain cultural, general historical, and present knowledge about different African countries, they broaden their sociopolitical understanding of the African/Black experience and more easily see themselves as Pan-African citizens in the world and how their actions connect to a larger community of African descendants (Kah, 2016). This connects to the essence of global citizenship inherent in Pan-Africanism and the idea that it is "a flexible, inclusive, dynamic and complex aspiration in identity making and belonging in the global community" that "[offers] a mental space for disparate identities to co-exist in freedom" (Nyamnjoh & Shoro, 2011, p. 40).

Within the club, African immigrant youth explored their sense of belonging and dual identity as both Africans and African Americans. For instance, during one session of the club, they were shown a video called "How Young Africans Found a Voice on Twitter." When asked their thoughts on the video one participant said:

> This video kind of reminds me of every single one of us in this room because . . . we all come from different countries and maybe a couple of us from two different African cultures and trying to merge with this whole American culture. Sometimes we try too hard to fit in over here and we end up forgetting where we come from or sometimes we don't try at all and hold on to our culture too much that we don't see what America is all about. (Year 2, Session 13)

Following the concept of Sankofa, the club encouraged students to make connections with the past, present, and future as they formulated civic identities within the context of multiple fluid ethnic and national identities. African immigrant youth's social relational learning stimulated ideas about how they should engage civically as Africans now living in America.

Ethnic club participation has been found to increase students' feelings of inclusion and belonging in school communities and their sense of cultural pride (Doucet & Kirkland, 2021). The experiences in the Africa Club improved students' conceptions of and pride in their culture and countries of origin, which added to their desires to help their community back in Africa. For example, one student who left their country in Africa mad and ashamed that it was poor became proud of their country as a result of the Africa Club.

> When I left my country, I didn't leave it in the [happiest way]. I learned my country is one of the poorest countries in the world. So inside myself, I was mad. I wanna [go] back and change that because people look down at the country because the country is poor. So I didn't really appreciate my country and my African origin as I was supposed to. But coming here and hearing about stories and hearing people talk about how they went through stuff is actually making me appreciate more of what I have and where I'm from. (Year 1, Session 15)

The Pan-African learning and belonging students experienced, translated to feelings of belonging not just to their countries of origin, but to Africa as a whole. This sense of Pan-Africanism and cultural pride promotes cooperation and sociopolitical problem solving.

The Africa Club also provided students the space to develop civic identities that incorporate indigenous African conceptions of civic education alongside American ones (see Chapter 7). Civic education within indigenous African societies aims to bring about social harmony and cohesion among diverse cultures and peoples within the African continent to ensure mutual coexistence with one another and nature (Mburu, 2012). Additionally, research suggests civic education should address the social, economic, and cultural development of a society (García-Cabrero et al., 2017). The Africa Club encouraged students to experience feelings of cultural belonging through *participatory communal civic learning*, which offered a platform for explicit discussion of issues that promote peace in the classroom and in broader society (Knight & Watson, 2014; Mburu, 2012). Through such discussions youth come to know themselves and their environment, history, and culture, which illuminates and develops understanding of themselves as community members situated in local and global knowledge, and the actions they will take on behalf of other community members.

Through conversations promoting social cohesion, African immigrant youth built upon their sociopolitical awareness as they raised concerns about issues that needed to be solved in Africa, America, and other parts of the world. They reflected on their historical and present knowledge and experiences in Africa and America to articulate and formulate ideas about personal civic commitments and broader civic responsibility in the contexts of their school, America, Africa, and the global community. For instance, many students shared their concern about military and police conduct that promotes insecurity and goes against social harmony. One student alluded to military and police issues in African and American communities as matters to be solved and thought of more globally.

> Back in my country, the military, they don't make me feel safe at all in my community. . . . They don't make me feel safe and at the same time they don't make me fear for my life, but they don't make me feel safe because . . . when you need them, they're not there. In America, people feel like here that police

brutality is a lot, people get killed, [and there's] racism. They don't understand what's going on outside of the world. Like in Brazil, Africa. (Year 1, Session 9)

Through conversations in the Africa Club, African immigrant youth engaged in social relational learning, positioning them to surface untapped knowledge of African people. It fostered a sense of Pan-Africanism that encouraged African immigrant youth to learn about themselves, from one another, and develop their civic identities. Through this, they identified social issues that are barriers to social harmony within and beyond U.S. and African national borders.

NAVIGATING RACIAL AWARENESS, ANTI-BLACKNESS, AND ECONOMIC REALITIES OF A SOCIETAL CURRICULUM

African immigrant youth who live in the United States navigate a societal curriculum that positions them as inferior in the contexts of Africa and the United States. This navigation entails reading and understanding how notions of anti-Blackness position them in society, especially how such notions inscribe inequities on the Black immigrant African body (Dumas & ross, 2016; Watson & Knight-Manuel, 2020).

During our initial and subsequent sessions with students in the Africa Club, they noted a lack of inclusion or misrepresentation of images of Africa/Africans in society, their civic life, and their schooling experiences (see Chapter 7). They highlighted societal stereotypes that they have encountered. For example, during the following conversation Kojo and Ihuoma discuss misperceptions about Africa and the United States.

> *Kojo:* There is a common misconception that Africa is poor, and that we live in trees.
> *Ihuoma:* People here say that Africa is full of huts and stuff.
> *Kojo:* The misinterpretations of Africa affects Africans' views of their own country. They see that it is beautiful but because many other countries view Africans as inferior, even the Africans are viewing themselves as inferior. When I found out that I was going to come here, I thought there was going to be money on the floor everywhere, and I would send it back home to Ghana. And when I came here, I saw a homeless man begging me for money. (Year 1, Session 1)

While youth recognized these stereotypes, the Africa Club provided space to challenge the misperceptions. They created collages that offered alternative perspectives to dominant narratives that they confronted in their neighborhoods, schools, and recreational spaces in the United States.

140 Participatory and Communal Approaches to Learning and Civic Engagement

For example, youth shared the juxtaposition between the ways in which Americans view Africa, and realities of life on the continent as it relates to social class, civic engagement, and everyday lives and activities.

> *Bintou:* One of our pictures is of child soldiers, and that's how Americans view Africans. They see child soldiers, civil war, animals, poverty. They think that Africa is very poor, but we are actually the richest continent in the world. They think of dirtiness, and some parts of Africa are much nicer and cleaner than parts of NYC. And they think we don't have houses. You go to some parts of Africa, and you would be surprised at how they are built. (Year 1, Session 5)

African immigrant youth's conversations of everyday civic life include a critical awareness of how those living in the United States view Africa, African children, and life in Africa. However, they challenge these views of African immigrant youth positioned as child soldiers situated within marginalization and disdain, with a comprehension that Africans are housed in structures and live in spaces that are much better than those of some Americans living in New York. While some of the African immigrant youth are navigating views of themselves and Africa, they simultaneously are questioning and grappling with how racism is experienced similarly or not by Africans and African Americans in the United States through the eyes of white people and the U.S. government.

Their conversation draws attention to African youth's sociopolitical awareness of how their civic lives and those of African Americans are integrally tied together and impacted through prevailing notions of anti-Blackness and racism. Specifically, in this conversation, youth grapple with and move to a positioning of Africans and African Americans as similar based on how they are both viewed by white people and how they are treated by the government as part of their civic life in the United States. Interestingly, the African immigrant youth live in spaces populated predominantly by people of color, whether they are Latinx or African American. The space where they physically encounter the most white people is within the schools they attend. Additionally, the treatment from the government does not distinguish between African immigrant youth and African American youth as the state-sanctioned body sees only skin color. This reading of African immigrant youth and African American youth highlights a "shared racial fate" (Hunter et al., 2017) and not the nuanced ways they experience civic life differently through their intersecting identities.

While African immigrant youth express a sociopolitical awareness of understanding of how racism works from "white people and the government" in everyday civic experiences, the youth participatory action research projects they completed in the Africa Club offered them insight into discriminatory practices they were experiencing and wanted to address. For example, one group of youth that included Kwame, Bintou, Emmanuel, and Abiodun used growing digital literacy skills to present their topic, "youth job/employment discrimination," on Google slides to members of the African Club, teachers, and an administrator within the school. Both Emmanuel and Abiodun chose this topic as they wanted to understand whether their experiences were similar to those of other youth (C. M. Abdi, 2012).

They shared how they were invited to come in for interviews, but after showing up, they either were told "to come back next year" or noted that their "interview was shorter" and that "they [the people hiring] did not put much time into [interviewing] me." The group decided on the following two questions: (1) What are the characteristics that hiring managers at McDonald's and Foot Locker in the borough look for in potential employees? (2) How do these characteristics affect young people at Treasure High School looking for employment at Foot Locker and McDonald's? They emphasized two major issues that came up during interviews. First, they highlighted how jobs were "easier [to get] for people who had the same ethnicity of the person hiring" and, second, that the person hiring did not focus on skills but rather who the hiring person was "more culturally [like] and comfortable with." For example, Stacy shared how "Hispanic hiring managers were hiring Hispanics. Caribbean people were hiring Caribbean people." Or another student, Abiodun, shared that when you go to different stores in different areas of the city, they hire "specific people . . . he's saying that they're hiring mostly Latino and not . . . not African, African American."

Thus, while living in civic spaces where predominantly people of color worked, African immigrant youth were not being hired by other Black or Latinx managers. Therefore, employment discrimination among people of color within spaces not dominated by white people was based on people hiring people of their own demographic community.

As the United States continues to engage in a browning of the nation (Blow, 2021), YPAR projects allowed youth to begin to read and unpack the treatment that they were receiving as they searched for jobs and how they might begin to navigate their employment futures going forward in a world where many people of color reside and work. This is significant for African immigrant youth, knowing that many of their families left their homes in Africa for better economic opportunities in the United States.

IMPLICATIONS AND CONCLUSION

Our study offers critical implications for teacher education and schooling to better meet educational needs of African immigrant youth. Given the growth of Black immigrant populations from Africa and the current climate

142   Participatory and Communal Approaches to Learning and Civic Engagement

in the United States, focusing on African immigrant youth's experiences in the Africa Club and how they made sense of civic identities, development, and engagement is timely and significant. The findings demonstrate that the Africa Club, as a culturally relevant "third" space, fostered students' sociopolitical consciousness for developing awareness about race and anti-Blackness by extending past-present-future learning with peers and educators (see Chapter 7, Chapter 11). Significantly, the Africa Club also supported participants in developing cultural competence and a collective identity of Pan-Africanism with a sense of belonging to their past, present, and future historical and cultural heritages.

We suggest that educators can benefit from ethnic clubs like the Africa Club to learn from and with immigrant youth who are already participating in civic learning opportunities as local and global citizens in and beyond the sphere of schools. Additionally, it may strengthen civic teaching and learning opportunities already present within schools and the curriculum. Complicating traditional constructions of youth engagement that prioritize skills or activities, the Africa Club supported social and relational learning opportunities of various modes of participatory communal civic learning and action-taking beyond one-time activities. Educators, including teachers, principals, school counselors, and teacher educators, can provide learning opportunities within schools and teacher education curriculum that affirm the knowledge and multiple identities African immigrant youth bring with them and can support their understandings and development of participatory citizenship. Collectively, such civic learning opportunities, dialogic space, and critical conversations can encourage youth to reflect on and take action against existing social structures that perpetuate larger issues of social injustices mediated by race, ethnicity, and immigrant status in order to support and advance diverse democratic societies.

TAKEAWAY QUESTIONS

1. How can schools create learning spaces, such as after-school programs, that build upon the cultural competence of immigrant students, especially African immigrant youth's language, literacy practices, and cultural knowledges?
2. How can the use of the concepts and ideas of Pan-Africanism and a sense of belonging support African immigrant youth's civic identity development?
3. In what ways can the civic concepts, understandings, and actions African immigrant youth bring with them into educational spaces be used in conjunction with U.S. civic concepts and actions to contribute to their civic literacies and engagement?

Part III

LITERACIES, LANGUAGES, AND LEARNING: TOWARD EMERGING PRACTICES AND APPROACHES

Patriann Smith

In Part III of this book, authors further build upon the *Framework for Educating African Immigrant Youth* (Chapter 1), inviting readers to interrupt Black people's knowing of their story "in ways that are partial and distorted" (King, 1992, p. 320). Building upon "diaspora literacy" as "an ability to read a variety of cultural signs of the lives of Africa's children at home and in the New World" and as Black people developing an understanding of their "story" of "cultural dispossession" (Busia, 1989, p. 197), the authors in Part III ask Black people to repossess this story and thus Black individuals' "cultural identity" as "Africa's children" so that "human consciousness permits [the retrieval of] humanity from distorted notions of the conceptual 'Blackness' which has long functioned as an alter ego of the socially constructed category of 'Whiteness'" (King, 1992, p. 321). In doing so, authors demonstrate how literacies and languaging of Black African immigrant youth function as necessary disruption of Westernized notions of normalcy, a longstanding project designed to make visible linguistic and literate richness of the Majority World (e.g., Henry, 1998; Ibrahim, 1999; P. Smith, 2023a; Smitherman, 1977).

David Bwire Wandera in Chapter 10 explores the role of education in a pluralistic world amid increasing global migration. Considering that immigrant students are becoming the fastest-growing student population in the United States, Wandera asks: "How might educators and related stakeholders and collaborators respond to achieve positive educational outcomes?" Challenging non-Western cultural epistemologies that tend to be analyzed using Western(ized) concepts and theories in the study of ethnoracially and linguistically diverse and immigrant students, Wandera takes aim at heritage resources shaping acculturation experiences in clarifying the cultural resources students bring, and how these resources might play a role in enabling successful acculturation. Wandera offers takeaways for educators and associated stakeholders to build cultural competence through demonstrable uptake of local epistemologies when working with immigrant youth.

Delving more deeply into ways in which Westernized notions of normalcy are embedded in languaging and literacies for African immigrant youth, Lakeya Afolalu in Chapter 11 draws from sociocultural perspectives of language and literacy use deployed in a critical ethnographic study to conceptually illustrate how one Nigerian girl agentively mediated colonial, racial, and linguistic tensions through multiliterate art practices. In conjunction, she demonstrates how lenses of raciolinguistics and postcolonial theories provide avenues to challenge talk-centric participation structures and offer multiliterate participation structures to help African immigrant youth mediate discrimination based on their talk. Afolalu calls for classroom and community educators to open multiliterate curricular spaces that honor, affirm, and integrate African immigrant youth, allowing them to engage in diverse languages, literacies, and multiliterate forms of communication and self-expression.

Functioning as a culminating climax to dynamic approaches presented in the book, Joel E. Berends, Vaughn W. M. Watson, and African immigrant youth Dinamic Kubengana, in Chapter 12, demonstrate possibilities of rightful literary presence as a productive framework for research and teaching with African immigrant youth. The authors conceptualize rightful literary presence as involving four complementary approaches: affirming, contextualizing, evoking and historicizing, and storyairing. To illustrate the four approaches, the authors share an extended narrative vignette coauthored with Dinamic, a high school student born in Uganda and living in the U.S. Midwest. The authors conclude with recommendations for envisioning rightful literary presence in teaching and learning, developed with Dinamic and illustrated through an example of teaching and research the authors discuss as participatory curriculum design.

As a researcher who has focused on Black immigrants from Africa and the Caribbean in the United States and as a former public school K–12 teacher of literacy in St. Lucia and Trinidad and Tobago, Patriann Smith also has worked as a teacher educator supporting literacy programs involving Black youth of multiple nationalities across Florida, Illinois, Texas, and the Organization of the Eastern Caribbean States. In Part III, Smith sees the authors' foci on heritage resources, raciolinguistically just, multiliterate practices, and the notion of rightful literary presence as critically extending conceptions of "diaspora literacy" (King, 1992, 2021), "transnational literacy" (Skerrett, 2015), "Black language pedagogy" (Baker-Bell, 2020), "Black immigrant literacies" (P. Smith, 2020a, 2023a), and "(transnational) Black language pedagogy" (Milu, 2021; Smitherman, 2000). With urgency, authors implore readers to consider epistemic, raciolinguistic (Alim, 2004a; Alim et al., 2016; Rosa & Flores, 2017), and literary impetus for affirming legitimate literacies and lives of African immigrant youth in ways that extend normalcy beyond monolithic notions of Americanness (P. Smith, 2020b), while bolstered by a centering of an established and emerging cadre of Black (African) voices.

CHAPTER 10

Unboxing Black Immigrant Youth's Heritage Resources

David Bwire Wandera

Global migration is not new. It has become a preeminent feature of our interconnected world and continues to re-contour various social domains. In the education domain, the contemporary classroom is the locus of ethnoracial, linguistic, and additional forms of diversity. Current trajectories show immigrant students are the fastest growing student population in the United States (Suárez-Orozco et al., 2010). What is the role of education in our pluralistic world? How might educators and related stakeholders and collaborators respond to achieve positive educational outcomes?

Although immigrant students experience migration, acculturative, and traumatic stress (Birman, 2002), research (Blommaert, 2010; C. C. Lee, 2019) has pointed to their multiliteracy competencies, including linguistic, cultural, and additional heritage assets they bring to the classroom. Scholarship abounds in research with and for ethnoracially and linguistically diverse and immigrant students, but their cultural epistemologies tend to be regarded as data that researchers analyze using Western(ized) concepts and theories. Immigrant students' worldviews promptly are translated to English, erasing cultural and heritage nuances.

This monocultural treatment diminishes opportunities for educators and stakeholders engaging with premigration resources that shape educational outcomes of immigrant youth. For example, a study might focus on immigrant youth literacy practices of Taiwanese or Ghanaian or Indonesian students, but Taiwanese or Ghanaian or Indonesian cultural practices and language feature only as data or are translated into English to be analyzed using exclusively Western epistemic traditions. Thus, Indigenous or immigrant youth tend to be evaluated and researched through theoretical lenses and understandings rooted in dominant norms and epistemologies (Petrone et al., 2021). This approach obscures roles specific heritage resources play in shaping acculturation experiences. The resultant paucity of non-Western sourced analytical tools in scholarship on immigrant youth and "an avoidance or ignorance of the burgeoning literature on Indigenous [immigrant]

148   Literacies, Languages, and Learning

ways of knowing" (Tierney, 2018, p. 405) permeate classrooms, whereby educators "lack the knowledge and strategies to address the cultural ways of knowing of the Indigenous [or immigrant] students they encounter" (p. 407).

In addressing this paucity, this chapter makes a case for the inadequacy of analytical apparatuses being drawn exclusively from some traditions; explores specific premigration heritage resources of immigrants from India, China, Nigeria, and Ghana; presents the empirical case of a Kenyan immigrant to illustrate how *interepistemic synergy* deploys culturally sourced apparatuses as metalanguage for analyzing acculturation; and offers takeaways for stakeholders to build cultural competence when working with immigrant youth.

LITERATURE REVIEW

Immigrant Trends

Behind every immigrant statistic is a human who has moved from their country or place of origin to a host place. The terms *immigrant, foreigner,* and *foreign born* tend to be used interchangeably in popular discourse and electronic and print media. Here, "immigrant" constitutes an umbrella term for foreign-born youth and first-generation youth from immigrant families (U.S. Census Bureau, 2012). This chapter adopts P. Smith's (2020a) definition of Black immigrants as "first-, second-, or third-generation immigrants to the U.S. who identify as Black, and who migrate to the U.S. from Africa, the Caribbean, or elsewhere" (p. 193). "Kenyan immigrant students" refer to students living with their immigrant parent(s) or who are citizens of or have transnational links with Kenya and who are in the United States on an immigration status and whose primary engagement is seeking education. Immigrants also are conceptualized as sojourners traversing global spaces (Fülöp & Sebestyén, 2012) due to myriad, complex factors that might not be fully accounted for through concepts such as "push and pull factors" of migration, as proposed by Franklin (2014).

Immigrant communities originate mainly from Mexico, India, China, and the Philippines. Migration correlates with increased multilingualism and multiculturalism. In the United States, Spanish, Chinese, Tagalog, Vietnamese, French, Korean, Arabic, German, and Russian are the most common languages in addition to English (Zong & Batalova, 2016). Originating from Jamaica and Trinidad and Tobago, Haiti, Cuba, Dominican Republic, and West and Sub-Saharan Africa, Black immigrants have increased by 56% in the past 10 to 15 years (J. Anderson, 2015). Immigration and Naturalization Services records show that although comparatively fewer than other immigrant groups, African immigrants increased from 109,733 between 1961 and 1980, to 531,832 between 1981 and 2000 (Takougang, 2003). In 2019, Yoruba, Twi, Igbo, and other West African languages accounted for 0.9% of non-English languages spoken by African immigrant students aged 5 and older (Esterline & Batalova, 2022).

Kenyan Immigrants

Kenyan immigrants started seeking educational opportunities in the United States in the late 1950s into the early 1960s, through "the airlift generation" or "Airlift Africa" initiatives. They came as scholarship recipients from U.S. and Canadian institutions (JFK Library records cited in Onwong'a et al., 2021). Despite prohibitively exorbitant migration-related costs, the 1965 Immigration and Naturalization Act led to increased immigration from Sub-Saharan Africa and Asia (Flahaux & de Haas, 2016).

More than 40 cultural groups inhabit Kenya, each with unique traditions and heritage. In addition to Kenyan English (normed toward received British pronunciation due to colonial history) and Swahili—the national language—Kenya is multilingual. The average Kenyan speaks English, Swahili, and their heritage language. Additionally, teenagers speak Sheng, a trendy generational urban linguistic mélange of Swahili, English, and Kenyan languages. Extant language ideologies position English, and increasingly Swahili, above heritage languages (Nabea, 2009). The Roman alphabet is the main orthography deployed for writing. Kenyan immigrants generally maintain transnational ties with Kenya (Onwong'a et al., 2021).

Heritage Resources

Like other immigrant youth, Black immigrant students bring cultural and experiential assets as they navigate myriad acculturative challenges in Western spaces. These challenges include invisibility through being subsumed into the "Black" population, having Englishes and accents perpetually marking them as outsiders, difficulties with academic English proficiency (Nero, 2014), placement in English remedial classes despite originating from spaces where English is the official language (Kajee, 2011), and being stereotyped (Kumi-Yeboah & Smith, 2017; Mas Giralt, 2015; P. Smith, 2020a). Historical differences of colonization in Kenya and slavery in the United States also complicate how Kenyan immigrants are racialized along *raciolinguistic hierarchies* (Baker-Bell, 2020).

Immigrant heritage resources result from premigration socialized worldviews internalized in countries of origin. These resources construct immigrant identity and shape acculturation, yet generally are unnoticed or unrecognized in daily classroom life (Kiramba, Kumi-Yeboah, & Mawuli Sallar, 2020). Notwithstanding this invisibility, these youth tap into cultural and experiential resources to navigate myriad acculturative challenges in and beyond classrooms (Watson & Knight-Manuel, 2017). Educators and stakeholders would benefit from collaborations with students or community members as cultural guides, to assist them in discerning these resources. For instance, C. C. Lee (2019) argues that multilingualism is a means of critical literacy as well as a resource. These resources comprise community cultural wealth, including aspirational, social, navigational, linguistic, resistant, and familial capital, together with resiliencies such as optimism, work ethic, value of education, cohesive extended families, perspective-taking, cross-cultural navigation, and adaptability (Sichra, 2017; Yosso, 2005). This chapter visualizes community-specific premigration cultural resources with Kenyan immigrants.

Exemplifying Premigration Cultural Resources

Concrete examples of premigration resources are described by Ghosh and Wang (2003), two Asian women, one from India and one from China, studying in Canada, who reflect on their identities. They highlight tensions as Ghosh navigates between a traditional Bengali *desi* identity versus becoming a Canadian *mem* (a Westernized woman), who would be perceived by fellow Bengalis as having shunned her culture after leaving home and going to *bidesh* (a foreign land). This study alludes to this *mem-bidesh* versus Bengali *desi* dichotomy, which can be deployed to make sense of Bengali immigrant transcultural navigations.

Additionally, Ping (2010), a Chinese international student reflecting on his acculturative choices, explains how heritage and culture shape specific classroom actions. He notes that "Chinese international students engaged in extensive self-monitoring . . . consistent with Confucian 'maxims of modesty'" (p. 208) and exemplifies how he feared "losing face in front of others because of [his] . . . face or miànzi culture— 面子" (p. 210). *Miànzi* (面子) is "the regard in which one is held by others or the light in which one appears" (p. 210). This specific concept can be deployed to make sense of literacy practices, acts of identity, or acculturative choices to better understand immigrant youth from cultures upholding Confucian maxims.

Considering immigrants from western Nigeria, of Yoruba origin, Adebisi (2015) and Adeniji-Neil and Ammon (2011) outline a premigration cultural philosophy instrumental in acculturation. The Yoruba concept of *Omoluabi* is defined as "a person of honor who believes in hard work, respects the rights of others, and gives to the community in deeds and in action . . . a person of personal integrity" (Adeniji-Neil & Ammon, 2011, p. 1). The authors, who identify, and are identified by family members, as cultural insiders, study eight Nigerian voluntary immigrant families in the United States and collaborate with participants to learn about acculturation choices in a manner emphasizing the community's strengths rather than reifying deficits. Keen observation was necessary since *Omoluabi* was not mentioned by researchers, but arose organically from participants. For instance, one might hear the *oriki* (a chant featuring panegyric praise-names of the child's progenitors as a reminder of noble ancestry), recited to encourage desirable *Omoluabi* behavior (Adebisi, 2015). *Omoluabi* socialization also happens through moonlight tales, proverbs, folktales, myths, and songs. *Omoluabi* entails:

> two basic tenets followed by five inalienable social values that motivate and guide social relations: *ajobí* (consanguinity/blood relations) and *àjogbé* (co-residence): (1) *ire àikú* (value of good health to old age), (2) *ire owó* (financial security), (3) *ire oko-aya* (the value of intimate companionship and love), (4) *ire omo* (the value of parenthood), and (5) *ire àborí òtá* (the value of assured self-actualization). (Adeniji-Neil & Ammon, 2011, p. 4)

Adebisi (2015) notes the antithesis of *Omoluabi* is *Omo ti a ko ko*, which translates into "the child that we failed to 'build up.'" A child who rejects cultural training is "*akoogba* (the one taught but refuses to heed the training)." Thus, *Omoluabi-omo ti a ko ko* can be deployed to illuminate acculturative choices and in- and out-of-class transcultural navigations by Yoruba immigrant youth.

A comparable concept applies with immigrant youth from the Akan community in Ghana. The term *Sankofa,* translated "from the Akan proverb, '*se wo were fin, Sankofa a yenkyi,*'" means, "it is not taboo to go back and fetch your past when you forget" (Yeboah, 2016, pp. 10–11). With roots in the Ghanaian nationalist movement, *Sankofa* is a popular idiom, philosophy, and practice for celebrating Akan cultural identity. The *Sankofa* sign, typically visualized as a bird with forward-facing feet and a backward-facing neck, carrying an egg in its beak (see Figure 10.1), is one among several *Adinkra* (symbols*)* for constructing Akan worldviews (Yeboah, 2016). For Ghanaian Akan immigrants, this philosophy affords a restorative stance to safeguard from cultural erosion, by finding ways to reawaken African roots through informing immigrant lives with teachings from Akan cultural heritage.

Given that *Adinkra* symbols are assimilated into material culture of Akan people (Yeboah, 2016), educators and stakeholders would need to collaborate with Akan immigrants to observe manifestations of *Sankofa* practices. Yeboah offers examples of immigrant youth telling stories in a narrative style aligning with the Akan storytelling tradition of *Anansesem* (featuring narrator-call-and-audience-response and references to ancient Egypt, etc.), or when youth adorn themselves in *kente* traditional clothing or colors. In a literacy classroom, a Ghanaian immigrant might appear to persistently misspell "Africa" as "Afrika." Yeboah explains how for many Ghanaians, *k* indexes resistance against *c*, which is associated with colonialism. Thus, *Sankofa* can be deployed to understand acculturative choices and Ghanaian immigrant literacy practices signaling an Afrikan identity.

Figure 10.1. Adobe Stock Image of *Sankofa*

Taken together, the *mem-bidesh* versus Bengali *desi* dichotomy, the Miànzi (面子) cultural philosophy, the *Omoluabi-omo ti a ko ko* cultural logic, and *Sankofa* are authentic apparatuses for data analysis and should not be "invisiblized" through being translated and interpreted through a Western lens.

RESEARCH QUESTIONS

Guided by the following research questions, this empirical study sought to discover, name, and deploy premigration resources to make sense of acculturative practices in the case of a Kenyan immigrant youth:

1. What specific premigration cultural resources do African immigrant youth bring to the host settings?
2. What insights might inservice and preservice teachers derive from these resources to understand school-related acculturation and better support immigrant students?

Overall, by confronting deleterious presuppositions through challenging invisiblization of premigration resources, this chapter presents educators and stakeholders an illustrative exposure to cultural assets.

METHODOLOGY

Participants and Setting

The main participant in this study, part of a year-long immigrant youth literacies project, is Wanjikũ (pronounced /wanjekoo/), nicknamed Ciku (pronounced /shekoo/), a 9-year-old, 4th-grade girl. Her 13-year-old, 7th-grade brother, Kimani (pronounced /kemʌne/), is a secondary participant. Both are siblings in a Kenyan immigrant family household from the Kikuyu community. The pseudonyms, from the Kikuyu community, are comparable to cultural nuances of real names. According to the Kikuyu myth of origin, the founders of the community, Gĩkũyũ and Mũmbi, had nine daughters, one called Wanjikũ, a founder of one of nine Kikuyu clans (Kenyatta, 1938). At the time of this study, Ciku's family was living in an urban midwestern city after immigrating from Kenya to the United States on an F1 student visa. Over time, her parents adjusted their immigration status to what the U.S. Citizenship and Immigration Services terms as "alien workers on an H1B visa." Ciku's dad held a job in the manufacturing industry, while her mother was a middle school teacher. Both parents spoke a combined five languages: Kikuyu, Swahili, English, Embu, and Kamba. Ciku and Kimani had some competence in Kikuyu and were highly proficient in Swahili and English. The family lived in a rented three-bedroom apartment in an ethnically diverse part of the city and kept social ties with fellow Kenyan immigrants.

The inside of Ciku's family apartment contrasted with the appearance of the surrounding U.S city. The parents proudly said in Swahili, *"huko nje ni America na hapa ndani tuko Kenya"* (outside there is America but in here we are in Kenya). Specifically, the family mixed Swahili, English, and Kikuyu, played Kenyan music, watched Kenyan news and programming through YouTube, and displayed Kenya- and Africa-shaped fridge magnets, artwork, and decorative wood carvings. A Kenyan flag was placed prominently in a living room corner. They sourced ingredients and condiments from the nearby "African Market" and prepared mainly Kenyan food such as *ugali* (corn-meal mush), *githeri* (corn and beans), *irio* (mashed dry beans, corn, and potatoes), *mukimo* (mashed green peas and potatoes), and *chapati* (an unleavened flatbread). This interior décor is a "black space . . . where black people imagine radical political futures, construct expansive meanings of blackness, and engage in the process of worldmaking" (Medford, 2021, pp. 915–916).

Located in a suburban setting with a student population of about 400, Ciku's school is a Pre-K–5 public school serving 51% Black/African American, 23% Hispanic, 14% white, 8% bi/multiracial, and 3% Asian students. Forty percent of students speak a home language other than English. The school has 26 equivalent full-time teachers with a 15:1

student-to-teacher ratio and offers lunch assistance. There is one full-time school counselor. The most prominent language spoken after English is Spanish, and there are West, Central, and East African immigrant students. Three episodes are examined through Ciku's cultural resources to offer an understanding of her school-related acculturation.

Data Collection

Focusing on Ciku, data were collected through observation notes, taken when the researcher was invited on weekends as a guest in the home or out and about with Ciku's family. Data also were excerpted from 30 hours of audio-recorded informal interviews with the family. Interview topics came up organically, including school-related acculturative experiences and aspects of Kenyan life. Data were then transcribed; thematic coding yielded categories such as social, economic, recreational, and academic stressors; coping strategies; cultural traditions; and acts of identity.

Analysis

A decolonizing methodologies approach (L. Smith, 2012) was preferred because it scrutinizes traditions of practice and amplifies questions of whose knowledge counts as knowledge. This scrutiny is central to this study examining three brief episodes, to understand Ciku's acculturative processes as she acclimates to school-based literacy competence. Being a Kenyan immigrant, I deployed insider–outsider knowledge (Banks, 1998) and emic member checking by ascertaining with Ciku's family where they were enacting Kenyan or Kikuyu cultural practices to cope with academic acculturation. Findings also were corroborated through examining related artifactual and ideational elements of Kenyan culture. The researcher, a close family friend, had known Ciku's family since they migrated.

Analysis was undertaken using an *interepistemic synergy approach*, whereby apparatuses from local culture and other scholarly traditions are applied for a comprehensive understanding of data (Wandera, 2019). This approach surfaced specific cultural tools for understanding how Ciku taps into premigration cultural heritage. In pursuit of scholarship that does not reproduce Western epistemological hegemony, interepistemic synergy insists on accounting for the positionality of a researcher's analytical tools to achieve a comprehensive understanding of phenomena as well as epistemic diversity (Wandera, 2019). This approach aligns with Mignolo's (2009) knowledge as pluriversal, Makoni's (2012) plural perspectives, A. A. Abdi's (2011) epistemically polycentric approach, and Tierney's (2018) global meaning-making. This chapter instantiates interepistemic synergy by engaging oft-neglected culturally sourced analytical tools, drawn from Ciku's Kenyan socialization.

FINDINGS

The following episodes instantiate interactions between Ciku and the researcher where premigration cultural resources become visible. In line with the research questions, these resources are deployed to understand her acculturation process.

Episode 1: Traditional Artifact

How might worn artifacts visualize practices of otherwise invisible cultural beliefs? Wherever she went, Ciku wore a diasporic artifact (Pechurina, 2020) on her left wrist called *bangili ya bendera* (beaded Kenya flag bracelet bangle, see Figure 10.2). The beads are colored like the Kenyan flag, where black represents native Kenyans, green represents agricultural productivity, red represents independence struggle, and white represents peace. Further, just like on the Kenya government coat of arms, the unisex *bangili* features a shield and spears. This shield (*ngao*) is echoed in the national anthem line, *"haki iwe ngao na mlinzi"* (service be our shield and defender).

Not only did this artifact hold sentimental value, having been given by her grandmother when the family visited Kenya, but Ciku also explained how she viewed the *ngao* (shield) as a sort of protective charm. Unlike the coat of arms, the *bangili* did not have the word *harambee*, the national

Figure 10.2. A Kenyan Flag *Bangili* Bracelet

156   Literacies, Languages, and Learning

philosophy for pulling together, which inspires Kenyans into collective effort and communal support. Yet, Ciku's family frequently used the proverb, *"Umoja ni nguvu,"* a shortened form of *"Umoja ni nguvu, utengano ni udhaifu"* (unity is strength, separation is weakness) to encourage service to others or doing household chores. Thus, Ciku's *bangili* artifact bears symbolic utility through signaling the *harambee* philosophy.

Additionally, Ciku uses the *bangili* for its ornamental utility (in an informal interview, she characterized it as a "beautiful" bracelet), and celebratory utility (she proudly explained to classmates that it is "worn by Kenyans"). Relatedly, Ciku used her *bangili* for a show-and-tell class assignment where she wrote about visiting Kenya and receiving the artifact from her grandmother:

> As we were about to leave, Cucu [Kikuyu word for "grandmother" (pronounced /shooshoo/)] called me and Kimani and said, I want to give you something. She handed us a bracelet each. My mum and dad also wear a similar one.

Ciku added that she felt proud wearing the bracelet with the Kenyan flag colors. When asked whether she was a proud Kenyan in America, she recalled a popular Swahili proverb that her parents use, *"muacha mila ni mtumwa"* (one who forsakes their culture is in servitude).

Episode 2: Sibling Tutoring

Why would a 13-year-old sibling internalize the compulsion to offer unsolicited regular peer tutoring and support to his 9-year-old, 4th-grade sister? *Harambee*-inspired collectivism was instantiated in Ciku's learning whereby her older brother, Kimani, embraced responsibility of home-tutoring her. Three times weekly, after school, they would spend an hour on reading and writing assignments employing English, Swahili, and some Kikuyu; math; and English syntax. Kimani also would generate some on-the-spot literacy tasks for Ciku. During an informal interview, Ciku stated:

> Kim always reminds me to study. Once I forgot. I came from school and was watching TV. Dad and mum were not at home. Kim came and said, Ciku it is time for studying and he told me to switch off the TV. [Kim, who was within earshot, interjected that he had reminded her "many times"]. Yes! (laughs) I think I forget sometimes. (laughs)

Ciku also described an occasion when she did not perform well on a writing assignment. She recalled her mother asking what had gone wrong and, as she was explaining that she did not understand some concepts, Kimani interjected, promising that they would both "work harder next time." She nodded in agreement. The "we" indexes a *harambee*-inspired collective responsibility and participation with deep roots in Kenya. Collectivism has existed since precolonial times and morphed into the postcolonial national *harambee* movement with the Swahili tagline, *"tuvute pamoja"* (let's pull/ work together). Kenyan diasporic communities enact this collectivist ontology through unifying to contribute toward projects or to attend to needs of community members.

Episode 3: Individual Impetus

What might account for the internal self-drive propelling a 9-year-old, 4th-grader despite myriad acculturative challenges? Although communal participation is encouraged, Kenyans are exhorted to play their part. This exhortation manifests through popular Swahili proverbs such as *"hakuna kitu kigumu kwa mtu mwenye bidii"* (there is nothing difficult for a determined individual) and *"achanikaye kwenye mpini hafi njaa"* (one who exerts themselves on a grinder won't die of hunger). In popular parlance, the word *kujituma* (pronounced /kojetooma/) translates into "send yourself" or "give yourself impetus." This popular cultural maxim motivates individual exertion and resilience and has inspired the production of hip-hop songs such as Ally Mahaba featuring Akeelah in "Ujitume" and Beebwoy in "Jitume." For Kenyan immigrants, *kujituma* provides mettle in the face of acculturative challenges.

For example, the school is a key site for acculturation, where some immigrant youth struggle to belong. During an informal interview, Ciku explained that she does not have many school friends and hence she does not like school:

> We were about to start a writing worksheet. Everyone was tired. I was tired. So, the teacher said that we take a break and play. Everyone suggested we play (hesitates, looking at Kim) that thing you do with the hands (waving her wrists) *Nîki gîkî*? (Kikuyu for "what is this?" Kim answered, "the rock-paper-scissors game"). Yes! That (waving her wrists and laughing). I did not know how to play. No one taught me and nobody wanted to play with me. So, the teacher came, and she was doing rock-paper-scissors (waving wrists) and I just stood there (stops moving wrists; long pause). Then I asked for a bathroom hallway pass.

Her lack of prior exposure to a game that was meant to rejuvenate the class, before they transitioned to a different activity during the literacy session, marked Ciku as an outsider. The *Nîki gîkî* Kikuyu request is directed at Ciku's brother and not the researcher, who is not Kikuyu. Ciku's embodied illustration, juxtaposing animated wrist movements by her teacher with stillness and the long pause, amplifies her alienation. During the interview, she reported requesting bathroom passes whenever she felt class activities were unfamiliar. Kimani added that Ciku's teacher informed their mother that Ciku was "going to the bathroom a lot." Although she still did not like attending school at the time of this study, Ciku said that her parents encouraged her with the Swahili maxim, *"mtu ni kujituma"* (one should have self-determination). *"Amka ujitume"* (get up and exert yourself) is ubiquitous around the household, used by her parents to encourage the siblings to work hard or not oversleep on school day mornings.

DISCUSSION AND TAKEAWAYS

Cultural Apparatuses for Analyzing Immigrant Youth Acculturation

Various scholars have highlighted immigrant youth's premigration socialization in action, using artifacts and cultural symbology as a signal of identity construction (Watson & Knight-Manuel, 2020), illustrating internalization of cultural values informed by heritage worldviews (Ghosh & Wang, 2003), and showcasing intrinsic motivation drawn from transnational connections (Skerrett & Omogun, 2020). Broadly, when examined through *harambee* and *kujituma* concepts, Ciku's school-based acculturation, featuring cultural artifacts, sibling tutoring, and self-determination, visualizes her Kenyan premigration socialization in action. *Harambee* indexes a collectivist impetus for pooling effort, and *kujituma* indexes self-determination for individual exertion. Together, they index a coconstitutive individual-in-community ontology.

Further, like Knight et al.'s (2006) example of an immigrant student wearing a bandana featuring the Puerto Rican flag, and Watson and Knight-Manuel's (2020) case of Kaya and Ade's Liberian and Nigerian multicolored attire and Chike's Nigerian bracelet, Ciku's flag-colored *bangili* artifact bears cultural resonances of identity and personhood. Specifically, the *harambee* lens crystalizes a situated multifunctionality of Ciku's *bangili* bracelet as a tangible manifestation of Kenyanness and a possession for cultural retention (Baffoe & Asimeng-Boahene, 2013), as well as an indicator of transnational connections with her Cucu (grandmother). The *harambee* lens also accounts for communal motivation and a sense of shared success/failure that informs sibling tutoring. This tutoring activity manifests a Kenyan aspect through tapping into the siblings' multilingual repertoire. Ciku's self-drive is vivified through *kujituma* philosophy entailing resilience despite acculturation challenges. Her familial connections are a consequential site for animating *harambee* and *kujituma* worldviews.

Additionally Ciku's cultural resources can be characterized as anonymously authored popular cultural wealth. These typically are present in oral traditions, stories, legends, riddles, songs, proverbs, folktales, recitation, demonstration, sports, epics, poetry, reasoning, praise, word games, puzzles, tongue twisters, dance, and music (Sichra, 2017). Generally, scholarship on immigrant youth tends to deploy cultural resources such as *mem-bidesh* versus Bengali *desi*, Miànzi (面子), *Omoluabi*, and *Sankofa* as data to be analyzed using exclusively apparatuses from Western(ized) research traditions. In the classroom, some educators might translate *harambee* and *kujituma* into English or seek their Western equivalents to make sense of Ciku's school-related acculturation. Although informative, such an approach does not confront Western exclusivity of frames and analytical tools for meaning-making (Tierney, 2018).

For example, the concept of funds of knowledge (FoK) (González et al., 2005), which could be applied to Ciku's case, is premised on the position that various competencies and experiences combine to afford people knowledge since no learner is a blank slate. In the case of immigrant youth and families with transnational ties, cultural resources can be considered as part of the funds. While useful in disrupting deficit perceptions of marginalized students' out-of-school practices, FoK has been criticized for being prone to imposition of cultural arbitraries by educators, and its terminology adopts a capitalistic un-Freirean metaphor while constructing learning as acquisition rather than as participation (Oughton, 2010). Importantly, FoK alone does not do the decolonizing work of foregrounding resourcefulness of cultural apparatuses for analyzing immigrant youth acculturative practices.

Understanding Immigrant Cultural Assets

For some time now, under banners of culturally relevant, responsive, and sustaining pedagogies, educators have been advised to adopt an asset-oriented approach to diversity as well as to become culturally competent (e.g., Ladson-Billings, 2001). By interrogating assumptions marginalizing non-Western cultures, stakeholders might enact attitudinal shifts from Western-centric Anglo normative postures toward globalizing stances (Tierney, 2018). *Interepistemic synergy* (Wandera, 2019) shows how such a shift would necessitate explicit uptake of cultural resources as metalanguage for sense-making, leading to diverse languacultures (Agar, 1994) playing a role in planning curricular support. A teacher-as-student posture would enable educators to bridge unfamiliar worldviews, with students and community members as languacultural guides. Future studies could illustrate unboxing of premigration resources in other cultural and host locations.

Importantly, immigrant students' psychosocial well-being depends on how supported they are to belong and flourish (Suárez-Orozco et al., 2010). However, evidence-based supports that have gaps in relation to immigrant cultural assets present a partial understanding. By collaborating with immigrant youth and communities through listening with, learning with, and self-scrutiny, inservice and preservice teachers can begin to develop a fuller understanding of premigration cultural assets shaping school-related acculturation.

TAKEAWAY QUESTIONS

1. What are some common challenges Black immigrant youth face when they navigate language, identity, and literacy in Western contexts?
2. How do Black immigrant youth leverage transnational connections and multiliteracies to construct identity?
3. What does it take to challenge popularized narratives about the resourcefulness of Black African immigrant youth cultures?
4. How might we carve out spaces and practices that allow us to understand immigrant youth acculturative practices?
5. How does including epistemic cultural concepts from the heritage of Black immigrant youth enrich how we teach and research for and with this population?

CHAPTER 11

Opening Space to Participate— One Nigerian Girl's Use of Visual Arts to Navigate School-Based Linguistic Discrimination

Lakeya Afolalu

In February 2019, I received an email from Ms. Graves, literacy coordinator of a Central Texas elementary school. We had developed a strong relationship 2 years prior through a university–school partnership where I taught preservice teachers a reading methods course in her school building. Ms. Graves, a middle-aged white woman, knew that I desired to work with African immigrant youth and families in their school, and she invited me to mentor a new 5th-grade student from Nigeria, Sarai Imasuen. Ms. Graves described Sarai as "amazing" but "having difficulty speaking in class and with her classmates." Weeks later, I met with the school principal, Mrs. Dawn, a Black American woman in her late 40s, who described Sarai similarly: "She's smart, but shy." Sarai's silence and perceived shyness led Mrs. Dawn to invite the *Black Panther* author to their school's cultural ceremony. She strategically sat Sarai in the front row so that she could "see and connect with aspects of African culture." This cultural event and my invitation to mentor Sarai were just two of the school's many attempts to help Sarai become more social. Still, Sarai remained quiet at school.

Interestingly, Mrs. Dawn's and Ms. Graves's descriptions contrasted with Sarai's mother's descriptions. Mrs. Imasuen and I met for coffee, and she told me that Sarai was "far from shy and quiet." She also told me that all four of her children—whose first language is Nigerian Standard English—had become less communicative since they moved to the United States just a year prior. The decrease in their willingness to talk, she explained, was due to differences between U.S. and Nigerian Standard English styles:

161

I've noticed that in Nigeria, the way we speak is different from you guys [in America]. So, that has been a challenge for them. They are trying to pick their languages, how they pronounce is different, what we mean is different. I tell them "Don't worry. You will get used to the system." Some of their friends can't really understand them. The accent is totally different. Give it time.

My conversation with Mrs. Imasuen drew my attention to a critical issue in school spaces—harmful language ideologies privileging dominant U.S.-accented English, and talk-centric participation structures.

In the past 4 decades, language and literacy scholars have examined perceptions of Black American and Black immigrant youths' language practices across school, home, community, and digital contexts. Dating back to the mid-1980s, renowned Black language scholar Geneva Smitherman indelibly contributed to the field of education, advocating for Black American children's languages. She defined Black English by highlighting its unique structure and distinctive lexicon and distinguished it from traditional English. During this time period, Shirley Brice Heath (1983) explored preschoolers' language development and usage across race, class, and culture—insights further rendering visible limitations of mainstream language practices in U.S. schools, particularly for Black American youth whose languages are shaped by familial and sociocultural contexts and discriminated against. Between the 1990s and the mid-2000s, language scholars continued to examine dispositions toward Black American youth cultural language practices, challenging intersectional ideas in relation to language, race, education, and power (Alim, 2004b; A. F. Ball, 1992; Haas-Dyson, 2013; Paris, 2011). Anne Haas-Dyson (2013) challenged language and literacy researchers and practitioners to (re)consider Black American students' language resources, expand social practices, and deconstruct the power associated with "what sounds better" (p. 167). Most recently, April Baker-Bell (2020) argued that Black language remains devalued and treated as "linguistically, morally, and intellectually inferior" (p. 8). She attributes this devaluation to the critical relationship between anti-Blackness and linguistic oppression, which results in the "linguistic violence, persecution, dehumanization, and marginalization that Black language speakers experience in school and everyday life" (p. 7).

In conjunction with scholarship on Black American youth cultural language practices, language scholars also have advocated for Black immigrant youth language practices in Western contexts. For instance, Cheryl McLean (2010) explored how a Trinidadian teenage girl, Zeek, spoke Trinidadian and U.S. dialects across social media platforms and, in turn, "nurtured relationships and friendships across sociocultural and geographical contexts" through multilingual practices (p. 19). Black immigrant language scholars have documented linguistic shifts and shedding that Black immigrant youth undergo when encountering racial and linguistic influences conflicting with their native language practices (Doucet, 2014; P. Smith, 2019, 2020c). Scholars also have used research as a tool to make Black immigrant youth languages more visible (Bauer & Sánchez, 2020; Kiramba & Oloo, 2020), pairing well with Black immigrant language scholars who have encouraged policymakers and educators to integrate Black immigrant youth languages into school curricula (Knight & Watson, 2014; Nalubega-Booker & Willis, 2020). As Allison Skerrett and Lakeya Omogun (2020) argue, it is critical to uncover and understand differences, similarities, and nuances existing between language practices.

While language scholars have advocated for Black immigrant youth, most scholarship has focused on Caribbean immigrant, Francophone African immigrant, and English-language-learning African immigrant youths. Thus, we know very little about the linguistic experiences of English-speaking African immigrant youths—a population with a less established immigration history in the United States (Rong & Brown, 2002)—in school and community spaces, given contexts of race, ethnicity, geography, and language. The invisibility of English-speaking African immigrant youth can be traced to a persistent failure to recognize the diversity in Black youth identities (Kumi-Yeboah et al., 2020).

I thus extend existing language scholarship focused on African immigrant youth languages, challenging talk-centric participation structures in schools, and offering multiliteracies as an alternative to create expansive, equitable, accessible, and inviting participation structures for English-speaking African immigrant youth facing linguistic discrimination. I call for classroom and community educators to open multiliterate curricular spaces honoring, affirming, and integrating African immigrant youths' diverse languages, literacies, and multiliterate forms of self-expression. I discuss invisibility of African immigrant youth in educational policy, research, and practice through an anti-Black linguistic racism, raciolinguistic, and colonial lens; and draw on insights from a critical ethnographic project (Duncan, 2005; Madison, 2011) to present the case of Okokho—a 10-year-old Nigerian girl using visual arts to navigate harmful language ideologies. I call for classroom and community educators to open multiliterate curricular spaces that invite youth to engage in diverse forms of communication and self-expression.

AFRICAN IMMIGRANT YOUTH INVISIBILITY IN EDUCATIONAL POLICY, RESEARCH, AND PRACTICE

When African immigrant youth move to Western societies like the United States, they often become subjected to monolithic, performative perceptions of Blackness (Ibrahim, 1999). These subjections can be attributed to static racial categories and racialization processes overlooking African immigrant youths' ethnic, cultural, and linguistic identities, which renders them a nearly invisible population in new host countries (Awokoya, 2012; Omi & Winant, 2014; Watson & Knight-Manuel, 2017). In response, African immigrant youth (re)construct identities to reflect dominant and more socially acceptable ones (Braden, 2020; Kiramba & Oloo, 2020). Although African immigrants continue to migrate to the United States at increasing rates, there remains an almost exclusive emphasis on Latinx and Asian immigrant youth in U.S. educational language policies, research, and practice (Bryce-Laporte, 1972; Guy, 2001; Schmidley & U.S. Census Bureau, 2001; Tamir, 2022; Traoré & Lukens, 2006). While English-speaking African immigrant youth are also a "highly stigmatized group within Western imagination and U.S. school curricula," their educational experiences rarely are included in scholarly and educational conversations (Awokoya, 2012, p. 257; see also Watson & Knight-Manuel, 2017).

African immigrant youth invisibility also was reflected in Sarai's Central Texas school through the school district's policies and academic initiatives. While mentoring Sarai, I frequently met with her principal, Mrs. Dawn, to discuss the district's political and curricular decisions. Mrs. Dawn told me that although the district comprised a diverse African student population, their immigrant policies and programs focused predominantly on Latinx immigrant students. She also shared that the district designed the African American Educational Achievement Plan (AAEAP) to "narrow the gap between white and Black students, particularly in literacy." Similar to the district's immigration policies, the AAEAP was not inclusive of African immigrant student needs. She argued that the district's omission of African immigrant students from policies and programs was due to limited experiences and understandings that "make people think that the African American and African immigrant experience is the same." In line with scholarship (Agyepong, 2013; Kumi-Yeboah et al., 2020), Mrs. Dawn possessed a nuanced understanding of race and ethnicity. This understanding stemmed from her undergraduate boarding experience with her Ghanaian roommate, which she described as "an unforgettable experience where she learned about the beautifully rich differences between their African American and Ghanaian cultural backgrounds."

Mrs. Dawn's nuanced racioethnic knowledge surfaced in her comments about varying linguistic practices among the Anglophone and Francophone African immigrant students in the school. Whereas Sarai and her siblings spoke English, the Francophone African immigrant students were offered dual-language opportunities that supported their "English-learning, French, and ethnic languages." The district's omission of English-speaking African immigrant students prompted Mrs. Dawn to create a school environment that made all immigrant families feel welcome through cultural nights, love and logic parenting classes, clothing closets, and a school-based mental healthcare center.

Based on my schooling experience as a first-generation Nigerian student in the United States, I was not shocked about the district's omission of English-speaking African immigrant students from its policies and initiatives. My observations of the district's omission of English-speaking African immigrant youth, coupled with the predominant focus on African refugees and African "English-language learner" student groups in educational research (Dabach & Fones, 2016; Dávila, 2015; Park, 2013), led me to interrogate how English-speaking African immigrant students participated in school spaces. While the needs of such learners are important, heavily focusing on these two populations does not fully capture African immigrant students' diverse linguistic repertoire and needs. In fact, I contend the overemphasis on African refugee and African English-language learner student populations is reflective of the single-story narrative commonly portraying African immigrant students' educational experiences as deficient, damage-centered, and in need of saving (Adichie, 2009; Tuck & Yang, 2014).

Narrow portrayals of African immigrant youth language practices can be further explained through an anti-Black linguistic racism, raciolinguistic, and colonial lens, as African youth migrations to Western countries include "[finding] themselves in a racially conscious society that asks them to racially fit somewhere" (Ibrahim, 1999, p. 353). Their language practices, as scholarship has shown, become critical in finding a sense of racial and social belonging (Dávila, 2019; Kiramba & Oloo, 2020). Not only do African immigrant youth identities become subjected to anti-Blackness, but they also experience anti-Black linguistic racism (Baker-Bell, 2020). Linguistic scholar Krystal Smalls (2020) argues that anti-Blackness compounds the symbolic weight of Black bodies, which shapes how African immigrant youth make meaning with others. A raciolinguistic (Flores & Rosa, 2015) perspective helps to explain the invisibility of African immigrant youth's diverse languages practices. Scholars Nelson Flores and Jonathan Rosa (2015) argue that when particular racialized bodies speak standardized forms of a language, it would be deemed appropriate if the speech emanated from a white-speaking privileged subject. However, when racialized bodies—in this case, African immigrant youth—speak "standardized forms of English," it is interpreted through a white listening gaze that deems the language deficient. This explains the racial and linguistic discrimination that silenced Sarai and her three siblings' "Nigerian-accented British English."

A colonial perspective provides a further historical explanation of African immigrant youths' linguistic portrayals. Colonial discourse (Ashcroft et al., 2013), commonly reflected in popular media narratives like *Feed the Children* commercials, the movie *Roots*, caricature drawings, and school textbooks, portrays African people and their languages as uncivilized, subhuman, and the Other (Césaire, 1972/2000; Fanon, 1967). Sarai and her siblings were aware of harmful linguistic and colonial ideologies—ideologies that coerced them into silence at their new Central Texas school.

Together, these three lenses—anti-Black linguistic racism, raciolinguistic, and colonial discourse—explicate the intersectional discrimination Sarai and her siblings faced. They also help to explain why African immigrant youths' language practices remain on the margins, in this particular school district and in national language policy, scholarly research, and educational practice writ large.

MORE THAN TALK: BROADENING PARTICIPATION STRUCTURES IN SCHOOL AND COMMUNITY SPACES THROUGH MULTILITERACIES

Undoing anti-Black linguistic racism, raciolinguistic, and colonial discourse perspectives in school and community spaces necessitates radical social and school transformations (Flores & Rosa, 2015). However, one way school and community learning spaces can resist these perspectives is by deprivileging Western, talk-centric participation structures in classrooms. While talk is a highly privileged indicator of communication and participation in most K–12 classrooms, participation structures need to be broadened to include more than oral speaking. This is especially important as English-speaking African immigrant youths' languages, dialects, and accents are embedded in damaging anti-Black and colonial ideologies. Because language and the self are interconnected (Doucet, 2014; Mahiri, 2017), positioning English-speaking African immigrant youths' Englishes as deficient can lead to bullying, isolation, and a lack of social acceptance (P. Smith, 2019, 2022). It also can negatively affect their well-being. Therefore, I offer multiliterate participation structures as an alternative to create expansive, equitable, accessible, inviting participation structures, particularly for English-speaking African immigrant youth. Broadly speaking, literacy is a form of communication. A sociocultural perspective of literacy, however, conceptualizes literacy not as a set of concrete cognitive skills, but rather as social practices privileging social, linguistic, and cultural identities as well as one's goals for engaging with literacy (Gee, 1991; Skerrett, 2018; Street, 1984). Multiliteracies, then, refer to *multiple* ways to communicate. A multiliterate approach proposes that communication occurs through diverse modes, including oral, aural, visual, spatial, gestural, linguistic, and multimodal (Hull & Schultz, 2002; New London Group, 1996). African immigrant youth experience identity, social, educational, and cross-cultural tensions through migrations (McLean, 2010), and communicative practices serve as essential tools in helping them navigate these tensions. Communicative practices that are multiliterate in nature are critical, as they privilege diverse modalities and purposes for which English-speaking African immigrant youth communicate.

As emphasized in foundational and contemporary language scholarship (Baker-Bell, 2020; Doucet, 2014; Smitherman, 1986; P. Smith, 2019), traditional and talk-centric participation structures have led educators to believe that students of color, particularly Black American and Black immigrant students, are linguistically deficient. Such participation structures have led educators to believe that English-speaking African immigrant youth like Sarai and her siblings are quiet and reluctant to participate in classrooms, resulting in labels such as nonparticipatory. Conversely, integrating multiliterate participation structures in school and community spaces illuminates diverse ways English-speaking African immigrant youth make meaning and participate in classrooms. For instance, in my research with Nigerian immigrant youth, I witnessed them joyfully text friends in Nigerian Pidgin English on digital apps. They shared with me their creative writing, dance, and voiceover videos on Tiktok and Snapchat. These multiliterate communicative forms (Lozenski & Smith, 2012; Simmons, 2021a) did not require oral talk and took place outside of school spaces that youth described as "safe" with "less judgment" in relation to their Nigerian-accented Englishes.

OKOKHO'S AGENTIVE MULTILITERATE PRACTICES

This case draws from an 11-month critical ethnographic project (Duncan, 2005; Geertz, 1973; Madison, 2011) where I partnered with six Nigerian immigrant youths in grades 5 through 9 in Central Texas to understand how U.S. racial constructs and racialization processes impacted their identity. I designed the project in three phases to make sense of youths' racio-ethnic and linguistic identity constructions through respective language and literacy practices across school, community, and digital spaces, using questionnaires, semistructured interviews, storytelling sessions, and observations. As a first-generation Nigerian graciously invited by youths' families to partake in various cultural practices in their home and social lives, I took on dual roles as researcher and Nigerian community member through visits to homes, churches, and community spaces. My positioning as a researcher–community member enabled me to identify insights that recognize, support, and honor African immigrant youth identities and their extensive language and literacy employment. I focus on one of the six youths, Okokho, who moved from Cross River State, Nigeria, to Pennsylvania at age 2. Her family later relocated to Central Texas, and she was 10 at the time of the project. I draw on data sources collected from the larger research project to narrate key moments in Okokho's school-based multiliterate practices: questionnaires; home and community space observations; semistructured interviews with Nigerian youths, parents, and youths' respective literacy teachers; literacy artifacts; and identity creative stories. In what follows, I discuss how Okokho navigated harmful perspectives at school—by abandoning her preferred Englishes and engaging in visual arts. Both protected her, made her feel more seen, fostered new friendships, and created a sense of community and belonging.

Abandoning Her Preferred Englishes

On a typical after-school day, Okokho did homework, helped her mother and father with domestic tasks, and cared for her younger brother and sister. She was vibrant and talkative at home, speaking three languages—Nigerian Standard English, Nigerian Pidgin English, and white middle-class English. Okokho excitedly spoke Nigerian Pidgin to bond with her grandmother and assert a sense of older sibling authority with younger siblings. Many times, she also spoke Nigerian Standard English and white middle-class English, especially during conversations with me and her parents. Okokho distinguished her languages, referring to them as her "African language" and "American language." When her family moved to a new part of town, she transferred to a new school for 5th grade. This switch was a big adjustment and resulted in her feeling ignored and isolated by most of her peers at school:

> Most of my like [classmates] ignore me, I guess. Umm, whenever I like get to class in the morning. I mean there's no like "hi" or "hello" or anything like that, but it's definitely different from my other classmates so. . . . It doesn't really make me feel like angry or sad because it's happened so many times like at the start of the year, I was surprised that they didn't say anything to me but I brushed it off and didn't say anything because I didn't wanna make a big deal out of it.

Here, Okokho is aware of social positioning in her school community. She had been ignored so many times that she numbed her feelings of sadness and anger, deciding that brushing it off was a better alternative. This was strikingly different from behavior at home, where she engaged in nonstop conversations with family members. I asked Okokho whether her multilingual practices played a role in her being ignored by her peers. She told me that she spoke only her "American language" and did not feel safe speaking her "African language" at school. She elaborated:

> Okay. Like, um, I, um, I'm kind of embarrassed about like talking, um, talking, uh, like talking in like, um, my, my, my African language because . . . like I didn't really want them to laugh and like, say, like, say stuff. . . . They . . . they didn't really understand these things.

While Okokho's Nigerian Standard English is esteemed in Nigeria (Ikime & Mafeni, 1972), she focuses only on her "African language." Her response reveals implicit understanding of how raciolinguistic (Flores & Rosa, 2015) and anti-Black linguistic racism (Baker-Bell, 2020) position not only Nigerian Pidgin, but also Nigerian Standard English in school contexts. Okokho also understands that her school is not a safe space to engage in multilingual practices as she does with ease at home. She knows that if she did exercise her multilingual practices, it would result in being humiliated with laughter. So, she abandons her preferred Englishes in exchange for white middle-class English and, in turn, sheds her Nigerian ethnic identity (Doucet, 2014).

Okokho's language abandonment was influenced by some textbooks in her school, which, as she explained, were filled with images of Africa that "made her classmates laugh." Her interview responses revealed her constant references to classmates as "they," which positions classmates as outside gazers who view both her language and accent as different from their own, although they all speak English. Their view of Okokho's English languages reflects colonial discourse (Ashcroft et al., 2013), which commonly positions African people as Other and sources of entertainment (Césaire, 1972/2000; Fanon, 1967). Okokho's awareness of classmates' and school curricula's perception of both African people and African languages led her to protect herself and resort to a communicative practice that felt most natural and comfortable for her—drawing.

Drawing Into Visibility, Friendships, and Community

Okokho told me she loves art and desires to practice as a professional artist before transitioning into a career as a medical doctor postcollege. She drew everywhere—at home, online, and at school. She loved art so much she joined her school's math club so that she could maintain art as her elective. Each week, she strengthened her drawing craft in art elective and at home. When I asked Okokho why she liked drawing so much, she said, "I like using my hands to make something look really good. Like something that's like really good to look at . . . something that other people like." Okokho's response reveals that she engages in artwork to bring aesthetic joy to herself and others. This contrasts with her reflections on Nigerian Englishes, which she strategically hid from classmates for the sake of protecting herself. Her school-based artwork, however, was suited for everyone. Unlike her Nigerian Englishes, the multiliterate nature of her artwork did not require her to talk. Her artwork was gestural and visual, strategically employed to guard herself and navigate harmful perspectives that discriminated against her talk.

By engaging in multiliterate visual arts, Okokho also became more visible over the academic year. Her increased visibility through her multiliterate artwork enabled her to foster friendships with several supportive and trustworthy 5th-grade girls who noticed Okokho's love for artwork and often encouraged her to remain committed to her art craft. Toward the middle of the school year, one of Okokho's illustrations was selected as the school's first-place art competition winner, and later placed on a T-shirt (see Figure 11.1). Okokho told me, "I made it for this project. I never really thought it would

Figure 11.1. Okokho's Illustrated School T-Shirt

be a T-shirt though." She further explained that her T-shirt was the thing for which she became known by teachers and peers. Okokho's T-shirt illustration was also multiliterate, as she drew on a range of modalities to create it—visual, gestural, written, and others. Similar to multiliterate art she enjoyed creating for herself and others, the T-shirt further fostered a sense of belonging, community, and identity. Okokho's multiliterate art practices facilitated the creation of nonjudgmental spaces where she felt safe enough to orally communicate using "her African accent" with trusted friends.

While Okokho's multiliterate art practices offered positive social and emotional benefits, her literacy teacher, Ms. Stunner, viewed her artwork quite differently. During an interview with Ms. Stunner, I learned she followed a scripted writing curriculum. I also learned Okokho frequently "doodled in the margins of her papers" of writing assignments. Although Ms. Stunner described Okokho as highly intelligent, she interpreted her doodling as a sign of nonparticipation and disengagement. In response to my questions about her doodling, Okokho told me that she desired more choice with writing assignments. Okokho confessed that her teacher often asked her to stop doodling, but explained why she did not stop: "Sometimes, when my mind begins to wander, I have these really good ideas and I just start drawing." Okokho's multiliterate art practices conflicted with Ms. Stunner's traditional, and arguably more narrow, understandings of classroom participation. They also reveal Ms. Stunner's lack of awareness of harmful language ideologies that made drawing—not speaking—a preferred form of classroom participation for Okokho. Finally, Okokho's art practices further affirm the need for multiliterate participation structures helping English-speaking African immigrant youth feel a sense of safety, belonging, and identity.

OPENING MULTILITERATE CURRICULAR SPACES
FOR AFRICAN IMMIGRANT YOUTH

I examined Okokho's agentive multiliterate art practices with the goal of making visible the intersectional harms of anti-Black linguistic racism, raciolinguistic, and colonial perspectives on English-speaking African immigrant youths' languages and sense of self. I offered multiliteracies as alternatives to create expansive, equitable, accessible, and inviting participation structures that can lessen linguistic discrimination. I illustrated how Okokho's multiliterate art practices helped her navigate harmful language and colonial ideologies, and also fostered a sense of safety, belonging, community, and identity.

It takes time to build community at a new school. While Okokho cheerfully and willingly spoke Nigerian Englishes at home, damaging linguistic and colonial perspectives led her to abandon these languages at school. Okokho was aware that her languages were embedded in these perspectives, which she revealed in her interview about her school textbook's colonial portrayals of African people and her classmates' perception of her Nigerian Englishes (Ashcroft et al., 2013; Césaire, 1972/2000; Subedi & Daza, 2008). The conjunction of these ideologies made her more hesitant to speak at school.

Because Okokho did not feel safe orally communicating at school, she communicated through another medium—visual artwork. Over time, Okokho's multiliterate art practices became instrumental in helping her navigate harmful language ideologies that had silenced her. Instead, she utilized a range of modalities, including but not limited to gestural, written, and visual, that made her more visible. Okokho's increased visibility positioned her to foster new trustworthy friendships and integrated her into self-selected parts of the larger school community. Okokho's art practices reveal the power of multiliteracies in African immigrant youths' schooling lives as well as their ability to shield the youths—to an extent—from racist and colonial discrimination against their languages.

Based on these insights, I recommend that classroom and community educators move beyond talk-centric forms of student participation. By expanding participation structures, educators can invite African immigrant youth to participate through communicative forms pointedly talk back to anti-African, anti-Black, colonial and raciolinguistic ideologies. Further, educators will be able to see how African immigrant youth already participate in the classroom and school environment through multiliterate communicative forms (see *Framework for Educating African Immigrant Youth*, Chapter 1). Critical to the expansion of participation structures is the exchange of narrow and traditional forms of literacy and communication for more accessible, equitable, and expansive ones that affirm African immigrant youth cultural, heritage, and language practices. Thus, I recommend school and community educators open multiliterate curricular spaces honoring, affirming, and integrating African immigrant youths' diverse languages, literacies, and identities. In cases where school and community educators need support with these curricular innovations, they could consider partnering with art instructors in school buildings or nearby community centers. A multiliterate approach to participation structures does not seek to further silence African immigrant youth but rather seeks to broaden ways they can participate. These approaches are meant to be coupled with traditional forms of participation. While I focus on African immigrant youth, opening multiliterate curricular spaces can and should recognize, honor, and integrate all youths' diverse forms of communication.

TAKEAWAY QUESTIONS

1. How can you invite African immigrant youth to participate in your school, classroom, or community environment in ways that extend beyond talk? What modalities could you incorporate (e.g., written, technological, visual arts, music, etc.)?
2. What already-present languages and literacies do African immigrant youth in your school, classroom, or community environment possess? How can you affirm them? How can you integrate them into larger teaching, learning, and social environments?
3. What curricular materials can you use that showcase depictions of African nations, African people, and African languages beyond colonialism?

CHAPTER 12

Theorizing Rightful Literary Presence and Participatory Curriculum Design With African Immigrant Youth

Joel E. Berends, Vaughn W. M. Watson,
and Dinamic Kubengana

Across our sessions in Lit Diaspora, the name given by Black African immigrant youth to our after-school, participatory collaboration in the U.S. Midwest, we asked youth to share digital collages using Padlet, an online whiteboard. Four weeks into the sessions, students were asked to compose "a list of 2 to 3 activities that you enjoy doing that you feel express who you are." Dinamic, born in the Democratic Republic of Congo, lived in Uganda and since 2017 has lived in the United States, recalled in his Padlet:

> I grew [up] knowing only one sport, soccer—football. I like everything about this sport. I remember a time back in Uganda when we had a school tournament, we had to walk for miles in order to get to the fields where the matches were going to be played.

African immigrant youth increasingly enact a range of literacy and learning practices and stances extending their dynamic racial, ethnic, gendered, cultural, linguistic, and geographic identities. Immigrant youth furthermore navigate contexts of adultism, and Eurocentric, colonial, anti-Black, anti-immigrant ideologies, undergirding theories, practices, and pedagogies in research and teaching in the United States and globally (e.g., Bertrand et al., 2020; de los Ríos et al., 2019; Watson & Petrone, 2020).

In Lit Diaspora, Dinamic, with peers, enacted what we theorize as *rightful literary presence*, a necessary stance-taking underscoring how immigrant youth make present the interplay of complex civic and literacy lives as contributors to schools and communities. We situate rightful literary presence as the ongoing work of designing and enacting frameworks, methodologies, and teaching approaches that disrupt dispiriting deficit narratives,

173

174   Literacies, Languages, and Learning

particularly of African immigrant communities, toward (re)envisioning what it may mean to more fully affirm, contextualize, historicize, and design transformative research and teaching approaches at the interplay of literacy and civic education for Black African immigrant students.

THEORETICALLY FRAMING RIGHTFUL LITERARY PRESENCE

Our theorizing of rightful literary presence builds on our ongoing research and teaching across 2 decades, rendering visible the varied civic learning and literacy experiences of African immigrant youth and communities (e.g., Knight et al., 2012; Watson et al., 2022). Vaughn identifies as Black and of African descent. His extensive teaching and learning with African immigrant youth and young adults across 2 decades includes teaching English with youth from Ghana and Nigeria at a public high school in New York City; working with researchers and community organizers with a center for African women and families in New York; facilitating participatory curriculum design with African immigrant youth in Lit Diaspora and English education with university collaborators in Pretoria, South Africa; and functioning as founding director of African Scholars in Education Research, a community of practice with African PhD students, supporting and advancing a range of African theoretical, epistemological, and methodological perspectives in education research. Joel identifies as white and of Dutch descent. His experiences teaching and learning with African immigrant youth include youth from Uganda, Angola, Senegal, Cameroon, Ghana, Kenya, Malawi, and Nigeria, within contexts of coaching soccer and teaching English language arts in public and private schools in Grand Rapids, MI, Baltimore, MD, and Jakarta, Indonesia.

In theorizing rightful literary presence, the university-based research team—including Vaughn, Joel, and Alecia Beymer and Lauren Elizabeth Reine Johnson (LJ), then PhD candidates in Curriculum, Instruction, and Teacher Education and currently university faculty—engaged a grounded theory analysis of three sets of collected data in the Lit Diaspora project: (1) transcripts of 18 Zoom literacy sessions attended by 11 youth; (2) transcripts of session chats; and (3) more than 135 multimodal entries featuring writing, art, photography, and music, posted by youth to Padlet. The analysis was informed by four areas of education and social science research:

1. Sociocultural perspectives prioritizing literacy and learning beyond texts and practices that center a monolingual, print-focused, white, cisgender male literary canon (e.g. , Moje & Lewis, 2020; New London Group, 1996; Perry, 2012; Price-Dennis & Sealey-Ruiz, 2021; Watson & Beymer, 2019).

Theorizing Rightful Literary Presence and Participatory Curriculum Design

2. Participatory communal civic learning and action, underscoring African immigrant youths' and young adults' civic contributions within and across contexts, such as with families and in informal learning spaces, and beyond one-time activities, such as voting, which delimit vast civic contributions of youth who are not yet 18 (de los Ríos & Molina, 2020; Knight & Watson, 2014).
3. A stance-taking of "literary presence" (Muhammad, 2020), to assert how Black youths and young adults have long accessed and participated in the range of social, civic, and political literary practices (e.g., Croom et al., 2021; Watson, 2018).
4. The theorizing of "rightful presence" in critical geographies (Squire & Darling, 2013) and informal STEM learning (Calabrese Barton et al., 2020) that envisions how youth engage in "making present" practices (Squire & Darling, 2013 p. 59) that vividly demonstrate histories of migration and relational connections to people and place.

CONCEPTUALLY ILLUSTRATING FOUR COMPLEMENTARY APPROACHES OF RIGHTFUL LITERARY PRESENCE

We conceptualize rightful literary presence as involving four complementary approaches that more fully recognize daily lived moments, literacies, and experiences of immigrant and refugee communities (see Figure 12.1).

To introduce each of the four approaches, which we discuss later in detail, we present an extended four-part narrative vignette, coauthored with Dinamic.

Approach 1: Affirming, Inviting, and Making Visible Complex Transnational Identities Through Literacy and Learning

Two years after Dinamic first talked about soccer, we met again via Zoom—Joel, Dinamic, and Vaughn, coauthoring this chapter as an enacting of rightful literary presence. Dinamic, now in 12th grade, continued his recollection of his time in Uganda. Affirming and making visible thus involved inviting Dinamic to co-narrate his interests, experiences, and identities across transnational contexts. Dinamic, chatting with Joel and Vaughn, recalled the school tournament:

> "The whole school came to watch. . . . The first time with a tournament this size." Teachers packed lunch for the entire 5th grade, beans and rice. "They came to have fun."
>
> No one complained about the 7-mile walk, and students played in their school uniforms—not team jerseys. "The other school came with this big bus.

Figure 12.1. Rightful Literary Presence: Four Complementary Approaches

Affirming	*Affirming* complex transnational identities through literacy and learning. By "affirming" we mean affirming, inviting in, and making who you are visible through the range of literacy activities youth engage in within and beyond home and schooling spaces.
Contextualizing	*Contextualizing* literacy and learning as informing and informed by transglobal social and cultural geographies. By "contextualizing," we mean ensuring that how we think about or enact literacy practices affirms and includes multiple and varied spaces and places that extend our identities, for example, home countries, learning across a range of (in)formal settings, etc.
Evoking and historicizing	*Evoking and historicizing* a connectedness to learning with places and elders past, present, and into the future. By "evoking and historicizing" we mean intentionally linking present literacy and learning with elders, places, and materials, past, present, and into the future.
Storyairing	By "storyairing" we mean youth and communities authoring, composing, and sharing tellings about literacy and learning that affirm, contextualize, and historicize in ways that youth and communities call forth as meaningful.

Our coach told us not to matter about that. It always only matters about the spirit of the game. We played and we even beat some of the teams, we got almost close to the finals."

Dinamic recalled the rain, that it was dark, and that the team walked back to school. He added, "That was one of the nights that even up to now I still remember everything that happened."

Approach 2: Contextualizing Literacy and Learning

When we first began Lit Diaspora sessions, the Champions League, one of the most anticipated European club soccer tournaments, was in full swing. Chelsea, a team from the English Premier League, was at the top of their table because of their stalwart defense. Knowing Dinamic had an interest in soccer, Joel mentioned the Champions League matches in an early Zoom session, and this was when Joel first learned that N'Golo Kanté, who played for Chelsea and France, was Dinamic's favorite player.

At the time, Chelsea made it through to the semifinals and was set to face Real Madrid. Chelsea went on to beat Manchester City, 1-0, in the Champions League final. When Joel, an avid fan, former coach, and player,

Theorizing Rightful Literary Presence and Participatory Curriculum Design

heard of Dinamic's appreciation for the play of N'Golo Kanté, he couldn't help but think of Kanté's leadership that held the midfield for Chelsea so that they could win the biggest cup in all of club football. Knowing Kanté was born in Paris, and that his parents migrated to France from Mali, Joel noticed Dinamic's preference for a player of African heritage who follows a long legacy of box-to-box midfielders such as Yaya Touré and Michael Essien.

Two weeks prior to naming activities expressing who you are, Dinamic, in our Lit Diaspora session, shared the song "Nyamunene Musica" and wrote, "The people who sang this song are from my Village. I like the way [they] are dressing up because it describes my culture." Contextualizing such literacy and learning involved Dinamic recalling to peers the range of his already-present transnational geographic, linguistic, embodied identities, extended within and across multiple and varied spaces and places (Skerrett & Omogun, 2020; P. Smith, 2019; Watson, 2018; Watson & Knight-Manuel, 2017).

Approach 3: Evoking and Historicizing

"My favorite player to watch is Kanté," Dinamic explained in our coauthoring meeting. "The reason is his vision."

> I just love to watch him play, so when he was not playing in the World Cup, I was just not into France as much. They had Mbappé, the speed guy, but I'm not an Mbappé fan. Now, he's a good player; he's fast, he can create, but to me he's the kind of player who would want to go through anybody to score the goal. Kanté is more like a creator, so they have different mindsets of the game.

Rightful literary presence, in *affirming, contextualizing, historicizing,* and *storyairing,* talks back to persistent deficit civic narratives of the social, civic, and educational lives of immigrant youth, what Squire and Darling (2013) refer to as benevolent hospitality—such as in the mere designation by a city council of a sanctuary city. Such storyairing is notable, as Watson and Knight-Manuel (2020) write, amid "the violence of separability evoked in the popularized narrative of Black immigrant bodies called to 'go back' to home countries" (para. 6). In this way, in Lit Diaspora sessions, evoking rightful literary presence involved youth and adult collaborators reading and discussing the work of Mejai Bola Avoseh.

For example, we shared with youth that Avoseh was born in Nigeria and is professor of adult and higher education at the University of South Dakota. We sought to pointedly affirm ways of being and knowing, and theorize with onto-epistemologies of Black African immigrant youth as a purposeful curriculum design, teaching practice, and research approach. We shared Avoseh's (2005) writing on the urgency of dialogue in many

178   Literacies, Languages, and Learning

African communities, that "dialogue as a method in . . . African pedagogy helped . . . the learners to think—usually from a known premise (concrete life situations) to an unknown—and to rely on their experiences and the environment as the foundation for knowledge" (p. 379). We shared, and listened, with Dinamic naming and storyairing with N'Golo Kanté, and with soccer as Dinamic's *making present* practice.

Dinamic recalled in a meeting over Zoom, talking and coauthoring:

> I've watched Kanté play for Chelsea, and France. Kanté—he has this way, he always has the mentality that I want it, I want that ball, if I get it I don't want to throw it away. Every time I was trying to play like Kanté—no matter how big a guy is, no matter what his mindset is, I want it, more than he does.

Approach 4: Storyairing—Sharing Tellings That Affirm, Contextualize, and Historicize

Dinamic later shared about his own recent game:

> This week Saturday, we had our first game. I scored my first goal of the season. But this is what happened: In the middle of the first half we got scored on—the first goal.
>
> That first goal, that's where you see the team, and that's where you see the separation of the team. That's where you see the agony. That's where it happens the first time. When we see the first goal, all our heads drop low. I don't think we are going to be able to score.

Our next week together, when we asked Dinamic to describe the way he plays, Dinamic shared:

> When I'm on the field, and say you're my striker or winger, I'm not going to yell what I'm going to do. I'm going to send the ball to the space you need to be in, so if you don't do it the first time, you'll know exactly what I'm doing the second time. I don't like to keep the ball on my feet. I *can*. I think it's fun to play with the team. Pass. Move. Keep it simple.

Returning, then, to that previous game, Dinamic's first game on a Saturday, his team down 1-0, Dinamic shared:

> I don't think we are going to be able to score. When the first half ended without us tying the game, the coach told us, get gutsy. You can win this game. Get in there and . . . have fun playing with your teammates. There is more work to do. . . . We doubted ourselves, but we got in there, we worked as a team, we started talking to each other, showing each other what to do.

I didn't even look at it, I just shot it, and the ball just ended up in the net. . . . That's the beauty of the game, you come from the lowest part, rising up, we was all crying, but we came out of that game happy.

Given lived realities African immigrant youth navigate, such as challenging adultism and contesting deficit narratives, envisioning rightful literary presence enacted across the four approaches—*affirming, contextualizing, historicizing,* and *storyairing*—prompts purposeful considerations of youth's complex civic engagement, and of how African immigrant youth story their literacy lives as contributors to schools and communities. As the ongoing work of "supporting activities in literacy teaching and research that acknowledge African immigrant youth as inquirers of their own lives" (Watson & Knight-Manuel, 2020, p. 22), we thus develop recommendations for enacting rightful literary presence in research, teaching, and teacher education through an example of research and teaching with Dinamic and peers, which we discuss in detail below as *participatory curriculum design*.

ENACTING RIGHTFUL LITERARY PRESENCE AS PARTICIPATORY CURRICULUM DESIGN

In previous and ongoing work, Vaughn, with faculty colleagues, educators, undergraduate students, and youth, codesigned and enacted a range of Youth Participatory Action Research (YPAR) inquiries (e.g., Watson & Marciano, 2015; Watson et al., 2020). Early on in a YPAR cycle, Vaughn and colleagues emphasized stances in YPAR, such as "youth and adult power sharing"—building with resources from the YPAR Hub (UC Regents, 2023)—that youth later returned to in designing, enacting, and sharing research projects that they named as important. In Lit Diaspora, adult collaborators—Vaughn, Joel, Alecia, and LJ—extended theoretical and methodological approaches in YPAR as a framework for curriculum design and teaching practice. We conceptualize and discuss this work as participatory curriculum design.

In participatory curriculum design, we recognize the limitations of enacting YPAR approaches in formal school settings (Brion-Meisels & Alter, 2018) and the possibilities in young people grappling with inequities and envisioning hope and goals for their future (Caraballo et al., 2017, Marciano & Vellanki, 2022; Mirra et al., 2015). Our conceptualizing of participatory curriculum design names and recognizes that adultism, and anti-Black, anti-immigrant ideologies, delimit research, teaching, and texts in the United States and globally across institutional levels (e.g., Bertrand et al., 2020; de los Ríos et al., 2019; Osei-Tutu, 2022; Watson & Petrone, 2020).

We understand participatory curriculum design as timely, necessary collaborative teaching practice—adult research and educator communities teaching and learning *with* youth. Moreover, we situate participatory curriculum design as particularly urgent at a time when for-profit textbook and test management interests in the United States and globally garner headlines undergirding opportunities and challenges of schooling for racially, linguistically, and culturally minoritized communities, including immigrant youth shaping and shaped by a neoliberal era (De Costa, 2019). Pearson, the textbook publisher, for example, recently adopted guidelines toward "tackling racism in higher education" (McKenzie, 2021), while the College Board significantly reduced the official curriculum for its Advanced Placement African American Studies course—dropping "names of many Black writers and scholars associated with critical race theory, the queer experience and Black feminism" (Hartocollis & Fawcett, 2023). Yet envisionings of youth learning appear less present (Bertrand & Lozenski, 2023; Kelly, 2023; Watson & Petrone, 2020).

In our intergenerational inquiry, we enacted rightful literary presence through an example of participatory curriculum design. Participatory curriculum design involves the collaborative work of adult educators teaching and learning with youth, jointly naming and enacting the what and how of curriculum design and teaching practice. We next detail a model of participatory curriculum design across three iterative phases of activities with youth (see Figure 12.2) and assert participatory curriculum design as a model educators may take up with a range of learners across contexts.

Figure 12.2. Three Iterative Phases of Participatory Curriculum Design

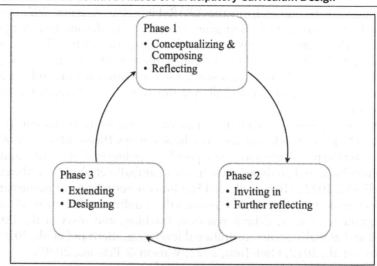

Enacting Rightful Literary Presence as Participatory Curriculum Design: Phase 1—Conceptualizing and Composing

To illustrate phase 1 of our participatory curriculum design work, we revisit the Lit Diaspora session where we discussed the prompt shared at the beginning of this chapter, with Dinamic recalling the school tournament in Uganda. In that session, we asked youth: (1) On your Padlet, make a list of 2 to 3 activities that you enjoy doing that you feel express who you are; (2) annotate your list by writing a sentence or two that describes how the activity expresses who you are.

Those first 10 weeks, our participatory curriculum design involved asking youth to compose responses to a range of prompts (see Figure 12.3).

Following youths' writing time, we asked Dinamic and peers to discuss their responses. We then concluded many sessions with Vaughn asking youths to join adult collaborators in drafting recommendations for curriculum design and teaching approaches, affirming and extending identities across literacy practices youths shared in their Padlets. To do so, we shared a Google doc with youths, and prompted students to list recommendations for teachers and teaching based on that day's activities.

Enacting Rightful Literary Presence as Participatory Curriculum Design: Phase 1 Continued—Reflecting. Yet in research team meetings that followed weekly sessions, adult collaborators discussed that students' engagement in drafting recommendations for teaching approaches was less generative than anticipated. On reflection, adult collaborators, and Joel and Vaughn as we engaged in the writing of this chapter, wondered whether students' drafting of recommendations was less generative given two inter-related factors: relational limitations of online teaching; and complications of relational power sharing in schools.

In online teaching, adult research team members and youth taught and learned together for the brief time of 10 Zoom sessions, with the COVID-19 pandemic and teaching via Zoom limiting relational teaching. For example,

Figure 12.3. Participatory Curriculum Design: Prompts for Composing Responses

Make a playlist of songs that express who you are.
Post found images that express who you are.
Share social media sites you visit for news or info that expresses who you are.
Describe a food, cuisine, or dish that reminds you of home.
Create or redesign a logo for an item you use that reflects your identity.
Compose a response that shares who inspires you or what place or places inspire you.
Share a photo or video that reminds you of languages you speak or that are spoken in your home.

students largely kept cameras turned off—and we did not require cameras to be turned on; and we recognized that students likely navigated Zoom fatigue after completing a day of online learning, as in-person schooling had not yet resumed. Adult collaborators did seek to prioritize relational learning in the online context (Marciano et al., 2020). Each week, as youth joined the virtual session, we asked students to share about their day, aloud or via Zoom's chat feature. At LJ's and Alecia's urging, we additionally invited youth to name a joy of their day or week. In the welcoming practice of naming joys, we connected with one another across present moments and shared interests. In this way, we first came to know of Dinamic's love of soccer; invited to share a joy, Dinamic said: "My soccer team starts practice next week."

Yet we reflected that while we envisioned Lit Diaspora as a space where youth and adults navigated relational power sharing, when we asked youth to name recommendations for curriculum design and teaching approaches affirming and extending African immigrant students' literacies and identities—based on ideas in their Padlets—youth named lingering power dynamics that complicate relational power sharing in schools. For example, in our ninth session, Vaughn asked:

> In your opinion, to what extent, . . . or how much are youth typically involved in selecting materials . . . books, teaching strategies, curriculum . . . the assessments, the things that you're assessed on? To what extent are youth involved in selecting materials that exist to support you? In other words, how much influence do youth have involving curriculum and teaching?

Moira, an 11th-grade student from Central African Republic, responded:

> So, I say the least involved . . . because they [teachers] just explain to you why you doing it, and why you gonna need it in the future, if you're gonna need it in the future. And, that's all. They don't really, like, for us, they, they, they prepare us for it, at, at some extent, but that's all.

We thus reflected on how we did not initially design our curriculum or teaching practice to introduce youth to instructional models on power sharing across youth and adult communities, such as the YPAR Hub model (UC Regents, 2023) that Vaughn typically engages when beginning a formal YPAR inquiry (e.g., Watson et al., 2020).

Enacting Rightful Literary Presence as Participatory Curriculum Design: Phase 2—Inviting in

Given our reflecting on teaching and research approaches with youth in phase 1, we (re)framed our teaching and research in Lit Diaspora in weeks

11 to 18. Specifically, in phase 2 of our participatory curriculum design approach (*inviting in; further reflecting*), the research team introduced Dinamic and four peers who continued in literacy sessions following the initial 10 weeks to writings of Paulo Freire and Mejai Bola Avoseh. In doing so, we took an approach of inviting youth into teaching and learning that Vaughn engaged in previous YPAR work (Watson et al., 2020), where he began each YPAR cycle by leading youth in shared reading of excerpts of Freire's *Pedagogy of the Oppressed* (1996), discussing the author's remarks that "problem-posing education bases itself on creativity and stimulates" reflection and action-taking (p. 84). In this way, adult and youth researchers in previous projects took up collaborative understandings of possibilities of community inquiry.

Enacting Rightful Literary Presence as Participatory Curriculum Design: Phase 2 Continued—Further Reflecting. In Lit Diaspora, in enacting our work as participatory curriculum design, we engaged a different shared reading with youth to facilitate our collaborative understanding and action-taking of possibilities of community inquiry, at the nexus of participatory approaches to curriculum design and teaching practice, and building with diverse onto-epistemologies of African immigrant youth.

For example, across weeks 11 and 12, adult research team members and youth read excerpts of Avoseh's (2005) article, "The Power of Voice: An Analysis of Dialogue as a Method in Both Elementary and Adult Education." Avoseh theorizes dialogue as methodology across elementary classrooms and adult education contexts, extending across Socratic, Freirean, and traditional African pedagogies and approaches. We read and discussed Avoseh's (2005) remarks that "dialogue as a method in African education is not limited to the spoken word. It is complex and all-involving. Dialogue in traditional education involves the whole of the people's culture, religion and other activities" (pp. 379–380; see also Avoseh, 2013). We discussed Avoseh's naming of possibilities for teaching that builds with "aspects of the learners' world":

> The teacher is in a better position to do this if the domains that give meaning to the learners' daily life are linked to the classroom activities. . . . Creating a room for [students'] voice is the first step to empowering them to become co-creators of knowledge. . . . Encouraging and allowing the voice of learners to be heard is a way of connecting to the best of the human-ness in them. (p. 382)

We invited Dinamic and peers to name connections, pose questions, and reflect on Avoseh's words in ways youth name as meaningful. Dinamic, across a range of response prompts, shared his adoration for the play of soccer midfielder N'Golo Kanté—as we recalled at the beginning of this chapter. Yet as Vaughn and Joel further reflected on our teaching and research across phase 1 and phase 2, we wondered how in enacting participatory curriculum design we might (re)envision entry points for youth, notably Dinamic in our present inquiry, to draft recommendations for teaching approaches at the interplay of youth's diverse onto-epistemologies, and that affirm, contextualize, evoke, and historicize youth's varied literacies and identities, underscoring Black African immigrant youth's rightful literary presence. As Dinamic shared in one of our last meetings, "I would love to see something that it's going to represent [ideas] that everyone [in Lit Diaspora] talked about, like their interests, and something that can represent a culture."

Enacting Rightful Literary Presence as Participatory Curriculum Design: Phase 3—Extending and Designing

Following our coauthoring of narrative vignettes with Dinamic, Joel and Vaughn shared our writing in a panel on African immigrant youth and language, literacy, and civic engagement, at the annual meeting of the American Educational Research Association. Across 2 weeks that followed, we continued coauthoring meetings via Zoom, conversations later rendered as the narrative vignette we shared to open this chapter. Vaughn, Joel, and Dinamic reflected on affirming, contextualizing, evoking, and historicizing complex trajectories and geographies of home spaces, languages, and schooling across Uganda, the Democratic Republic of Congo, France, and the United States, as Dinamic complicated meanings of soccer as N'Golo Kanté's *making present* practice, and his own.

In our fifth coauthoring meeting, to enact a participatory curriculum design that more fully builds with diverse onto-epistemologies of African immigrant youth, we posed a question to Dinamic, extending his recollections with soccer: "How would you teach rightful literary presence?" Our collaborative, intentional engagement sought to provide opportunities to author, compose, and share, and that affirm, contextualize, and historicize in ways authors name as meaningful, comprising phase 3 of the participatory curriculum design approach (*extending and designing*).

In our question to Dinamic—"How would you teach rightful literary presence?"—we underscore possibilities in rightful literary presence as a generative research, methodological, curricular, and teaching lens, in the ongoing work of talking back to curriculum design and teaching practice steeped in adultism and persistent popularized narratives that do not fully illuminate the range of cultural, linguistic, and civic participatory strengths of African immigrant youth and communities (Amaize, 2021; Onwuegbuzie & Frels, 2015; Simmons, 2021a; Watson et al., 2022). In our fifth Zoom coauthoring meeting, we (Vaughn and Joel) first (re)familiarized Dinamic with the framing of rightful literary presence and the four approaches (see Figure 12.1).

Then, returning to a practice we engaged with Dinamic and peers in Lit Diaspora when we read the work of Avoseh (2005, 2013), we collaboratively read excerpts of several news articles. Vaughn and Joel previously had selected each article to connect to one of the four rightful literary presence approaches. For example, as an example of evoking and historicizing in rightful literary presence, we discussed Attiah's (2018) article, "Why Calling France 'the Last African Team' in the World Cup Is Problematic," published in *The Washington Post*. Now, to focus our discussion of each article, we engaged Dinamic in conversation across three questions that we think of as prompts for participatory curriculum design (see Figure 12.4). We created an article discussion chart to keep track of the title, author, and source of each of the four news articles; to refer to the rightful literary presence approach to which the article content connected; and to write notes as we discussed the article using each of the three prompts for participatory curriculum design (see example in Figure 12.5).

We next share from our discussion of the four articles using the *prompts for participatory curriculum design*. We situate Dinamic's extended responses as draft recommendations for curriculum design and teaching approaches at the interplay of Black African immigrant youth's diverse onto-epistemologies and their rightful literary presence (see *Framework for Educating African Immigrant Youth*, Chapter 1).

Affirming as Participatory Curriculum Design. In deliberating with *affirming* as the approach, we (Joel, Vaughn, and Dinamic) read excerpts of Vejar's (2019) article, "Meet African Stars FC, Utah's Newest Soccer Franchise," in *The Salt Lake Tribune*. The author of the article shared remarks from Matt Khala, director of the United Professional Soccer League (UPSL), who welcomed the African Stars FC franchise owned and run by members of the African immigrant community, stating: "Diversity of club ownership is one of the strengths of the UPSL, and to have a club that has come together to represent their heritage is a movement we will always support" (para. 3).

Dinamic offered recommendations for teaching practice, as we discussed the article using a prompt for participatory curriculum design—"How would you have students interact with this article?" Dinamic recalled what he described as his multicultural class, and how his teacher once shared that the U.S. Men's National Soccer Team comprised a range of players born in

Figure 12.4. Prompts for Participatory Curriculum Design

Prompt 1:	If you were to teach about the ideas in this article, what's a question or two you would ask students to respond to?
Prompt 2:	If you were to teach about the ideas in this article, what do you think students would need to know?
Prompt 3:	How would you have students interact with this article?

Figure 12.5. Article Discussion Chart

News article title:	"Meet African Stars FC, Utah's Newest Soccer Franchise"
Article author:	Alex Vejar
Article source:	*The Salt Lake Tribune*
Rightful literary presence approach that connects to the article:	*Affirming, inviting, and making visible* complex transnational identities through literacy and learning. By "affirming" we mean affirming, inviting in, and making who you are visible through the range of literacy activities you engage in and beyond home and schooling spaces.
Prompt 1 for participatory curriculum design: If you were to teach about the ideas in this article, what's a question or two you would ask students to respond to?	[Add notes while discussing the article and the prompt for participatory curriculum design]
Prompt 2 for participatory curriculum design: If you were to teach about the ideas in this article, what do you think students would need to know?	[Add notes while discussing the article and the prompt for participatory curriculum design]
Prompt 3 for participatory curriculum design: How would you have students interact with this article?	[Add notes while discussing the article and the prompt for participatory curriculum design]

various countries. Dinamic explained, "When you look at the U.S. team, a lot of folks are from different countries." As a curricular or teaching approach, Dinamic noted, a teacher might ask youth to study a player or, in the example of African Stars FC, explore a team's social media presence to consider nuanced expressions of players' complex transnational identities, stories of migration, or cultural identities publicly shared.

Contextualizing as Participatory Curriculum Design. As an example of *contextualizing* as the rightful literary presence approach, we read excerpts of Attiah's (2018) article in *The Washington Post*, "Why Calling France 'the Last African Team' in the World Cup Is Problematic." Attiah, born in the United States and self-identifying as of Ghanaian and Nigerian heritage, wrote in the opinion article:

> France should not be allowed to claim distinction and separation from Africa so casually, because France owes Africa everything. Not just the resources it

continues to pillage, not just the labor force it shamelessly taps into, not just the art it appropriates as it has for centuries: France owes Africa its very soul. (para. 8)

Dinamic connected discussion of French colonization in the article to legacies of colonialism in language. He emphasized that students should gain awareness of the depth of a country's richness. Dinamic's extended response provided recommendations for teaching practice, as we considered the article using a prompt for participatory curriculum design—"If you were to teach about the ideas in this article, what's a question or two you would ask students to respond to?"

Dinamic shared that he would ask students, "Why is French taught? Who colonized the Congo and why?" Dinamic continued, reflecting with a prompt for participatory curriculum design—"If you were to teach about the ideas in this article, what do you think students would need to know?" Dinamic shared:

> If you look at it in the Congo, we do not learn English, we learn in French. I would ask the kids, "Why is that? Why is it French that's taught?" If I were to teach about ideas in this article, because it mentions something about labor and the riches, so if I were to teach those ideas, I'd dig deep into the countries riches, which is something that the country has. My country, Congo, is known for its gold mines, a lot of gold mines, and diamonds, all this good stuff. When we look at it, in the labor force of it, the people who do it, who fight or kill each other . . . they're going to work themselves, and dig deep into the ground.

Dinamic reflected and shared about the interplay of a global mining market for such minerals as cobalt, diamonds, and gold, and people in Congo working in mines, facing low pay and dangerous working conditions (e.g., Sawasawa, 2021): "They make way more money than they give out."

Evoking and Historicizing as Participatory Curriculum Design. As an example of *evoking and historicizing*, we read excerpts of Carotenuto's (2021) article, "What I Learned From Teaching African Sport History to American Students." The author noted, reflecting on a seminar taught at St. Lawrence University: "Presenting material in the common language of sports allows students to find a personal connection to topics far removed from their contemporary life" (para. 5). Moreover, Carotenuto wrote, teaching activities "challenged students to think about the way Africa is represented in the west. They showed how sport could be used to study social history" (para. 11). We share Dinamic's extended response as a recommendation for teaching practice, as we discussed the article using the participatory curriculum design prompt: "If you were to teach about the ideas in this article, what's a question or two you would ask students to respond to?" Dinamic shared that he would ask students:

What do you think Africa is about? What do you think it is like? I liked when [the author] talked about the 2010 World Cup. That was a big event in South Africa. As a teacher, if I'm a teacher, I would love to set up a random question to students: What do you think Africa is about? When you ask certain questions, you could find a different way to think of Africa.

I was talking to a friend, he asked me, "What was the country that you came from like? I didn't respond "bad" or "good." I was like, "What do you think it is?" He was like, "They tell me that's it really bad. The roads are really bad. Everything is terrible." I was like "You're right. Not everything is good in Africa, but when you get to visit Africa you might see that some countries in Africa are better than some states in the United States."

I gave him the example of the capital city of Congo. The capital of Congo is a blast. It's the one place that anybody is gonna want to visit. By responding to his question, I twisted it a little bit by telling him, that's not how *everything* is. My friend only knows what he reads, on the media, what he sees, and thinks, "Oh, that country is horrible, it's really bad." But with more explaining—I've been there, I've lived there. I came here for a better life—but I was like, "All the minerals come from us; we've got gold mines, diamonds, and all the good resources, if only we could know how to use them. We would be one of the richest countries in the world."

He was like, "Well, why don't you use them?" Then I was like trying to give him more history, enlighten him.

Storyairing as Participatory Curriculum Design. In relation to *storyairing* as an approach, we read excerpts of Hirsi's (2018) article in *MinnPost*, "For Minnesota Immigrants With Dreams of Playing Pro Soccer, Club Fees Are a Major Hurdle." An 11th-grade student, Yimer, born in Ethiopia and attending school in Minneapolis, shared in the article: "We have the talent . . . but we just don't have the chance to make it big because we don't have money" (para. 27). Dinamic, reflecting, shared:

This article reminds me of myself, like, when I came here. The first club they took us to, me and my brother, we practiced with them, but at the end, the woman who took us was like, "It's really expensive, like 2k for just a year to join the club." That's when I started to just play for my high school soccer team. And this year, the club that I play for costs $1,625, and if I wasn't on a scholarship, I wouldn't play. Then I was like, it's ok, I'm gonna see if I can apply for a scholarship. The clubs are expensive. You have to pay for your own jersey, own ball, travel and hotels. In America, playing club sports is just too expensive.

In discussing the article using the prompt for participatory curriculum design, "How would you have students interact with this article?" Dinamic

Theorizing Rightful Literary Presence and Participatory Curriculum Design   189

named recommendations for teaching practice and student work. For example, a teacher might envision assignments such as evaluating pay-to-play, or engage students in sharing their experiences; as Dinamic noted, "I would tell it in a story, create a story, make the students try to capture the story in a picture."

NEXT STEPS FOR TEACHING AND RESEARCH COMMUNITIES

Educators and research communities may take up participatory curriculum design with intergenerational youth and adult teaching and research collaborations and in a range of schooling contexts. Such work asks educator communities to (re)imagine and enact the what and how of collaborative curriculum design and teaching practice. For example, shared reading and discussion with African immigrant youth in Lit Diaspora supported understanding and action-taking toward possibilities of community inquiry, at the nexus of participatory approaches to curriculum design, teaching practice, and affirming and extending onto-epistemologies of Black African immigrant youth.

Thinking with Dinamic through a lens of rightful literary presence for Black African immigrant youth underscores the urgency of the four complementary approaches (see Figure 12.1). Moreover, Dinamic and peers demonstrate the value of rightful literary presence and participatory curriculum design as generative approaches for illuminating the multiple ways that African immigrant youth and communities affirm, contextualize, and historicize their lived schooling experiences in ways that youth call forth as meaningful.

TAKEAWAY QUESTIONS

- How may you include the four rightful literary presence approaches in teaching and learning in your varied contexts? For example, how may you engage Black African immigrant and refugee youth and their peers with more pointed affirming, contextualizing, and historicizing stances?
- How, in your contexts, are youth's tellings called forth and shared on youth's terms to shape meaningful teaching and learning?
- How, specifically, may teachers and community educators build with youth and their interests as a participatory curriculum design approach?
- What additional teaching practices and approaches to curriculum design may affirm Black African immigrant and refugee youth in your learning communities?

ACKNOWLEDGMENTS

Authors Berends, Watson, and Kubengana contributed equally to the manuscript. The authors gratefully acknowledge Lit Diaspora youth participants, families, elders, and community educators; the Mt. Hope United Methodist Church community; and Lauren Elizabeth Reine Johnson and Alecia Beymer for Lit Diaspora curriculum design and teaching, data collection, and early conversations preceding writing. This work was supported by the National Academy of Education/Spencer Foundation Postdoctoral Fellowship.

CHAPTER 13

Conclusion

Vaughn W. M. Watson, Michelle G. Knight-Manuel,
and Patriann Smith

The urgent, vital storying of and with Black African immigrant youth and communities in *Educating African Immigrant Youth: Schooling and Civic Engagement in K–12 Schools* prompts important insights for productive frameworks and approaches in teaching, teacher education, and research. In Chapter 1, we as coeditors built with and across three waves of robust scholarship examining schooling and civic lives of African immigrant youth to conceptualize one such generative cross-disciplinary framework, the *Framework for Educating African Immigrant Youth*. As shown, the framework comprehensively addresses the scope and heterogeneity of African immigrant youth and their schooling and civic engagement experiences across four complementary approaches: (1) emboldening tellings of diaspora narratives; (2) navigating pasts, presence, and futures of literacy, language, teaching, and learning; (3) envisioning and enacting social civic literacies and learning to extend complex identities; and (4) affirming and extending cultural, heritage, and embodied knowledges, languages, and practices. Chapter authors illuminated the four approaches in rendering visible, in Part I, *schooling and classroom perspectives and contexts*; in Part II, *participatory and communal approaches to learning and civic engagement*; and in Part III, *emerging practices and approaches to literacies, languages, and learning*. In (re)centering perspectives and possibilities of the vibrant schooling and civic lives of Black African youth and communities in the United States and Canada, we worked to forward understandings of an ongoing envisioning, a type of speculative seeing, telling, affirming, and building with lived past, presence, and future possibilities.

In advancing the notion of *speculative seeing*, we reference the unpublished story *The Princess Steel*, authored between 1908 and 1910 by W.E.B. Du Bois. In the 14-page manuscript, located in 2015 in Du Bois's collections by Adrienne Brown and Brett Rusert, Du Bois composed the character of a Black sociologist who invented the "megascope," a viewfinder shaped to

191

resemble a "shining trumpet," affixed with "head and eye and ear and hand pieces" through which a viewer glimpsed across space and time (Du Bois et al., ca. 1908/2015, p. 824). The story's protagonist, peering through the megascope, viewed an African princess, hair made of steel, "who has been kidnapped and separated from her mother: a metaphor of colonization and exploitation of Africa" (Esteve, 2016, para. 3). Brown and Rusert observed that "Du Bois's genre work does more than challenge stereotypes with its royal black characters. It also reveals . . . racial archetypes propping up these genres" (Du Bois et al., ca. 1908/2015, p. 820).

Returning, in our work, to Chapter 1, we recalled that Àsìkò, the Nigerian photographer living and working in London, shared on Instagram photographs reenvisioning Black youth as lead characters in *Black Panther*. The following Monday, the Smithsonian National Portrait Gallery unveiled the official portrait of former U.S. President Barack Obama, son of a Kenyan immigrant, painted by Kehinde Wiley, whose father is Nigerian. As a CNN reporter recounted, President Obama purposefully selected Wiley to paint the official portrait—"a Yale University–trained painter famous for his depiction of African Americans posed in the style of Old Master paintings, regal, formal and filled with pops of color" (K. Bennett, 2018, para. 3). Wiley explained in promotional materials accompanying a Brooklyn Museum exhibit of his work that he undertakes such (re)envisioning of "specific paintings by Old Masters, replacing the European aristocrats depicted in those paintings with contemporary Black subjects, drawing attention to the absence of African Americans from historical and cultural narratives" (Brooklyn Museum, n.d., para. 2). In this way, Wiley's reimagined work displayed at the Brooklyn Museum, titled "Napoleon Leading the Army Over the Alps," portrays a young Black man as a warrior riding on horseback, contemporarily clothed in baggy camouflage-print pants, Starter-brand athletic wristbands, Timberland boots, his head adorned with a white bandana (Wiley, 2005).

As such speculative seeing, Wiley painted President Obama, in the portrait on permanent display in the Smithsonian National Portrait Gallery's "America's Presidents" exhibit, seated against a backdrop of foliage (see Cascone, 2018). In this portrait, white jasmine flowers symbolize Hawaii, Obama's birth state; chrysanthemums reflect the official flower of the city of Chicago; and African blue lilies appear, illustrative of Obama's father's "Kenyan heritage" (Dingfelder, 2018). At the unveiling of the portrait, President Obama told the gathered crowd of journalists and politicians:

> What I was always struck by whenever I saw [Kehinde's] portraits, was the degree to which they challenged our conventional views of power, wealth, privilege and the way that he would take extraordinary care and precision and vision in recognizing the beauty and the grace and the dignity of people, and put them on a grand stage. (D. Clark, 2018, para. 14; see also CNN Newsroom, 2018)

Brown and Rusert, introducing *The Princess Steel*, Du Bois's 14-page unpublished story, noted that Du Bois offered ways of "imagining historical change, a creative mode ready to be used in the present . . . to disrupt the nationalist tenor" (Du Bois et al., ca. 1908/2015, p. 820; see also R. Anderson, 2016; Asim, 2016; Okorafor, 2019; S. R. Toliver, 2020), a stance-taking and approach we acknowledge as part of this ongoing work of speculative seeing, which undergirds Parts I, II, and III of this book.

In Part I: "Schooling and Classroom Perspectives and Contexts," authors invited meanings of the *Framework for Educating African Immigrant Youth* (Chapter 1), simultaneously navigating present and past teaching and learning, making visible Black African immigrant youths' and young adults' multifaceted identities, and complexities of race, culture, and language, in schooling settings. Authors illuminated pressing narratives at the interplay of lived schooling experiences of Black African immigrant youths and young adults, and those emerging in disciplinary contexts of STEM, mathematics, and history in secondary and university classrooms. Authors across Part I demonstrated how they build with and extend histories of research literature at the nexus of schooling, classroom contexts, and rendering visible lived experiences of Black African immigrant youths and young adults (e.g., Dei, 2012; Harushimana & Awokoya, 2011; P. Smith, 2023a; Ukpokodu & Otiato Ojiambo, 2017; Watson & Knight-Manuel, 2017). These explorations provoke meaningful envisionings as speculative seeing, and storying of varied and multifaceted navigations of schooling in the United States and Canada, narrated by and with Black African immigrant youth. Such work evokes possibilities of engaging diverse culturally informed frameworks with Black African immigrant youths and young adults; and extends narrative approaches as types of methodological journeying, underscoring artistic and disciplinary dimensions of teaching, teacher education, and research.

For example, Omiunota Nelly Ukpokodu in Chapter 2 reckons with and affirms the full humanity of Black African immigrant youth in P–12 schools; Oyemolade Osibodu and Nyimasata Damba Danjo's analysis in Chapter 3 of the protagonist in the novella *Binti* functions simultaneously as a study of mathematical literacies and a necessary enacting of African Indigenous Knowledges and lived experiences with African immigrant women, navigating and talking back to ontological and epistemological queries undergirding Western fixtures of mathematics and STEM education. James Oloo and Priscila Dias Corrêa in Chapter 5 traverse and (re)frame narratives of STEM learning via nuanced first-person storying of multiple strengths the African immigrant collegians draw on and leverage, underscoring the cultural assets and community cultural wealth that university students Hera and Achieng bring to their schooling experiences. Irteza Anwara Mohyuddin in Chapter 4 conveys possibilities in Kabeera's reimagining of teaching and learning with peers and a teacher as speculative seeing in an African American history class; Kabeera asks how she may meaningfully navigate potentials of racial spacemaking that bring forward experiences of Black African immigrant communities in the broader conversation and action-taking of the global Black Lives Matter movement.

In Part II: "Participatory and Communal Approaches to Learning and Civic Engagement," authors extended the *Framework for Educating African Immigrant Youth* (Chapter 1) by engaging the language and literacies of African immigrant youth as strengths in their schooling and civic engagement. Authors highlighted distinctive meanings of teaching and learning in the context of African immigrant youth's schooling and civic engagement, while also arguing that the integration of their past, present, and future lives disrupts negative dominant narratives, challenges existing inequitable structures, and illuminates new truths that educators can take up. In doing so, this authoring within the book makes two key contributions: First, utilizing a range of theoretical lenses from transnational social fields and diasporic networks, affective and indigenous frameworks, critical digital literacy, and *Sankofa* to frame their research with African immigrant youth, the authors draw attention to new ways of viewing and participating in schooling, civic literacies, and engagement. Second, exploring notions of belonging and anti-Blackness in relation to teaching and learning opens up possibilities for the schooling and civic engagement of African immigrant youth in collaboration with families, peers, and educators in a world where youth and people of color have become the future.

Patrick Keegan in Chapter 6 and Michelle Knight-Manuel, Natacha Robert, and Sibel Akin-Sabuncu in Chapter 9 take educators on a journey revealing the ongoing sanctioned violence in the African diaspora, specifically France and the United States (Bordonaro, 2023; Noel, 2022), where African (immigrant) youth are looking back and forward as diasporic speculative movements of hope as they leverage their strengths in reading and acting in a world where anti-Blackness, the dehumanization of Black people, tries to derail their very lives. The authors ask educators to grapple with a speculative seeing into a more just world that could be, but is not yet present, as African immigrant youth grapple with societal ills of racism and anti-Blackness and anti-Muslim narratives of their Black bodies (R. Anderson, 2016). Educators can build on the already-present ways that African immigrant youth are leading the way in fighting back against negative dominant narratives through their focus on utilizing their civic literacies and identities as well as uniting in solidarity with other African youth through a focus on Pan-Africanism and a sense of belonging.

Equally important, Liv T. Dávila and Susan A. Ogwal in Chapter 7 and Maryann J. Dreas-Shaikha, OreOluwa Badaki, and Jasmine L. Blanks Jones in Chapter 8 reflect the emotional struggles of parents to nurture African values, languages, and literacies, and youth's activism through their digital literacies (Price-Dennis & Sealey-Ruiz, 2021). Their languages and literacies bear witness to their humanity and views of learning and civic

Conclusion

engagement that challenge presumed authorities of their lives and futures (R. Anderson, 2016). The varied embodied expressions of Black African immigrant girls' and family experiences in diverse schooling contexts challenge norms of who can be the teacher and the learner, which, in turn, upend dehumanizing language and literacy notions of who African immigrant youth are, who they can be, and who they want to be.

We cannot close this discussion without noting the interpretive gazes of the researchers and how they position all of us who seek to teach, collaborate with, and work with African immigrant youth. The authors invite us to consider how we engage in humanizing research with African immigrant youth and families as cocreators of knowledge in the research process, and in turn we encourage teachers, teacher educators, and community workers to imagine new ways of centering and building upon the strengths of African immigrant youth as creators and teachers of varied literacies and as already involved civically in acting on their worlds for the betterment of all humankind.

In Part III: "African Immigrant Youth Literacies, Languages, and Learning: Toward Emerging Practices and Approaches," authors built upon the *Framework for Educating African Immigrant Youth* (Chapter 1), inviting readers to interrupt Black people's knowing of their story "in ways that are partial and distorted" (King, 1992, p. 320). Deploying the notion of speculative seeing, the authors built upon "diaspora literacy" as "an ability to read a variety of cultural signs of the lives of Africa's children at home and in the New World" and as Black people developing an understanding of their "story" of "cultural dispossession" (Busia, 1989, p. 197). In turn, the authors invited Black students to repossess this "story" and thus Black people's "cultural identity" as "Africa's children" so that "human consciousness permits [the retrieval of] humanity from distorted notions of the conceptual 'Blackness' which has long functioned as an alter ego of the socially constructed category of 'Whiteness'" (King, 1992, p. 321). In doing so, the authors demonstrate how literacies and languaging of Black African immigrant youth function as a necessary disruption of Westernized notions of normalcy, a longstanding project designed to make visible the linguistic and literate richness of the Majority World (e.g., Henry, 1998; Ibrahim, 1999; P. Smith, 2023b; Smitherman, 1977).

Even as David Bwire Wandera in Chapter 10 explored the role of education in a pluralistic world amid increasing global migration, Lakeya Afolalu, in Chapter 11, noted that African immigrant youth often experience racial, linguistic, and colonial ideologies that discriminate against their languages, accents, and dialects and accented English, resulting in a hesitancy to speak in school and community spaces. Functioning as a culminating climax to the dynamic approaches presented in the book, and offering a methodological vision for engaging with African immigrant and other youth in the art of speculative seeing, Joel E. Berends, Vaughn W. M. Watson, and African immigrant youth, Dinamic Kubengana, in Chapter 12, demonstrated possibilities of rightful literary presence as a productive framework for research and teaching with African immigrant youth.

Creating a pathway for speculative seeing, the authors in Part III highlighted the significance of attending to heritage resources and raciolinguistically just multiliterate practices, even as they advanced the notion of rightful literary presence. In doing so, they critically extend conceptions of "diaspora literacy" (King, 1992, 2021), "transnational literacy" (Skerrett, 2015), "Black language pedagogy" (Baker-Bell, 2020), "Black immigrant literacies" (P. Smith, 2020a, 2023a), and "(transnational) Black language pedagogy" (Milu, 2021; Smitherman, 2000). With urgency, the authors implored readers to consider the epistemic, raciolinguistic (Alim, 2004b; Alim et al., 2016; Rosa & Flores, 2017), and literary impetus for affirming the legitimate literacies and lives of African immigrant youth in ways that extend normalcy beyond monolithic notions of Americanness (Smith, 2020b) and that are bolstered by a centering of an established and emerging cadre of Black (African) voices.

References

Abdi, A. A. (2002). *Culture, education, and development in South Africa: Historical and contemporary perspectives*. Bergin & Garvey.

Abdi, A. A. (2011). African philosophies of education: Deconstructing the colonial and reconstructing the indigenous. *Counterpoints, 379*, 80–91.

Abdi, C. M. (2012). The newest African-Americans? Somali struggles for belonging. *Bildhaan: An International Journal of Somali Studies, 11*(12), 90–107.

Abu El-Haj, T. R. (2015). *Unsettled belonging: Educating Palestinian American youth after 9/11*. University of Chicago Press.

Abu-Ras, W., & Abu-Bader, S. H. (2008). The impact of the September 11, 2001 attacks on the wellbeing of Arab Americans in New York City. *Journal of Muslim Mental Health, 3*, 217–239.

Achebe, C. (1959). *Things fall apart*. Penguin.

Achebe, C. (1987). *Anthills of the Savannah*. Penguin.

Addams, J. (1930). *The second twenty years at Hull-House: September 1909 to September 1929 with a record of growing consciousness*. Macmillan.

Adebisi, A. (2015). Yoruba traditional education philosophy in the evolution of a 'total man.' *International Journal of Humanities and Cultural Studies, 2*(2), 33–45.

Adenekan, O. K. (2021). Navigating the linguistic terrain: Immigrants' personal stories of aspiration, access, identity, and acclimation. *Journal of Language and Literacy Education, 16*(2), 1–35.

Adeniji-Neil, D., & Ammon, R. (2011). Omoluabi: The way of human being: An African philosophy's impact on Nigerian voluntary immigrants' educational and other life aspirations. *A Journal of African Migration, 5*, 1–28.

Adichie, C. N. (2009). *The danger of a single story*. https://www.ted.com/talks/chimamanda_adichie_the_danger_of_a_single_story

African Union Youth Charter. (2006). https://www.youthpolicy.org/library/documents/african-youth-charter/

Agar, M. (1994). *Language shock. Understanding the culture of conversation*. William Morrow.

Agyepong, M. (2013). Seeking to be heard: An African-born, American-raised child's tale of struggle, invisibility, and invincibility. In I. Harushimana, C. Ikpeze, & S. Mthethwa-Sommers (Eds.), *Reprocessing race, language and ability: African-born educators and students in transnational America* (pp. 155–168). Peter Lang.

Agyepong, M. (2017). The struggles of invisibility: Perception and treatment of African students in the United States. In O. N. Ukpokodu & P. Otiato Ojiambo

(Eds.), *Erasing invisibility, inequity and social injustice of Africans in the diaspora and the continent* (pp. 155–168). Cambridge Scholars.

Agyepong, M. (2018). Discourse, representation, and "othering": Postcolonial analysis of Donald Trump's education reform. In R. Winkle-Wagner, J. Lee-Johnson, & A. N. Gaskew (Eds.), *Critical theory and qualitative data analysis in education* (pp. 177–192). Routledge.

Alaazi, D. A., Ahola, A. N., Okeke-Ihejirika, P., Yohani, S., Vallianatos, H., & Bukola, S. (2020, July 27). Immigrants and the Western media: A critical discourse analysis of newspaper framings of African immigrant parenting in Canada. *Journal of Ethnic and Migration Studies, 47*(19), 4478–4496.

Alim, H. S. (2004a). Hearing what's not said and missing what is: Black language in white public space. In S. F. Kiesling & C. B. Paulston (Eds.), *Intercultural discourse and communication: The essential readings* (pp. 180–197). Blackwell.

Alim, H. S. (2004b). *You know my steez: An ethnographic and sociolinguistic study of styleshifting in a Black American speech community.* Stanford University.

Alim, H. S., Rickford, J. R., & Ball, A. F. (Eds.). (2016). *Raciolinguistics: How language shapes our ideas about race.* Oxford University Press.

Allen, K. M., Jackson, I., & Knight M. G. (2012). Complicating culturally relevant pedagogy: Unpacking West African immigrants' cultural identities [Special issue]. *International Journal of Multicultural Education, 14*(2), 1–28.

Alvarez, P. (2022). White House plans to allow up to 125,000 refugees into US for 2023 fiscal year. https://www.cnn.com/2022/09/09/politics/refugees-fiscal-year-2023/index.html

Alvarez, S. (2017). *Brokering tarejas: Mexican immigrant families translanguaging homework literacies.* SUNY Press.

Amaize, O. (2021). The "social distance" between Africa and African-Americans. https://daily.jstor.org/the-social-distance-between-africa-and-african-americans

American Civil Liberties Union. (n.d.). For Black immigrants, police and ICE are two sides of the same coin. https://www.aclu.org/news/criminal-law-reform/for-black-immigrants-police-and-ice-are-two-sides-of-the-same-coin

American Community Survey (ACS). (2009). *Place of birth of the foreign-born population: 2009.* Accessed from Grieco, E. M. & Trevelyan, E. N. http://www.census.gov/prod/2010pubs/acsbr09-15.pdf

American Community Survey. (2012). Retrieved from https://www2.census.gov/programs-surveys/acs/tech_docs/accuracy/ACS_Accuracy_of_Data_2012.pdf

American Psychological Association. (2021). Apology to people of color for APA's role in promoting, perpetuating, and failing to challenge racism, racial discrimination, and human hierarchy in US. https://www.apa.org/about/policy/racism-apology

Amonyeze, C. (2017). Writing a new reputation: Liminality and bicultural identity in Chimamanda Adichie's Americanah. *Journal of Black Studies, 7*(2), 1–9.

Anderson, M. (2015). *African immigrant population in the U.S. steadily climbs.* Pew Research Center. https://www.pewresearch.org/short-reads/2017/02/14/african-immigrant-population-in-u-s-steadily-climbs/

Anderson, R. (2016). Afrofuturism 2.0 & the Black speculative arts movement: Notes on a manifesto. *Obsidian, 42*(1/2), 228–236.

Apple, M. W. (2004). *Ideology and curriculum* (3rd ed.). Routledge Falmer.

References

Aroian, K. J. (2012). Discrimination against Muslim American adolescents. *Journal of School Nursing, 28,* 206–213.

Arthur, J. A. (2000). *Invisible sojourners: African immigrant diaspora in the United States.* Praeger.

Asante, M. K. (1987). *The Afrocentric idea.* Temple University Press.

Asante, M. K. (1988). *Afrocentricity.* Africa World.

Ashcroft, B., Griffiths, G., & Tiffin, H. (2013). *Post-colonial studies: The key concepts* (Eds.). (3rd ed.) Routledge.

Àsìkò Fine Art Photography. (2018, February 7). *Why Black Panther matters. As a kid who read comics Black Panther was one of the very few superheroes I came across* [Image attached] [Status update]. Facebook. https://www.facebook.com /asiko.artist/photos/a.10155268570864814/10156074751599814/?type =3&theater

Asim, J. (2016). Afro-futurism. *The Crisis, 123*(2), 22–28.

Attewell, P., Lavin, D., Domina, T., & Levey, T. (2006). New evidence on college remediation. *The Journal of Higher Education, 77*(5), 886–924.

Attiah, K. (2018). Why calling France "the last African team" in the World Cup is problematic. *The Washington Post.* https://www.washingtonpost.com/news /global-opinions/wp/2018/07/10/why-calling-france-the-last-african-team-in -the-world-cup-is-problematic

Avoseh, M.B.M. (2000). Adult education and participatory research in Africa: In defence of tradition. *Canadian Journal of Development Studies, 21,* 565–578.

Avoseh, M.B.M. (2001). Learning to be active citizens: Lessons of traditional Africa for lifelong learning. *International Journal of Lifelong Learning, 20,* 479–486.

Avoseh, M.B.M. (2005). The power of voice: An analysis of dialogue as a method in both elementary and adult education. *International Journal of Case Method Research & Application, 17*(3), 374–384.

Avoseh, M.B.M. (2011). Informal community learning in traditional Africa. In S. Jackson (Ed.), *Innovations in lifelong learning: Critical perspectives on diversity, participation and vocational learning* (pp. 34–49). Routledge.

Avoseh, M.B.M. (2013). Proverbs as theoretical frameworks for lifelong learning in indigenous African education. *Adult Education Quarterly, 63*(3), 236–250.

Awokoya, J. (2009). "I am not enough of anything": The racial and ethnic identity construction s and negotiations of one-pint-five- and second-generation Nigerian immigrants. Unpublished doctoral dissertation, University of Maryland, College Park, MD.

Awokoya, J. T. (2012). Identity constructions and negotiations among 1.5- and second-generation Nigerians: The impact of family, school, and peer contexts. *Harvard Educational Review, 82,* 255–281.

Badaki, O. (2020). Embodied learning and community resilience. *Penn GSE Perspectives on Urban Education, 18*(1)

Badaki, O. (2023). Seeds of the diaspora. In E. E. Schell, D. Winslow, & P. Shrestha (Eds.), *Food justice activism and pedagogies: Literacies and rhetorics for transforming food systems in local and transnational contexts* (p. 85–108). Lexington Books.

Baffoe, M., & Asimeng-Boahene, L. (2013). Using cultural artifacts, positions, and titles as retentions of cultural attachments to original homelands: African immigrants in the diaspora. *Academic Journal of Interdisciplinary Studies, 2*(2), 85–92.

Bajaj, M., Argenal, A., & Canlas, M. (2017). Socio-politically relevant pedagogy for immigrant and refugee youth. *Equity & Excellence in Education, 50*(3), 258–274.

Bajaj, M., & Bartlett, L. (2017). Critical transnational curriculum for immigrant and refugee students. *Curriculum Inquiry, 47*(1), 25–35.

Bakar, A. (2023). *A narratological inquiry into US African refugee youths' educational experiences.* [Doctoral dissertation, University of Missouri-Kansas City.]

Baker-Bell, A. (2020). *Linguistic justice: Black, language, literacy, identity, and pedagogy.* Routledge.

Balogun, O. M. (2011). No necessary tradeoff: Context, life course, and social networks in the identity formation of second-generation Nigerians in the U.S. *Ethnicities, 11*, 436–466.

Ball, A. F. (1992). Cultural preference and the expository writing of African-American adolescents. *Written Communication, 9*(4), 501–532.

Ball, D. L. (2018, April 15). *Just dreams and imperatives: The power of teaching in the struggle for public education* [Presidential address]. American Educational Research Association Annual Meeting, New York, NY, United States. https:// deborahloewenbergball.com/news-archive/2018/4/19/deborah-loewenberg-ball -delivers-presidential-address-at-aera-annual-meeting

Banks, J. A. (1998). The lives and values of researchers: Implications for educating citizens in a multicultural society. *Educational Researcher, 27*(7), 4–17.

Banks, J. A. (2008). Diversity, group identity, and citizenship education in a global age. *Educational Researcher, 37*(3), 129–139.

Banks, J. A. (Ed.). (2017). *Citizenship education and global migration: Implications for theory research, and teaching.* American Educational Research Association.

Baruch College, W. C. for I. B. (2019). *NYCdata: Foreign Born Population—by Country of Birth.* Cuny.edu. https://www.baruch.cuny.edu/nycdata/population -geography/foreign-birthcountry.htm

Basford, L. (2010). From mainstream to East African charter: Cultural and religious experiences of Somali youth in U.S. schools. *Journal of School Choice, 4*, 485–509.

Bauer, E. B., & Sánchez, L. (2020). Living nan lonbraj la: Haitian immigrant young people writing their selves into the world. *Teachers College Record, 122*(13), 1–36.

Bayeck, R. Y. (2020). The meaning of video gameplay: A case study of three Black African immigrant students in the US. *Journal of Underrepresented & Minority Progress, 4*(1), 109–126.

Beaman, J. (2012). But madam, we are French also. *Context, 11*(3), 46–51.

Bennett, C. I. (1990). *Comprehensive multicultural education: Theory and practice.* Pearson.

Bennett, K. (2018, February 12). Obamas' official portraits unveiled. CNN. https:// www.cnn.com/2018/02/12/politics/obama-portrait-unveiling/index.html

Bertrand, M., Brooks, M. D., & Dominguez, A. D. (2020). Challenging adultism: Centering youth as educational decision makers. *Urban Education*, pp. 1–28.

Bertrand, M., & Lozenski, B. D. (2023). YPAR dreams deferred? Examining power bases for YPAR to impact policy and practice. *Educational Policy, 37*(2), 437–462.

References

Bhattacharya, K. (2018). Coloring memories and imaginations of "home": Crafting a de/colonizing autoethnography. *Cultural Studies↔Critical Methodologies, 18*(1), 9–15.

Bigelow, M. (2008). Somali adolescents' negotiation of religious and racial bias in and out of school. *Theory Into Practice, 47*(1), 27–34.

Binte-Farid, I. A. (2022). *Narratives of Islamic self-making: Black Muslim youth in a Philadelphia public school* [Doctoral dissertation, University of Pennsylvania].

Birman, D. (2002). *Refugee mental health in the classroom: A guide for the ESL teacher.* Spring Institute for Intercultural Learning.

Bitew, G., & Ferguson, P. (2010). Parental support for African immigrant students' schooling in Australia. *Journal of Comparative Family Studies, 41*, 149–165.

Black Alliance for Just Immigration. (n.d.). https://baji.org

Blanks Jones, J. L. (2015). Staging and streaming: Murder in the cassava patch performed 'live' in its 50th year. *Liberian Studies Journal, 40*, 55–73.

Blanks Jones, J. L. (2018). Flipping the panopticon. In A. Rapoport (Ed.), *Competing frameworks: Global and national in citizenship education* (p. 137–144). Information Age.

Blizzard, B., & Batalova, J. (2019). Refugees and asylees in the United States. Migration Information Source. Retrieved from https://www.migrationpolicy.org/article/refugees-and-asylees-united-states

Blommaert, J. (2010). *The sociolinguistics of globalization.* Cambridge University Press

Blow, C. (2021, November 14). The impact of the browning of America on anti-Blackness. *The New York Times.* https://www.nytimes.com/2021/11/14/opinion/latinos-colorism-anti-blackness.html

Boal, A. (1979). *Theater of the oppressed.* Pluto Press.

Boal, A. (2002). *Games for actors and non-actors.* (3rd ed.) Routledge

Bogdan, R. C., & Biklen, S. K. (2007). *Qualitative research for education: An introduction to theory and methods.* Pearson Education.

Bordonaro, A. (2023, March 3). Confronting antiblackness in France. https://faculty.dartmouth.edu/artsandsciences/news/2023/03/confronting-antiblackness-france

Boutte, G., & Bryan, N. (2021). When will Black children be well: Interrupting antiviolence in early childhood education classrooms and schools. *Contemporary Issues in Early Childhood Education, 22*(3), 23.

Boutte, G., Johnson, G. L., & Muki, A. (2019). Revitalization of indigenous African knowledges among people in the African diaspora. In L. L. Johnson, G. Boutte, G. Greene, & D. Smith (Eds.), *African diaspora literacy: The heart of transformation in K–12 schools and teacher education* (pp. 13–42). Lexington Books.

Boutte, G., Johnson, G. L., Wynter-Hoyte, K., & Uyoata, U. E. (2017). Using African diaspora literacy to heal and restore the souls of young Black children. *International Critical Childhood Policy Studies Journal, 6*(1), 66–79.

Boveda, M., & Annamma, S. (2023). Beyond making a statement: An intersectional framing of the power and possibilities of positioning. *Educational Researcher, 52*(5), 306–314.

Boyte, H. C. (2004). *Everyday politics: Reconnecting citizens and public life.* University of Pennsylvania Press.

Braden, E. G. (2020). Navigating Black racial identities: Literacy insights from an immigrant family. *Teachers College Record, 122*(13), 1–26.

Braden, E. G., Boutte, G., Gibson, V., & Jackson, J. (2022). Using Afrocentric praxis as loving pedagogies to sustain Black immigrant racial identities. *International Journal of Qualitative Studies in Education, 35*(6), 569–587.

Bredell, K. H. (2013). *Black panther high: Racial violence, student activism, and the policing of Philadelphia public schools* [Doctoral dissertation, Temple University]. ProQuest Dissertations.

Brion-Meisels, G., & Alter, Z. (2018). The quandary of youth participatory action research in school settings: A framework for reflecting on the factors that influence purpose and process. *Harvard Educational Review, 88*(4), 429–454.

Brooklyn Museum. (n.d.). *Kehinde Wiley: A new republic.* https://www.brooklyn museum.org/ exhibitions/kehinde_wiley_new_republic

Browdy, R., & Milu, E. (2022). Global Black rhetorics: A new framework for engaging African and Afro-diasporic rhetorical traditions. *Rhetoric Society Quarterly, 52*(3), 219–241.

Brunet, S., & Galarneau, D. (2022). Profile of Canadian graduates at the bachelor level belonging to a group designated as a visible minority, 2014 to 2017 cohorts. *The Daily.* https://www150.statcan.gc.ca/n1/pub/81-595-m/81-595-m2022003-eng .htm

Bryan, K. (2020). "I had to get tougher": An African immigrant's (counter)narrative of language, race, and resistance. *Teachers College Record, 122*(13).

Bryce-Laporte, R. S. (1972). Black immigrants: The experience of invisibility and inequality. *Journal of Black Studies, 3*(1), 29–56.

Bucholtz, M., Casillas, D. I., & Lee, J. S. (2018). *Feeling it: Language, race, and affect in Latinx youth learning.* Routledge.

Burger, B. (2020). Math and magic: Nnedi Okorafor's Binti trilogy and its challenge to the dominance of Western science in science fiction. *Critical Studies in Media Communication, 37*(4), 364–377.

Busia, A. P. (1989). Silencing Sycorax: On African colonial discourse and the unvoiced female. *Cultural Critique*, 81–104.

Calabrese Barton, A. C., Kim, W. J., & Tan, E. (2020). Co-designing for rightful presence in informal science learning environments. *Asia-Pacific Science Education, 6*(2), 285–318.

Cammarota, J., & Fine, M. (2008). Youth participatory action research: A pedagogy for transformational resistance. In J. Cammarota & M. Fine (Eds.), *Revolutionizing education: Youth participatory action research in motion* (pp. 1–12). Routledge.

Campano, G., Ghiso, M. P., & Welch, B. J. (2016). *Partnering with immigrant communities: Action through literacy.* Teachers College Press.

Campbell, D. D. (1996). *Choosing democracy. A practical guide to Multicultural Education.* Prentice-Hall Inc.

Capps, R., McCabe, K., & Fix, M. (2011). *New streams: Black African migration to the United States.* Migration Policy Institute. https://www.migrationpolicy.org /research/new-streams-black-african-migration-united-states

Caraballo, L., Lozenski, B. D., Lyiscott, J. J., & Morrell, E. (2017). YPAR and critical epistemologies: Rethinking education research. *Review of Research in Education, 41*(1), 311–336.

References

203

Carnegie Endowment for International Peace. (2021). *Racial reckoning in the United States: Expanding and innovating on the global transitional justice experience.* https://carnegieendowment.org/2021/10/26/racial-reckoning-in-united-states-expanding-and-innovating-on-global-transitional-justice-experience-pub-85638

Carotenuto, M. (2021). What I learned from teaching African sport history to American students. https://theconversation.com/what-i-learned-from-teaching-african-sport-history-to-american-students-162366

Carr, W., & Kemmis, S. (1986). *Becoming critical: Education, knowledge and action research.* Falmer.

Carroll, K. K. (2014). An introduction to African-centered sociology: Worldview, epistemology, and social theory. *Critical Sociology, 40*(2), 257–270.

Cascone, S. (2018, October 4). Kehinde Wiley and Amy Sherald's blockbuster Obama paintings nearly doubled the National Portrait Gallery's attendance in 2018. *Artnet News.* https://news.artnet.com/art-world/national-portrait-attendance-1363435

Césaire, A. (2000). *Discourse on colonialism.* Monthly Review Press. (Original work published 1972)

Chareka, O., & Sears, A. (2006). Civic duty: Young people's conceptions of voting as a means of political participation. *Canadian Journal of Education, 29,* 521–540.

Chikkatur, A. P. (2012). Difference matters: Embodiment of and discourse on difference at an urban public high school. *Anthropology & Education Quarterly, 43,* 82–100.

Chilisa, B. (2019). *Indigenous research methodologies* (2nd ed.). Sage.

Chilisa, B., & Ntseane, G. (2014). Resisting dominant discourses: Implications of indigenous, African feminist theory and methods for gender and education research. In J. Ringrose (Ed.), *Rethinking gendered regulations and resistances in education* (pp. 23–38). Routledge.

Clandinin, D. J. (2013). *Engaging in narrative inquiry.* Left Coast Press.

Clark, D. (2018, February 12). Obama portraits unveiled at National Portrait Gallery. NBC News. https://www.nbcnews.com/politics/politics-news/barack-obama-s-presidential-portrait-be-unveiled-n847111

Clark, M. K. (2008). Identity among first and second generation African immigrants in the United States. *African Identities, 6,* 169–181.

Clark, V. A. (2009). Developing diaspora literacy and marasa consciousness. *Theatre Survey, 50*(1), 9–18.

Clarke, K. M., & Thomas, D. A. (Eds.). (2006). *Globalization and race: Transformations in the cultural production of Blackness.* Duke University Press.

Clay, K. L., & Turner, D. C., III. (2021). "Maybe you should try it this way instead": Youth activism amid managerialist subterfuge. *American Educational Research Journal, 58*(2), 386–419.

CNN Newsroom. (2018). Obamas back on public stage for portrait unveiling. http://transcripts.cnn.com/TRANSCRIPTS/1802/12/cnr.04.html

Cochran-Smith, M., & Lytle, S. L. (2009). *Inquiry as stance: Practitioner research for the next generation.* Teachers College Press.

Coe, I. (2015). A degree in STEM can land you your dream job. https://www.huffpost.com/archive/ca/entry/a-degree-in-stem-can-land-you-your-dream-job_b_8455866

Coles, J. A., & Kingsley, M. (2021). Blackness as intervention: Black English outer spaces and the rupturing of antiblackness and/in English education. *English Teaching: Practice & Critique, 20*(4), 454–484.

Colletti, R. (2014). African boys attacked at Bronx school, called "Ebola": Advocacy group. https://www.nbcnewyork.com/news/local/senegal-boys-attacked-bullying-is-318-tremont-nyc/863666/#:~:text=Their%20father%2C%20Ousame%20Drame%2C%20said,for%20two%20weeks%20over%20Ebola.

Collins, S. (2008). *Hunger games*. Scholastic Press.

Cooper, H. (2015, December 10). Liberia's shunned "Ebola burners." *The New York Times*, p. A1.

Corrêa, P. D., & Oloo, J. A. (2022). Racialized mathematics narratives of Black undergraduate students in Ontario. In C. Fernández, S. Llinares, A. Gutiérrez, & N. Planas (Eds.), *Proceedings of the 45th Conference of the International Group for the Psychology of Mathematics Education* (Vol. 4, p. 194). PME.

Corrêa, P. D., & Oloo, J. A. (2023). Racialized mathematics learning experiences of Black undergraduate students. *International Educational Review, 1*(1), 41–55.

Council on American Islamic Relations. (2012). Retrieved from www.cair.com.

Countryman, M. (2007). *Up south: Civil rights and Black power in Philadelphia*. University of Pennsylvania Press.

Covington-Ward, Y. (2017). "Back home, people say America is heaven": Pre-migration expectations and postmigration adjustment for Liberians in Pittsburgh. *Journal of International Migration and Interactions, 18* (4), 1013–1031.

Croom, M., Wynter-Hoyte, K., Watson, V. W., Gadsden, V. L., Hucks, D. C., Lee, C. D., & Bauer, E. B. (2021). Black Lives Matter panel: A generous invitation to the archive. *Literacy Research: Theory, Method, and Practice, 70*(1), 62–85.

Curry-Stevens, A., & Coalition of Communities of Color. (2013). *The African immigrant and refugee community in Multnomah County: An unsettling profile*. Portland State University.

Dabach, D. B., & Fones, A. (2016). Beyond the "English learner" frame: Transnational funds of knowledge in social studies. *International Journal of Multicultural Education, 18*(1), 7–27.

Dallavis, C. (2013). Qualifying sociopolitical consciousness: Complicating culturally responsive pedagogy for faith-based schools. *Education and Urban Society, 45*(2), 266–284.

Danielle, B. (2018, February 12). An artist recreated the "Black Panther" film poster with kids, and it's amazing. *Essence*. https://www.essence.com/entertainment/black-panther-film-poster-kids

Dattatreyan, E. G., & Marrero-Guillamón, I. (2019). Introduction: Multimodal anthropology and the politics of invention. *American Anthropologist, 121*(1), 220–228.

Dávila, L. T. (2015). Diaspora literacies: An explanation of what reading means to young African immigrant women. *Journal of Adolescent & Adult Literacy, 58*, 641–649.

Dávila, L. T. (2019). Multilingualism and identity: Articulating "African-ness" in an American high school. *Race, Ethnicity and Education, 22*(5), 634–646.

Dávila, L. T. (2021). Newcomer refugee and immigrant youth negotiate transnational civic learning and participation in school. *British Educational Research Journal, 47*(4), 855–871.

References

Dávila, L. T., & Doukmak, N. (2022). Immigration debated: Central African immigrant youth's discourses of fairness and civic belonging in the United States. *Equity & Excellence in Education, 55*(1–2), 118–132.

De Costa, P. (2019). Elite multilingualism, affect and neoliberalism. *Journal of Multilingual and Multicultural Development, 40*(5), 453–460.

de los Ríos, C. V., Martinez, D. C., Musser, A. D., Canady, A., Camangian, P., & Quijada, P. D. (2019). Upending colonial practices: Toward repairing harm in English education. *Theory Into Practice, 58*(4), 359–367.

de los Ríos, C. V., & Molina, A. (2020). Literacies of refuge: "Pidiendo posada" as ritual of justice. *Journal of Literacy Research, 52*(1), 32–54.

Dei, G.J.S. (2000). Rethinking the role of indigenous knowledges in the academy. *International Journal of Inclusive Education, 4*(2), 111–132.

Dei, G.J.S. (2012). Indigenous anti-colonial knowledge as 'heritage knowledge' for promoting Black/African education in diasporic contexts. *Decolonization: Indigeneity, Education & Society, 1*(1), 102–119.

Dei, G.J.S. (2017). *Reframing Blackness and Black solidarities through anti-colonial and decolonial prisms.* Springer.

Dernikos, B. P., Ferguson, D. E., & Siegel, M. (2020). Possibilities for "humanizing" posthumanist inquiries. An intra-active conversation. *Cultural Studies, Critical Methodologies, 20*(5), 433–447.

Diallo, R. (2021, April 21). France's latest vote to ban hijabs shows how far it will go to exclude Muslim women. *The Washington Post.* https://www.washingtonpost.com/opinions/2021/04/21/france-hijab-ban-vote-exclusion

Dillard, C. B., & Neal, A. (2020). I am because we are: (Re)membering Ubuntu in the pedagogy of Black women teachers from Africa to America and back again. *Theory Into Practice, 59*(4), 370–378.

Dingfelder, S. (2018, February 12). Decoding the symbolism in the new Obama portraits. *The Washington Post.* https://www.washingtonpost.com/express/wp/2018/02/12/decoding-the-symbolism-in-the-new-obama-portraits/?utm_term=.5b636cdd34fb

Dinishak, J. (2016). The deficit view and its critics. *Disability Studies Quarterly, 36*(4).

Dixon-Román, E. J., Everson, H. T., & McArdle, J. J. (2013). Race, poverty and SAT scores: Modeling the influences of family income on Black and white high school students' SAT performance. *Teachers College Record, 115*(4), 1–33.

Dlamini, S. N., & Anucha, U. (2009). Trans-nationalism, social identities, and African youth in the Canadian diaspora. *Social Identities, 15,* 227–242.

Doucet, F. (2014). Panoply: Haitian and Haitian-American youth crafting identities in U.S. schools. *Trotter Review, 22*(1), 3.

Doucet, F., & Kirkland, D. E. (2021). Sites of sanctuary: Examining Blackness as "something fugitive" through the tactical use of ethnic clubs by Haitian immigrant high school students. *Journal of Adolescent Research, 36*(6), 615–653.

Dozono, T. (2020). The passive voice of White supremacy: Tracing the epistemic and discursive violence in world history curriculum. *Review of Education, Pedagogy, and Cultural Studies, 42*(1), 1–26.

Dryden-Peterson, S. (2010). Bridging home: Building relationships between immigrant and long-time resident youth. *Teachers College Record, 112,* 2320–2351.

Dryden-Peterson, S. (2018). Family–school relationships in immigrant children's well-being: The intersection of demographics and school culture in the experiences of Black African immigrants in the United States. *Race Ethnicity and Education, 21*(4), 486–502.

Du Bois, W.E.B. (2008). *The souls of Black folk* (B. H. Edwards, Ed.). Oxford University Press. (Original work published 1903)

Du Bois, W.E.B., Brown, A., & Rusert, B. (2015). The princess steel. *PMLA, 130*(3), 819–829. (Original work written ca. 1908)

Dumas, M. J., & ross, k. m. (2016). "Be real Black for me": Imagining BlackCrit in education. *Urban Education, 51*(4), 415–442.

Duncan, G. A. (2005). Critical race ethnography in education: Narrative, inequality and the problem of epistemology. *Race ethnicity and Education, 8*(1), 93–114.

Dyrness, A., & Abu El-Haj, T. R. (2019). Reflections on the field: The democratic citizenship formation of transnational youth. *Anthropology & Education Quarterly, 51*(2), 165–177.

Echeverria-Estrada, C., & Batalova, J. (2019). Sub-Saharan African immigrants in the United States. Migration Information Source. https://www.migrationpolicy.org/article/sub-saharan-african-immigrants-united-states-2018

Emerson, R. M., Fretz, R. I., & Shaw, L. L. (2011). *Writing ethnographic fieldnotes.* University of Chicago Press.

Enriquez, G., Johnson, E., Kontovourki, S., & Mallozzi, C. A. (Eds.). (2015). *Literacies, learning, and the body: Putting theory and research into pedagogical practice.* Routledge.

Esterline, C., & Batalova, J. (2022). Frequently requested statistics on immigrants and immigration in the United States. *Migration Information Source*, pp. 1–32.

Esteve, F. (2016, March 22). Afrofuturism, science fiction, and African identity. CCCB Lab. http://lab.cccb.org/en/afrofuturism-science-fiction-and-african-identity

Falola, T., & Oyebade, A. (Eds.). (2017). *The new African diaspora in the United States.* Routledge.

Fanon, F. (1961). *The wretched of the earth.* Grove Atlantic.

Fanon, F. (1967). *Black skin, white mask.* Grove Press.

Fasheh, M. (2015). Over 68 years with mathematics: My story of healing from modern superstitions and reclaiming my sense of being and well-being. In *Proceedings of the Eighth International Mathematics Education and Society Conference* (Vol. 1, pp. 33–60).

Feinberg, R., & Petrie, B. (2019, June 20). African migrants are becoming a new face of the U.S. border crisis. NPR. https://www.npr.org/2019/06/20/733682502/african-migrants-are-becoming-a-new-face-of-the-u-s-border-crisis

Fernandez, M. (2019, June 16). A new migrant surge at the border, this one from Central Africa. *The New York Times.* https://www.nytimes.com/2019/06/16/us/border-africanscongo-maine.html

Ferris, R. (2015). World population: Quarter of Earth will be African in 2050. CNBC. https://www.cnbc.com/2015/07/30/world-population-quarter-of-earth-will-be-african-in-2050.html

Flahaux, M., & de Haas, H. (2016). African migration: Trends, patterns, drivers. *Comparative Migration Studies, 4*(1), 1–25.

References

207

Flores, N., & Rosa, J. (2015). Undoing appropriateness: Raciolinguistic ideologies and language diversity in education. *Harvard educational review*, *85*(2), 149–171.

Flowers, D. (2003). An Afrocentric view of adult learning theory. In L. M. Baumgartner, M.-Y. Lee, S. Birden, & D. Flowers, *Adult learning theory: A primer*. https://eric.ed.gov/?id=ED482337

Frankenstein, M. (2010). Developing critical mathematical numeracy through real real-life word problems. In *Proceedings of the Sixth International Mathematics Education and Society Conference* (pp. 248–257).

Franklin, B. (1749). Proposals relating to the education of youth in Pennsylvania. In J. A. Lemay (Ed.). *Writings* (pp. 152–153). New York: Library of America.

Franklin, R. (2014). Crossing the U.S./Mexico border: Push and pull factors for migration. *Righting Wrongs: A Journal of Human Rights, 4*(2), 1–23.

Freeman, K. (2023). Foreword. In V. B. Bush, C. R. Chambers, & M. B. Walpole (Eds.), *From diplomas to doctorates: The success of Black women in higher education and its implications for equal educational opportunities for all.* (pp. i–iii). Taylor & Francis.

Freire, P. (1970). *Pedagogy of the oppressed*. Continuum.

Freire, P. (1978). *Pedagogy in process*. Seabury Press.

Freire, P. (1996). *Pedagogy of the oppressed*. Continuum.

Fülöp, M., & Sebestyén, N. (2012). Being a student abroad. The sojourner experience: USA meets Hungary. In S. Goncalves & M. Carpenter (Eds.), *Intercultural policies and education* (pp. 141–171). Peter Lang.

Gallagher, K., Starkman, R., & Rhoades, R. (2016). Performing counter-narratives and mining creative resilience: Using applied theatre to theorize notions of youth resilience. *Journal of Youth Studies, 20*(2), 216–233.

Garcia, P., Fernández, C., & Okonkwo, H. (2020). Leveraging technology: How Black girls enact critical digital literacies for social change. *Learning, Media and Technology, 45*(4), 345–362.

García-Cabrero, B., Sandoval-Hernández, A., Treviño-Villarreal, E., Diazgranados Ferráns, S., & Guadalupe Pérez, M. (2017). *Civics and citizenship: Theoretical models and experiences in Latin America.* Brill.

Gay, G. (2018). *Culturally responsive teaching: Theory, research, and practice* (2nd ed.). Teachers College Press.

Gee, J. P. (1991). What is literacy? In C. Mitchell & K. Weiler (Eds.), *Rewriting literacy: Culture and the discourse of the other* (pp. 3–11). Bergin & Garvey.

Geertz, C. (1973). *The interpretation of cultures*. Basic Books.

Ghaffar-Kucher, A., Abu El-Haj, T., Ali, A., Fine, M., & Shirazi, R. (2022): "Muslims are Finally waking up": Post-9/11 American immigrant youth challenge conditional citizenship. *Ethnic and Racial Studies, 45*(6), 1054–1074.

Ghong, M., Saah, L., Larke, P. J., & Webb-Johnson, G. (2007). Teach my child, too: African immigrant parents and multicultural educators sharing culturally responsive teaching tips. *Journal of Praxis in Multicultural Education, 2*(1), 61–69.

Ghosh, S., & Wang, L. (2003). Transnationalism and identity: A tale of two faces and multiple lives. *Canadian Geographer/Le Géographe Canadien, 47*(3), p. 269–282.

Gilroy, P. (1993). *The Black Atlantic: Modernity and double consciousness*. Harvard University Press.

Girls Write Now. (n.d.). *About Girls Write Now*. https://girlswritenow.org/about

Glaude, E. S., Jr. (2020). *Begin again: James Baldwin's America and its urgent lessons for our own*. Crown.

Glick-Schiller, N., Basch, L., & Blanc-Szanton, C. (1992). Transnationalism: A new analytical framework for understanding migration. *Annals of the New York Academy of Sciences, 645*(1), 1–24.

Global Migration Group. (2014). Migration and youth: challenges and opportunities. Global Migration Group. https://publications.iom.int/system/files/pdf/mrs_59.pdf

Godreau, I. P. (2015). *Scripts of Blackness: Race, cultural nationalism, and U.S. colonialism in Puerto Rico*. University of Illinois Press.

González, N., Moll, L., & Amanti, C. (2005). *Funds of knowledge: Theorizing practices in households, communities, and classrooms*. Erlbaum.

Goodwin, A. L. (2010). Curriculum as colonizer: (Asian) American education in the current U.S. context. *Teachers College Record, 112*(12), 3102–3138.

Gordon, A. (1998). The new diaspora—African immigration to the United States. *Journal of Third World Studies, 15*(1), 79–103.

Grant, C. A., Woodson, A., & Dumas, M. (Eds.). (2020). *The future is Black: Afropessimism, fugitivity, and radical hope in education*. Routledge.

Greene, G. (2019). A call for "work woke" educators: Actuating diaspora literacy to raise critical consciousness. In L. L. Johnson, G. Boutte, G. Greene, & D. Smith (Eds.), *African diaspora literacy: The heart of transformation in K–12 schools and teacher education* (pp. 91–106). Lexington Books.

Grinage, J. (2019). Reopening racial wounds: Whiteness, melancholia, and affect in the English classroom. *English Education, 51*(2), 126–150.

Grumet, M. R. (1985). Bodyreading. *Teachers College Record, 87*(2), 175–193.

Gustavo, S. (2019, July 28). Little Africa Festival returns with first-ever parade. *Minnesota Spokesman-Recorder*. https://spokesman-recorder.com/2019/07/28/little-africa-festival-returns-with-first-ever-parade/

Gutstein, E. (2016). "Our issues, our people—Math as our weapon": Critical mathematics in a Chicago neighborhood high school. *Journal for Research in Mathematics Education, 47*(5), 454–504.

Guy, T. C. (2001). Black immigrants of the Caribbean: An invisible and forgotten community. *Adult Learning, 13*(1), 18–21.

Haas-Dyson, A. H. (2013). *Rewriting the basics: Literacy learning in children's cultures*. Teachers College Press.

Haddix, M., & Price-Dennis, D. (2013). Urban fiction and multicultural literature as transformative tools for preparing English teachers for diverse classrooms. *English Education, 45*(3), 247–283.

Hailu, M. F., & Simmons, M. C. (2022a). A collaborative auto-ethnographic examination of Black immigrant women's journeys to and in doctoral education. *Race Ethnicity and Education*, pp. 1–20.

Hailu, M. F., & Simmons, M. C. (2022b). Considering race, culture, and gender in P–16 education: A film-based inquiry of Black African immigrant girls' and women's experiences. In R. D. Mayes, M. C. Shavers, & J. L. Moore III (Eds.), *African American young girls and women in pre-K–12 schools and beyond* (pp. 137–159). Emerald Publishing.

References

Hansler, J., & Alvarez, P. (2020) Trump administration sets refugee cap at 15,000, a new historic low. Retrieved from https://www.cnn.com/2020/10/01/politics/us-refugee-cap-fy21/index.html

Hartocollis, A., & Fawcett, E. (2023, February 1). The College Board strips down its A.P. curriculum for African American studies. *The New York Times*. https://www.nytimes.com/2023/02/01/us/college-board-advanced-placement-african-american-studies.html

Harushimana, I. (2011). Mutilated dreams: African-born refugees in US. Secondary schools. *Journal of Peace and Justice Studies, 21,* 23–41.

Harushimana, I., & Awokoya, J. (2011). African-born immigrants in U.S. schools: An intercultural perspective on schooling and diversity. *Journal of Praxis in Multicultural Education, 6*(1), 34–48.

Hatoss, A. (2012). Where are you from? Identity construction and experiences of 'othering' in the narratives of Sudanese refugee-background Australians. *Discourse & Society, 23*(1), 47–68.

Hauslohner, A. (2017, July 21). 'Muslim Town': A look inside Philadelphia's thriving Muslim culture. *The Washington Post*. https://www.washingtonpost.com/news/post-nation/wp/2017/07/21/muslim-town-how-one-american-city-embraced-a-muslim-community-in-decline

Heath, S. B. (1983). *Ways with words: Language, life and work in communities and classrooms*. Cambridge University Press.

Henry, A. (1998). "Speaking up" and "speaking out": Examining "voice" in a reading/writing program with adolescent African Caribbean girls. *Journal of Literacy Research, 30*(2), 233–252.

Hersi, A. A. (2012). Transnational immigration and education: A case study of an Ethiopian immigrant high school student. *Creative Education, 3*(1), 149–154.

Hirsi, I. (2018). For Minnesota immigrants with dreams of playing pro soccer, club fees are a major hurdle. *MinnPost*. https://www.minnpost.com/new-americans/2018/07/minnesota-immigrants-dreams-playing-pro-soccer-club-fees-are-major-hurdle

Holsey, B. (2008). *Routes of remembrance: Refashioning the slave trade in Ghana*. University of Chicago Press.

Hotchkins, B. K., & Smith, P. (2020). Translanguaging as a gateway to Black immigrant collegians' leadership literacies. *Teachers College Record, 122*(13), 1–29.

Hoye, S., & Hayes, A. (2011). 7 teens arrested in recorded beating of bullying victim. CNN. http://www.cnn.com/2011/CRIME/02/01/pennsylvania.teen.beating/index.html

Hull, G. A., & Schultz, K. (Eds.). (2002). *School's out: Bridging out-of-school literacies with classroom practice*. Teachers College Press.

Human Rights First. (2022). CERD: Anti-Black discrimination within US immigration, detention, and enforcement systems. https://humanrightsfirst.org/library/cerd-anti-black-discrimination-within-us-immigration-detention-and-enforcement-systems

Hunter, C. D., Case, A. D., Joseph, N., Mekawi, Y., & Bokhari, E. (2017). The roles of shared racial fate and a sense of belonging with African Americans in Black immigrants' race-related stress and depression. *Journal of Black Psychology, 43*(2), 135–158.

Ibrahim, A.E.K.M. (1999). Becoming Black: Rap and hip-hop, race, gender, identity, and the politics of ESL learning. *TESOL Quarterly, 33*(3), 349–369.

Ibrahim, A.E.K.M. (2005). "Whassup, homeboy?" Joining the African diaspora: Black English as a symbolic site of identification and language learning. In S. Makoni, G. Smitherman, A. F. Ball, & A. K. Spears (Eds.), *Black linguistics: Language, society and politics in Africa and the Americas* (pp. 181–197). Routledge.

Ibrahim, A. (2008). Operating under erasure: Race/language/identity. *Comparative and International Education, 37*(2).

Ibrahim, A. (2013). The new flâneur: Subaltern cultural studies, African youth in Canada and the semiology of in-betweenness. In K. Tomaselli & H. Wright (Eds.), *Africa, cultural studies and difference* (pp. 62–81). Routledge.

Ibrahim, A. (2014). *The rhizome of Blackness: A critical ethnography of hip-hop culture, language, identity, and the politics of becoming.* Peter Lang.

Ibrahim, A. (2017). Don't call me Black! Rhizomatic analysis of Blackness, immigration, and the politics of race without guarantees. *Educational Studies, 53*(5), 511–521.

Ibrahim, A. (2019). *Black immigrants in North America: Essays on race, immigration, identity, language, hip-hop, pedagogy, and the politics of becoming Black.* Myers Education Press.

Ighodaro, E., & Wiggan, G. (2011). *Curriculum violence: America's new civil rights issue.* Nova Science.

Ikhane, P. A., & Ukpokolo, I. E. (Eds.). (2023). *African epistemology: Essays on being and knowledge.* Routledge.

Ikime, O., & Mafeni, B.O.W. (1972). *The Isoko People: A historical survey.* Ibadan University Press.

Ikpeze, C., Harushimana, I., & Mthethwa-Sommers, S. (2013). *Reprocessing race, language and ability: African-born educators and students in transnational America.* Peter Lang.

Imoagene, O. (2015). Broken bridges: An exchange of slurs between African Americans and second generation Nigerians and the impact on identity formation among the second generation. *Language Sciences, 52,* 176–186.

Ip, C. (2015). *60 Minutes' Africa problem.* https://www.cjr.org/analysis/60_minutes.php

Jackson, J. L., Jr. (2012). Ethnography is, ethnography ain't. *Cultural Anthropology, 27*(3), 480–497.

Jackson, S. A. (2005). *Islam and the Blackamerican: Looking toward the third resurrection.* Oxford University Press.

Jaffee, A. T., Watson, V.W.M., & Knight, M. G. (2014). Toward enacted cosmopolitan citizenship: New conceptualizations of African immigrants' civic learning and action in the United States. *Journal of Global Citizenship & Equity Education, 4*(1).

Jaji, T. (2014). *Africa in stereo: Modernism, music, and pan-African solidarity.* Oxford University Press.

Jensen, E., Jones, N., Rabe, M., Pratt, B., Medina, L., Orozco, K., & Spell, L. (2021). 2020 U.S. population more racially and ethnically diverse than measured in 2010. https://www.census.gov/library/stories/2021/08/2020-united-states-population-more-racially-ethnically-diverse-than-2010.html

References

Johnson, E., & Vasudevan, L. (2012). Seeing and hearing students' lived and embodied critical literacy practices. *Theory into Practice, 51*(1), 34–41.

Johnson, L. B. (1966). State of the Union Address. https://www.infoplease.com/primary-sources/government/presidential-speeches/state-union-address-lyndon-b-johnson-january-12-1966

Johnson, L. J., Boutte, G., Greene, G., & Smith, D. (Eds.). (2018). *African diaspora literacy: The heart of transformation in K–12 schools and teacher education.* Lexington Books.

Joseph, G. G. (1987). Foundations of Eurocentrism in mathematics. *Race & Class, 28*(3), 13–28.

Kah, H. (2016). Kwame Nkrumah and the panAfrican vision: Between acceptance and rebuttal. *Austral: Brazilian Journal of Strategy & International Relations, 5*(9).

Kajee, L. (2011). Literacy journeys: Home and family literacy practices in immigrant households and their congruence with schooled literacy. *South African Journal of Education, 31*, 434–446.

Kamya, H. A. (2005). African immigrant families. In M. McGoldrick, J. Giordano, & N. Garcia-Preto (Eds.), *Ethnicity and family therapy* (pp. 101–116). Guilford Press.

Kebede, K. (2019). The African second generation in the United States—identity and transnationalism: An introduction. *African and Black diaspora: An International Journal, 12*(2), 119–136.

Keegan, P. (2019). Migrant youth from West African countries enacting affective citizenship. *Theory & Research in Social Education, 47*(3), 347–373.

Keegan, P. (2023). Migrant youths' creation of visual counternarratives to expand the boundaries of civic belonging. *International Journal of Qualitative Studies in Education, 36*(9), 1891–1911.

Kelland, Z., & Sanchez, E. (2018). Debunking common myths and misconceptions about Africa. https://www.globalcitizen.org/en/content/africans-are-all-poor-and-15-other-myths

Kelly, L. L. (2023). "It's what we're about": Youth epistemologies in the design of social and educational futures. *Equity & Excellence in Education*, pp. 1–14.

Kendi, I. X. (2023). *How to be an antiracist.* One World.

Kenyatta, J. (1938). *Facing Mount Kenya.* Secker & Warburg.

Khabeer, S.A.A. (2016). *Muslim cool: Race, religion, and hip hop in the United States.* New York University Press.

Kim, J. H. (2015). *Understanding narrative inquiry: The crafting and analysis of stories as research.* Sage.

King, J. E. (1992). Diaspora literacy and consciousness in the struggle against miseducation in the Black community. *The Journal of Negro Education, 61*(3), 317–340.

King, J. (2006). "If justice is our objective": Diaspora literacy, heritage knowledge, and the praxis of critical studyin' for human freedom. *Yearbook of the National Society for the Study of Education, 105*(2), 337–360.

King, J. E. (2015). Dysconscious racism: Ideology, identity, and the miseducation of teachers. In *Dysconscious racism, Afrocentric praxis, and education for human freedom: Through the years I keep on toiling* (pp. 111–125). Routledge.

King, J. E. (2021). Diaspora literacy, heritage knowledge and revolutionary African-centered pedagogy in Black studies curriculum theorizing and praxis.

In W. H. Schubert & M. F. He (Eds.), *Oxford encyclopedia of curriculum studies* (pp. 415–441). Oxford University Press.

King, J. E., & Swartz, E. E. (2016). The Afrocentric praxis of teaching for freedom: *Connecting culture to learning*. Routledge.

Kiramba, L. K., Kumi-Yeboah, A., & Mawuli Sallar, A. (2020). "It's like they don't recognize what I bring to the classroom": African immigrant youths' multilingual and multicultural navigation in United States schools. *Journal of Language, Identity & Education*, pp. 1–16.

Kiramba, L. K., Kumi-Yeboah, A., Smith, P., & Mawuli Sallar, A. (2021). Cultural and linguistic experiences of immigrant youth: Voices of African immigrant youth in United States urban schools. *Multicultural Education Review*, pp. 43–63.

Kiramba, L. K., & Oloo, J. A. (2019). "It's OK. She doesn't even speak English": Narratives of language, culture, and identity negotiation by immigrant high school students. *Urban Education, 58*(3). https://doi.org/10.1177/0042085919873696

Kiramba, L. K., & Oloo, J. A. (2020). Identity negotiation in multilingual contexts: A narrative inquiry into experiences of an African immigrant high school student. *Teachers College Record, 122*(13).

Kiramba, L. K., Onyewuenyi, A. C., Kumi-Yeboah, A., & Sallar, A. M. (2020). Navigating multiple worlds of Ghanaian-born immigrant adolescent girls in U.S. urban schools. *International Journal of Intercultural Relations, 77*, 46–57.

Kiramba, L. K., Traore, H. M., & Trainin, G. (2022). "At school, it's a completely different world": African immigrant youth agency and negotiation of their adaptation processes in U.S. urban schools. *Urban Education*. https://doi.org/10.1177/00420859221140407

Knight, M. (2011). "It's already happening": Learning from civically engaged transnational immigrant youth. *Teachers College Record, 113*, 1275–1292.

Knight, M. (2013). Living the legacies and continuing the struggle: Immigration, pre-K–16 education, and transnationalism. *Texas Education Review, 1*, 225–233.

Knight, M., Bangura, R., & Watson, V.W.M. (2012). (Re)framing African immigrant women's civic leadership: A case study of the role of families, schooling, and transnationalism. *Global Studies Journal, 4*, 135–148.

Knight, M. G., Dixon, I. R., Norton, N. E., & Bentley, C. C. (2006). Critical literacies as feminist affirmations and interventions: Contextualizing Latina youth's construction of their college-bound identities. In D. Delgado Bernal, C. A. Elenes, F. E. Godinez, & S. Villenas (Eds.), *Chicana/Latina education in everyday life: Feminista perspectives on pedagogy and epistemology* (pp. 39–58). State University of New York Press.

Knight, M. G., Roegman, R., & Edstrom, L. (2015). My American dream: The interplay between structure and agency in West African immigrants' educational experiences in the United States. *Education and Urban Society, 48*, 827–851.

Knight, M. G., & Watson, V.W.M. (2014). Toward participatory communal citizenship: Rendering visible the civic teaching, learning, and actions of African immigrant youth and young adults. *American Educational Research Journal, 51*, 539–566.

Koyama, J. P., & Subramanian, M. (2014). *U.S. education in a world of migration: Implications for policy and practice*. Routledge.

References

Kress, G., & Van Leeuwen, T. (2001). *Multimodal discourse: The modes and media of contemporary communication.* Arnold.

Kumi-Yeboah, A. (2016). Educational resilience and academic achievement of immigrant students from Ghana in an urban school environment. *Urban Education, 55*(5). https://doi.org/10.1177/0042085916660347

Kumi-Yeboah, A. (2018). The multiple worlds of Ghanaian-born immigrant students and academic success. *Teachers College Record, 120*(9), 1–48.

Kumi-Yeboah, A., Brobbey, G., & Smith, P. (2020). Exploring factors that facilitate acculturation strategies and academic success of West African immigrant youth in urban schools. *Education and Urban Society, 52*(1), 21–50.

Kumi-Yeboah, A., & Smith, P. (2017). Cross-cultural educational experiences and academic achievement of Ghanaian immigrant youth in urban public schools. *Education and Urban Society, 49*(4), 434–455.

Kumi-Yeboah, A., Tsevi, L., & Addai-Mununkum, R. (2017). Parental aspirations and investments in the educational achievements of African immigrant students. *Multicultural Learning and Teaching, 13*(2). https://doi.org/10.1515/mlt-2016-0009

Ladson-Billings, G. (2001). *Crossing over to Canaan: The journey of new teachers in diverse classrooms.* San Francisco, CA: Jossey-Bass.

Ladson-Billings, G. (2004). Culture versus citizenship: The challenge of racialized citizenship in the United States. In J. A. Banks (Ed.), *Diversity and citizenship: Global perspectives* (pp. 99–126). Jossey-Bass.

Ladson-Billings, G. (2009). *The dreamkeepers: Successful teachers of African American children.* (2nd ed.) John Wiley & Sons.

Ladson-Billings, G. (2014). Culturally relevant pedagogy 2.0: aka the remix. *Harvard Educational Review, 84*(1), 74–84.

Larnell, G. V. (2016). More than just skill: Examining mathematics identities, racialized narratives, and remediation among Black undergraduates. *Journal for Research in Mathematics Education, 47*(3), 233–269.

Leander, K. M., & Ehret, C. (Eds.). (2019). *Affect in literacy learning and teaching. Pedagogies, politics and coming to know.* Routledge.

Lee, C. C. (2019). Invite their languages in: Community-based literacy practices with multilingual African immigrant girls in New York City. *International Journal of Multicultural Education, 21*(2), 1–22.

Lee, C. C. (2020). "I have a voice": Reexamining researcher positionality and humanizing research with African immigrant girls. *Multicultural Perspectives, 22*(1), 46–54.

Lee, C. C., Desai, K., & Knight-Manuel, M. (2016). Fostering a humanizing pedagogy: Imagined possibilities for African immigrant girls. *Education Leadership Review, 16*(3), 34–43.

Lee, C. D. (2008). The centrality of culture to the scientific study of learning and development: How an ecological framework in education research facilitates civic responsibility. *Educational Researcher, 37*(5).

Lee, S. (2001). More than "model minorities" or "delinquents": A look at Hmong American high school students." *Harvard Educational Review, 71*, 505–529.

Lee, W. (2016, June 30). Africa-born US residents embrace politics to bring about change. Voice of America. http://www.voanews.com/content/africa-born-united states-residents-embrace-politics-bring-about-change/3399834.html

Levitt, P., & Glick-Schiller, N. (2004). Conceptualizing simultaneity: A transnational social field perspective on society. *International Migration Review, 38*(3), 1002–1039.

Literacy Futurisms Collective-in-the-Making. (2021). "We believe in collective magic": Honoring the past to reclaim the future(s) of literacy research. *Literacy Research: Theory, Method, and Practice, 70*(1), 428–447.

Liu, K., & Ball, A. F. (2019). Critical reflection and generativity: Toward a framework of transformative teacher education for diverse learners. *Review of Research in Education, 43*(1), 68–105.

Lorenzi, J., & Batalova, J. (2022). Sub-Saharan African immigrants in the United States. https://www.migrationpolicy.org/article/sub-saharan-african-immigrants-united-states-2019

Lozenski, B., & Smith, C. (2012). Pen 2 paper 2 power: Lessons from an arts-based literacy program serving Somali immigrant youth. *Equity & Excellence in Education, 45*(4), 596–611.

Luke, A. (1992). The body literate: Discourse and inscription in early literacy training. *Linguistics and Education, 4*(1), 107–129.

Lukose, R. (2007). The difference that diaspora makes: Thinking through the anthropology of immigrant education in the United States. *Anthropology and Education, 38*(4), 405–418.

Luttrell, W. (2020). *Children framing childhoods: Working class kids' visions of care.* Policy Press.

Madison, D. S. (2011). *Critical ethnography: Method, ethics, and performance.* Sage Publications.

Maestripieri, L. (2021). The COVID-19 pandemics: Why intersectionality matters. *Frontiers in Sociology, 6*, 1–6. https://doi.org/10.3389/fsoc.2021.642662

Mahiri, J. (2017). *Deconstructing race: Multicultural education beyond the colorblind.* Teachers College Press.

Makoni, S. B. (2012). Language and human rights discourses in Africa: Lessons from African experience. *Journal of Multicultural Discourses, 7*(1), 1–20.

Mandela, N. (July 2003). Lighting your way to a better place. Speech delivered at a launch of Mindset Network. University of Witwatersrand, Johannesburg, South Africa. http://db.nelsonmandela.org/speeches/pub_view.asp?pg=item&ItemID=NMS909&txtstr=education %20is%20the%20most%20powerful

Mann, H. (1848). *Twelfth annual report: In annual reports of the secretary of the board of Massachusetts for the years 1845–1848.* Boston: Lee and Shephard.

Marciano, J. E., Peralta, L. M., Lee, J. S., Rosemurgy, H., Holloway, L., & Bass, J. (2020). Centering community: Enacting culturally responsive-sustaining YPAR during COVID-19. *Journal for Multicultural Education, 14*(2), 163–175.

Marciano, J. E., & Vellanki, V. (2022). Generating new narratives: Examining youths' multiliteracies practices in youth participatory action research. *Research in the Teaching of English, 56*(3), 245–274.

Martin, D. B., Gholson, M. L., & Leonard, J. (2010). Mathematics as gatekeeper: Power and privilege in the production of knowledge. *Journal of Urban Mathematics Education, 3*(2), 12–24.

Mas Giralt, R. (2015). Socio-cultural invisibility and belonging: Latin American migrants in the north of England. *Emotion, Space and Society, 15*, 3–10.

References

Masinda, M. T., Jacquet, M., & Moore, D. (2014). An integrated framework for immigrant children and youth's school integration: A focus on African Francophone students in British Columbia, Canada. *International Journal of Education, 6*, 90–107.

Maswabi, K. (2016). The big African tree. https://www.poemhunter.com/poem/the-big-african-tree

Matza, M., & Duchneskien, J. (2013, December 23). Southwest Phila., a 'little Africa' is growing. *Philadelphia Inquirer.* https://www.inquirer.com/philly/news/20131223_In_Southwest_Phila___a_quot_little_Africa_quot__is_growing.html

Mazrui, A. (1986a). *The Africans: A triple heritage.* Little, Brown.

Mazrui, A. (Narrator). (1986b). The nature of a continent. In *The Africans: A triple heritage* [Documentary series]. PBS.

Mburu, W. (2012). Indigenous conceptions of civic education. In A. Asabere-Ameyaw, G.J.S. Dei, K. Raheem, & J. Anamuah-Mensah (Eds.), *Contemporary issues in African sciences and science education* (pp. 175–193). Sense.

McCabe, K. (2011a). African immigrants in the United States. *Migration Information Source, July 2011.* http://www.migrationinformation.org/issue_jul11.cfm

McCabe, K. (2011b). *African immigrants in the United States in 2009.* Migration Policy Institute. https://www.migrationpolicy.org/article/african-immigrants-united-states-2009

McKenzie, L. (2021). Tackling racism in textbook publishing. https://www.insidehighered.com/news/2021/02/26/publisher-pearson-tries-tackle-systemic-racism-higher-ed

McLean, C. A. (2010). A space called home: An immigrant adolescent's digital literacy practices. *Journal of Adolescent & Adult Literacy, 54*(1), 13–22.

McLean, C. A. (2020). Racialized tensions in the multimodal literacies of Black immigrant youth. *Teachers College Record, 122*(13), 1–22.

Medford, M. (2021). Jamaican cultural symbols as transethnic artifacts: How Black immigrant vendors construct boundaries of racial consciousness at a Caribbean festival. *Ethnicities, 21*(5), 912–933.

Medina, C., & Campano, G. (2006). Performing identities through drama and teatro practices in multilingual classrooms. *Language Arts, 83*(4), 332–341.

Mentor, M., & Sealey-Ruiz, Y. (2021). Doing the deep work of antiracist pedagogy: Toward self-excavation for equitable classroom teaching. *Language Arts, 99*(1), 19–24.

Mignolo, W. D. (2007). Delinking: The rhetoric of modernity, the logic of coloniality and the grammar of de-coloniality. *Cultural Studies, 21*(2–3), 449–514.

Mignolo, W. D. (2009). *The idea of Latin America.* Wiley.

Migration Policy Institute. (2019). Sub-Saharan African immigrants in the United States. https://www.migrationpolicy.org/article/sub-saharan-african-immigrants-united-states-2018

Milner, H. R., IV. (2007). Race, culture, and researcher positionality: Working through dangers seen, unseen, and unforeseen. *Educational Researcher, 36*(7), 388–400.

Milner, H. R., IV. (2020). Fifteenth annual AERA Brown lecture in education research: Disrupting punitive practices and policies: Rac(e)ing back to teaching, teacher preparation, and Brown. *Educational Researcher, 49*(3), 147–160.

Milu, E. (2021). Diversity of raciolinguistic experiences in the writing classroom: An argument for a transnational Black language pedagogy. *College English, 83*(6).

Mims, M. J., Mims, G. A., & Newland, L. A. (2009). Career counselling an African immigrant student in a USA school setting: Merging transition theory with a narrative approach. *South African Journal of Higher Education, 23*, 590–607.

Mirra, N., Garcia, A., & Morrell, E. (2015). *Doing youth participatory action research: Transforming inquiry with researchers, educators, and students.* Routledge.

Mkabela, Q. (2005). Using the Afrocentric method in researching indigenous African culture. *Qualitative Report, 10*(1), 178–189.

Moje, E. B., & Lewis, C. (2020). Examining opportunities to learn literacy: The role of critical sociocultural literacy research. In C. Lewis, P. E. Enciso, & E. B. Moje (Eds.), *Reframing sociocultural research on literacy* (pp. 15–48). Routledge.

Moll, L. C., Soto-Santiago, S., & Schwartz, L. (2013). Funds of knowledge in changing communities. In K. Hall, T. Cremin, B. Comber, & L. C. Moll (Eds.), *International handbook of research on children's literacy, learning and culture* (pp. 172–183). Wiley Blackwell.

Monea, B. (2022). Sharing the screen: Reconfiguring participatory methodologies for digitally mediated literacy research. In C. Lee, C. Bailey, C. Burnett, & J. Rowsell (Eds.), *Unsettling literacies: Directions for literacy research in precarious times* (pp. 33–49). Springer Singapore.

Morton, T. R., Gee, D. S., & Woodson, A. N. (2019). Being vs. becoming: Transcending STEM identity development through Afropessimism, moving toward a Black X consciousness in STEM. *The Journal of Negro Education, 88*(3), 327–342.

Moses, R., & Cobb, C. E. (2002). *Radical equations: Civil rights from Mississippi to the Algebra Project.* Beacon Press.

Movement for Black Lives. 2024. "Vision for Black Lives." https://m4bl.org/policy-platforms/

Muhammad, G. (2020). *Cultivating genius: An equity framework for culturally and historically responsive literacy.* Scholastic.

Munasinghe, V. (1997). Culture creators and culture bearers: The interface between race and ethnicity in Trinidad. *Transforming Anthropology, 6*(1–2), 72–86.

Muwanguzi, S., & Musambira, G. W. (2012). Communication experiences of Ugandan immigrants during acculturation to the United States. *Journal of Intercultural Communication, 30*, 71–86.

Mwangi, C. (2017). Being Black (and) immigrant students: When race, ethnicity and nativity collide. *International Journal of Multicultural Education, 19*(2), 100–120.

Nabea, W. (2009). Language policy in Kenya: Negotiation with hegemony. *The Journal of Pan African Studies, 3*(1), 121–139.

Nabwire, N. S. (2021). *Navigating the U.S. educational system: Perspectives of Kenyan immigrant students labeled with dis/abilities and their families* [Doctoral dissertation, University of Kansas].

Nalubega-Booker, K., & Willis, A. (2020). Applying critical race theory as a tool for examining the literacies of Black immigrant youth. *Teachers College Record, 122*(13), 1–24.

National Council for the Social Studies (n.d.). *College, Career, and Civic life (C3). Frameworks for social studies standards.* https://www.socialstudies.org/standards/c3

Ndemanu, M. T., & Jordan, S. (2018). Culturally responsive pedagogy for African immigrant children in U.S. P–12 schools. *Journal of Black Studies, 49*(1), 71–84.

References

Nero, S. (2014). Classroom encounters with Caribbean Creole English: Language, identities, pedagogy. In A. Mahboob & L. Barratt (Eds.), *Englishes in multilingual contexts: Language variation and education* (pp. 33–46). Springer.

New London Group. (1996). A pedagogy of multiliteracies: Designing social futures. *Harvard Educational Review, 66*(1), 60–93.

The New York Times. (2020). Black Lives Matter may be the largest movement in US history. https://www.nytimes.com/interactive/2020/07/03/us/george-floyd-protests-crowd-size.html

Ngugi Wa Thiong'o. (1967). *A grain of wheat.* Heinemann.

Ngugi wa Thiong'o, N. W. (1986). *Decolonising the mind: The politics of language in African literature.* James Currey.

Nieto, S. (2018). *Language culture, and teaching: Critical perspectives for a new century.* Erlbaum.

Njue, J., & Retish, P. (2010). Transitioning: Academic and social performance of African immigrant students in an American high school. *Urban Education, 45*, 347–370.

Nkemka, A. (2022). *Educators' descriptions of academic engagement strategies for recent Sub-Saharan immigrants* [Doctoral dissertation, Capella University].

Noah, T. (2016). *Born a crime: Stories from a South African childhood.* Hachette UK.

Noel, F. (2022). *Solidarity in translation: Anti-Blackness from the U.S. to France.* Black Youth Project.

Noy Meir, U. Y., & Larcher, A. (2020). Joker exchange online—Meeting the risks and opportunities of the COVID-19 crisis. *Pedagogy and Theatre of the Oppressed Journal, 5*(17).

Nsangou, A., & Dundes, L. (2018). Parsing the gulf between Africans and African Americans. *Social Sciences, 7*(2), 24.

Nyamnjoh, F. B., & Shoro, K. (2011). Language, mobility, African writers and pan-Africanism. *African Communication Research, 4*(1), 35–62.

Obiakor, F. E., & Afolayan, M. O. (2007). African immigrant families in the United States: Surviving the sociocultural tide. *The Family Journal, 15*, 265–270.

Ogbu, J. (1978) *Minority education and caste: The American system in cross-cultural perspective.* New York: Academic Press.

Ogwal, S. (2020). African mobility: A historical perspective of immigration in the U.S. *International Journal of Social Policy & Education, 2*(2), 13–29.

Ohuche, R. O. (1978). Change in mathematics education since the late 1950's—Ideas and realisation Nigeria. *Educational Studies in Mathematics, 9*(3), 271–281.

Okonofua, B. A. (2013). "I am Blacker than you": Theorizing conflict between African immigrants and African Americans in the United States. *Sage Open.* https://doi.org/10.1177/2158244013499162

Okorafor, N. (2015). *Binti.* Tor.

Okorafor, N. (2019, October). *Africanfuturism defined.* Nnedi's Wahala Zone Blog. http://nnedi.blogspot.com/2019/10/africanfuturism-defined.html

Okpalaoka, C. L., & Dillard, C. B. (2012, Winter-Spring). (Im)migrations, relations, and identities of African peoples: Toward an endarkened transnational feminist praxis in education. *Educational Foundations*, pp. 121–142.

Oloo, J. A. (2022). Understanding and enhancing academic experiences of culturally and linguistically-diverse international students in Canada. In C. Smith &

G. Zhou (Eds.), *Handbook of research on teaching strategies for culturally and linguistically diverse international students* (pp. 61–74). IGI Global.

Oloo, J. A., & Kiramba, L. K. (2019). A narrative inquiry into the experiences of indigenous teachers during and after teacher preparation. *Race, Ethnicity & Education*. pp. 331–350.

Omi, M., & Winant, H. (2014). *Racial formation in the United States: From the 1960s to the 1990s*. (3rd ed.) Routledge.

Omogun, L., & Skerrett, A. (2021). From Haiti to Detroit through Black immigrant languages and literacies. *Journal of Literacy Research, 53*(3), 406–429.

Omolewa, M., Adeola, O. A., Adekanmbi, G., Avoseh, M.B.M., & Braimoh, D. (1998). *Literacy, tradition and progress: Enrolment and retention in an African rural literacy programme*. UNESCO.

Onwong'a, J., Slaten, C., & McClain. S. (2021). "AmeriKenyan": Lived acculturation and ethnic identification of Kenyan natives during their youth. *Journal of Black Psychology, 48*(5), 1–33.

Onwuegbuzie, A. J., & Frels, R. K. (2015). A framework for conducting critical dialectical pluralist focus group discussions using mixed research techniques. *Journal of Educational Issues, 1*(2), 159–177.

Onyenekwu, I. U. (2017). Providing culturally relevant services for international Black African collegians in the United States: A guide for student affairs professionals. *Journal of International Students, 7*(4), 1113–1125.

Oropeza, M. V., Varghese, M. M., & Kanno, Y. (2010). Linguistic minority students in higher education: Using, resisting, and negotiating multiple labels. *Equity & Excellence in Education, 43*, 216–231.

Osei-Tutu, A. A. (2022). Developing African oral traditional storytelling as a framework for studying with African peoples. *Qualitative Research, 23*(6). https://doi.org/10.1177/14687941221082263.

Osibodu, O. (2021). Necessitating teacher learning in teaching mathematics for social justice to counter anti-Black racism. *For the Learning of Mathematics, 41*(1), 18–20.

Osibodu, O., & Cosby, M. D. (2018). Shades of Blackness: Rehumanizing mathematics education through an understanding of Sub-Saharan African immigrants. In I. Goffney & R. Gutiérrez (Eds.), *Annual perspectives in mathematics 2018: Rehumanizing mathematics for Black, Indigenous, and Latinx students* (pp. 39–49). National Council of Teachers of Mathematics.

Osunde, E. O., Tlou, J., & Brown, N. (1996). Persisting and common stereotypes in U.S. students' knowledge of Africa: A study of preservice social studies teachers. *The Social Studies*, pp. 119–125.

Oughton, H. (2010). Funds of knowledge—A conceptual critique. *Studies in the Education of Adults, 42*(1), 63–78.

Pangrazio, L. (2016). Reconceptualising critical digital literacy. *Discourse: Studies in the Cultural Politics of Education, 37*(2), 163–174.

Paris, D. (2011). *Language across difference: Ethnicity, communication, and youth identities in changing urban schools*. Cambridge University Press.

Paris, D., & Alim, H. S. (2017). *Culturally sustaining pedagogies: Teaching and learning for justice in a changing world*. Teachers College Press.

Park, J. Y. (2013). Becoming academically literate: A case study of an African immigrant youth. *Journal of Adolescent & Adult Literacy, 57*(4), 298–306.

References

Parslow, K. A. (2023). *A narrative study of an African immigrant high school student* [Doctoral dissertation, University of Wisconsin–Madison].

Pechurina, A. (2020). Researching identities through material possessions: The case of diasporic objects. *Current Sociology, 68*(5), 669–683.

Perry, K. H. (2012). What is literacy?—A critical overview of sociocultural perspectives. *Journal of Language & Literacy Education, 8*(1), 50–71.

Persaud, F. J. (2020). Remembering the Black men and immigrants killed by U.S. police. https://amsterdamnews.com/news/2020/06/04/remembering-black-men-and-immigrants-killed-us-pol

Peshkin, A. (1988). In search of subjectivity—One's own. *Educational Researcher, 17*(7), 17–21.

Petrone, R., Ybarra, A., & Rink, N. (2021). Toward an indigenizing, anti-colonial framework for adolescent development research. *Journal of Adolescent Research, 36*(6), 584–614.

Pew Research Center. (2019). *Defining generations: Where millennials end and generation Z begins.* https://www.pewresearch.org/short-reads/2019/01/17/where-millennials-end-and-generation-z-begins

Pew Research Center. (2020). *Philadelphia 2020: State of the city.* https://www.pewtrusts.org/-/media/assets/2020/04/state_of_the_city_2020.pdf

Pew Research Center. (2022). Key findings about Black immigrants in the U.S. https://www.pewresearch.org/short-reads/2022/01/27/key-findings-about-black-immigrants-in-the-u-s

Pew Research Center. (2022). *The growing diversity of Black America.* https://www.pewresearch.org/social-trends/2021/03/25/the-growing-diversity-of-black-america

Pew Research Center. (2023). *Support for the Black Lives Matter movement has dropped considerably from its peak in 2020.* https://www.pewresearch.org/social-trends/2023/06/14/support-for-the-black-lives-matter-movement-has-dropped-considerably-from-its-peak-in-2020

Philadelphia rocked by fresh unrest after police shooting. (2020, October 28). BBC News. https://www.bbc.com/news/world-us-canada-54710244

Pierre, J. (2013). *The predicament of Blackness: Postcolonial Ghana and the politics of race.* University of Chicago Press.

Pierre, J. (2020). Slavery, anthropological knowledge, and the racialization of Africans. *Current Anthropology, 61*(S22), S220–S231.

Ping, W. (2010). A case study of an in-class silent postgraduate Chinese student in London Metropolitan University: A journey of learning. *TESOL Journal, 2*, 207–214.

Price-Dennis, D. (2016). Developing curriculum to support Black girls' literacies in digital spaces. *English Education, 48*(4), 337–361.

Price-Dennis, D., & Sealey-Ruiz, Y. (2021). *Advancing racial literacies in teacher education: Activism for equity in digital spaces.* Teachers College Press.

Ramos-Zayas, A. Y. (2012). *Street therapists: Race, affect and neoliberal personhood in Latino Newark.* University of Chicago Press.

Rana, J. (2011). *Terrifying Muslims: Race and labor in the South Asian diaspora.* Duke University Press.

Reisman, A., Enumah, L., & Jay, L. (2020). Interpretive frames for responding to racially stressful moments in history discussions. *Theory & Research in Social Education, 48*(3), 321–345.

Reuters Staff. (2018, February 12). Guinean government warns against ethnic violence after polls. https://www.reuters.com/article/guinea-politics-idINKBN1FW2CA

Rich, A. (1994). *Blood, bread, and poetry: Selected prose, 1979–1985.* Norton.

Ríos-Rojas, A. (2011). Beyond delinquent citizenships: Immigrant youth's (re) visions of citizenship and belonging in a globalized world. *Harvard Educational Review, 81,* 64–95.

Roberts, L., Migueliz Valcarlos, M., Nkrumah, T., & Agosto, V. (2021). Expanding and expounding upon forum theater to engage spect-actors in virtual spaces. *Pedagogy and Theatre of the Oppressed Journal, 6*(10).

Roberts, S. (2005, February 21). More Africans enter U.S. than in days of slavery. *The New York Times.* http://www.nytimes.com/2005/02/21/nyregion/more-africans-enter-us-than-in-days-of-slavery.html?_r=0

Roegman, R., Knight, M., Taylor, A., & Watson, V.W.M. (2016). From microscope to mirror: Doctoral students' evolving positionalities through engagement with culturally sensitive research. *International Journal of Qualitative Studies in Education, 29*(1), 44–65.

Rong, X. L., & Brown, F. (2002). Socialization, culture, and identities of Black immigrant children: What educators need to know and do. *Education and Urban Society, 34*(2), 247–273.

Rosa, J., & Flores, N. (2017). Unsettling race and language: Toward a raciolinguistic perspective. *Language in Society, 46*(5), 621–647.

Roth, V. (2011). *Divergent.* Katherine Tegen Books.

Roubeni, S., De Haene, L., Keatley, E., Shah, N., & Rasmussen, A. (2015). "If we can't do it, our children will do it one day": A qualitative study of West African immigrant parents' losses and educational aspirations for their children. *American Educational Research Journal, 52*(2), 275–305.

Roy, L., & Roxas, K. (2011). Whose deficit is this anyhow? Exploring counter-stories of Somali Bantu refugees' experiences in "doing school." *Harvard Educational Review, 81,* 521–542.

Rumbaut, R. G., & Ima, K. (1988). *The adaptation of southeast Asian refugee youth: A comparative study.* U.S. Department of Health and Human Services, Family Support Administration, Office of Refugee Resettlement.

Salami, B., Alaazi, D.A., Yohani, S., Vallianatos, H., Okeke-Ihejirika, P., Ayalew, T., & Nsaliwa, C. (2020). Parent–child relationships among African immigrant families in Canada. *Family Relations: An Interdisciplinary Journal of Applied Family Studies, 69*(4), 743–755.

Sánchez, P. (2007). Urban immigrant students: How transnationalism shapes their world learning. *The Urban Review, 39*(5), 489–517.

Sanders, F. C. (2009). *A curricular policy forty years in the making: The implementation of an African American history course in the Philadelphia school district.* Pennsylvania State University.

Sawasawa, M. (2021). *Price of gold: DRC's rich soil bears few riches for its miners* [Photo essay]. https://www.theguardian.com/global-development/2021/may/12/price-of-gold-drcs-rich-soil-bears-few-riches-for-its-miners-photo-essay

Schmidley A. D., & U. S. Census Bureau. (2001). *Profile of the foreign-born population in the United States, 2000.* U.S. Department of Commerce, Economics and Statistics Administration, U.S. Census Bureau.

References

Schmidt, S. J. (2021). Merging landscapes: Socio-spatial intersections and formations of belonging among African migrant youth in the US. *Visual Studies, 38*(3–4), 351–365.

Schmidt, S. J. (2022). "We don't live in jungles": Mediating Africa as a transnational socio-spatial field. *Teachers College Record, 124*(6), 38–61.

Schmidt, S. J. (2023). Merging landscapes: Socio-spatial intersections and formations of belonging among African migrant youth in the US. *Visual Studies, 38*(3–4), 351–365.

Schön, D. A. (1995). Knowing-in-action: The new scholarship requires a new epistemology. *Change: The Magazine of Higher Learning, 27*(6), 27–34.

Scribner, S., & Cole, M. (1981). *The psychology of literacy.* Harvard University Press.

Shizha, E., Abdi, A. A., Wilson-Forsberg, S., & Masakure, O. (2020). African immigrant students and postsecondary education in Canada: High school teachers and school career counsellors as gatekeepers. *Canadian Ethnic Studies, 52*(3), 67–86.

Sichra, I. (2017). Language diversity and indigenous literacy in the Andes. In B. Street & B. May (Eds.), *Literacies and language education* (pp. 235–248). Springer International.

Siegel, M. (2015). Inscription, erasure, embodiment: Literacy research and bodies of knowledge. In G. Enriquez, E. Johnson, S. Kontovourki, & C. A. Mallozzi (Eds.), *Literacies, learning, and the body: Putting theory and research into pedagogical practice* (pp. 20–37). Routledge.

Silko, L. M. (1977). *Ceremony.* Penguin.

Silverstein, J. (2021). The global impact of Goerge Floyd: How Black Lives Matter protests shaped movements around the world. https://www.cbsnews.com/news/george-floyd-black-lives-matter-impact/

Simmons, M. C. (2021a). *(Re)claiming and (re)framing: Exploring how Black West African immigrant girls depict their understandings of self-identity and representations through multimodal literacy.* [Doctoral dissertation, Georgia State University].

Simmons, M. C. (2021b). "There's more than one way to be Black": The literary experiences of Black African immigrant girls in the United States. In D. Petra Dennis & G. E. Muhammad (Eds.), *Black girls' literacies* (pp. 98–112). Routledge.

Sims, D. (2018, February 20). The game-changing success of Black Panther. *The Atlantic.* https://www.theatlantic.com/entertainment/archive/2018/02/the-game-changing-success-of-black-panther/553763

60 Minutes. (2013). The lost boys who beat the odds. https://www.cbsnews.com/news/the-lost-boys-of-sudan-12-years-later-02-04-2013/

Skerrett, A. (2015). *Teaching transnational youth: Literacy and education in a changing world.* Teachers College Press.

Skerrett, A. (2018). Learning music literacies across transnational school settings. *Journal of Literacy Research, 50*(1), 31–51.

Skerrett, A., & Omogun, L. (2020). When racial, transnational, and immigrant identities, literacies, and languages meet: Black youth of Caribbean origin speak. *Teachers College Record, 122*(13), 1–24.

Smalls, K. A. (2014). The proverbial monkey on our backs: Exploring the politics of belonging among transnational African high school students in the US. In

J. Koyama & M. Subramanian (Eds.), *U.S. education in a world of migration: Implications for policy and practice* (pp. 19–37). Taylor & Francis.

Smalls, K. A. (2020). *Race, SIGNS, and the body: Towards a theory of racial semiotics*. Oxford University Press.

Smith, L. (2012). *Decolonizing methodologies* (2nd ed.). Zed Books.

Smith, P. (2019). (Re)positioning in the Englishes and (English) literacies of a Black immigrant youth: Towards a transraciolinguistic approach. *Theory Into Practice, 58*(3), 292–303.

Smith, P. (2020a). The case for translanguaging in Black immigrant literacies. *Literacy Research: Theory, Method, and Practice, 69*, 192–210.

Smith, P. (2020b). "How does a Black person speak English?" Beyond American language norms. *American Educational Research Journal, 57*(1), 106–147.

Smith, P. (2020c). Silencing invisibility: Toward a framework for Black immigrant literacies. *Teachers College Record, 122*(13), 1–42.

Smith, P. (2022). Black immigrants in the United States: Transraciolinguistic justice for imagined futures in a global metaverse. *Annual Review of Applied Linguistics, 42*, 109–118.

Smith, P. (2023a). *Black immigrant literacies: Intersections of race, language, and culture in the classroom*. Teachers College Press.

Smith, P. (2023b). *How Black immigrant literacies can reinstate Black language and transcend the global myth of invented illiteracy and Black brokenness*. LSE USAPP Blog.

Smitherman, G. (1977). *Talkin and testifyin: The language of Black America* (Vol. 51). Wayne State University Press.

Smitherman, G. (1986). *Talkin and testifyin: The language of Black America* (Vol. 51). Wayne State University Press.

Smitherman, G. (1998). Word from the hood: The lexicon of African-American vernacular English. In S. S. Mufwene, J. R. Rickford, G. Bailey, & John Baugh (Eds.), *African-American English: Structure, history, and use* (pp. 203–225). Routledge.

Solomon, D. B. (2019). U.S. dream pulls African migrants in record numbers across Latin America. Reuters World News.

Sparks, D. M. (2023). Analyzing the intersectional and bicultural experiences of Black immigrant women STEM students at a diverse urban university: A phenomenological study. *The Urban Review, 55*(2), 269–292.

Squire, V., & Darling, J. (2013). The "minor" politics of rightful presence: Justice and relationality in city of sanctuary. *International Political Sociology, 7*(1), 59–74.

Statistics Canada. (2020). Black history month 2022 . . . by the numbers. *The Daily*. https://www.statcan.gc.ca/en/dai/smr08/2022/smr08_259

Statistics Canada. (2023). Immigration and ethnocultural diversity in Canada. https://www12.statcan.gc.ca/nhs-enm/2011/as-sa/99-010-x/99-010-x2011001-eng.cfm

Stebleton, M. J. (2007). Career counseling with African immigrant college students: Theoretical approaches and implications for practice. *Career Development Journal, 55*, 290–312.

Stebleton, M. J. (2012). The meaning of work for Black African immigrant adult college students. *Journal of Career Development, 39*, 50–75.

References

223

Stebleton, M. J., Diamond, K. K., & Rost-Banik, C. (2020). Experiences of foreign-born immigrant undergraduate women at a U.S. institution and influences on career–life planning. *Journal of Career Development, 47*(1), 11–28.

Stornaiuolo, A., & Thomas, E. E. (2018). Restorying as political action: Authoring resistance through youth media arts. *Learning, Media and Technology, 43*(4), 345–358.

Street, B. (1984). *Literacy in theory and practice*. Cambridge University Press.

Strong, K. (2018). Do African lives matter to Black Lives Matter? Youth uprisings and the borders of solidarity. *Urban Education, 53*(2), 265–285.

Strong, K., & Blanks Jones, J. (2023). Come correct: Itineraries of discovery in Black women's ethnographic practice. *Feminist Anthropology, 4*(1), 54–61.

Suárez-Orozco, C., Suárez-Orozco, M., & Todorova, I. (2010). *Learning a new land: Immigrant students in American society*. Harvard University Press.

Subedi, B., & Daza, S. L. (2008). The possibilities of postcolonial praxis in education. *Race Ethnicity and Education, 11*(1), 1–10.

Sue, D. W., Capodilupo, C.M., Torino, G.C., Bucceri, J.M., Holder, A, M. B., Nadal, K.L., & Esquilin, M. (2007). Racial microaggressions in everyday life: Implications for clinical practice. *American Psychologist, 62* (4), 271–286.

Taarnby, M. (2005). *Recruitment of Islamist terrorists in Europe: Trends and perspectives* [Research report]. http://www.investigativeproject.org/documents/testimony/58.pdf

Tadesse, S. (2014). Parent involvement: Perceived encouragement and barriers to African refugee parent and teacher relationships. *Childhood Education, 90*, 298–305.

Takougang, J. (2003). Contemporary African immigrants to the United States. *Irinkerindo: A Journal of African Migration, 2*, 1–15.

Takyi, B. K. (2002). The making of the second diaspora: On the recent African immigrant community in the United States of America. *Western Journal of Black Studies, 26*, 32–43.

Tamir, C. (2022, January 27). Key findings about Black immigrants in the U.S. Pew Research Center. https://www.pewresearch.org/fact-tank/2022/01/27/key-findings-about-black-immigrants-in-the-u-s

Tamir, C., & Anderson, M. (2022). One-in-ten Black people living in the U.S. are immigrants. https://www.pewresearch.org/race-ethnicity/2022/01/20/one-in-ten-black-people-living-in-the-u-s-are-immigrants

Temple, C. N. (2010). The emergence of Sankofa practice in the United States: A modern history. *Journal of Black Studies, 41*, 127–150.

Tesfa, E., & Lowenhaupt, R. (2023). Caring through crisis: Supporting African immigrant students and educators during the COVID-19 pandemic. *VUE (Voices in Urban Education), 51*(1).

Thelamour, B., & Mwangi, C.A.G. (2021). "I disagreed with a lot of values": Exploring Black immigrant agency in ethnic-racial socialization. *International Journal of Intercultural Relations, 85*, 26–36.

Thomas, E. E., & Stornaiuolo, A. (2016). Restorying the self: Bending toward textual justice. *Harvard Educational Review, 86*(3), 313–338.

Thomas, K.J.A. (2012). Race and school enrollment among the children of African immigrants in the United States. *International Migration Review, 46*, 37–60.

Tierney, R. J. (2018). Toward a model of global meaning making. *Journal of Literacy Research, 50*(4), 397–422.

Toliver, R. (2014, Sept. 28). What are the children who grew up to become police officers learning in school?. *The New Republic.* https://newrepublic.com/article/119593/surprising-lessons-philadelphias-african-american-history-course

Toliver, S. R. (2020). Can I get a witness? Speculative fiction as testimony and counterstory. *Journal of Literacy Research, 52*(4), 507–529.

Tran, N., & Birman, D. (2019). Acculturation and assimilation: A qualitative inquiry of teacher expectations for Somali Bantu refugee students. *Education and Urban Society, 51*(5), 712–736.

Traoré, R. L. (2004). Colonialism continued: African students in an urban high school in America. *Journal of Black Studies, 34*, 348–369.

Traoré, R. L. (2006). Voices of African students in America. *Multicultural Perspectives, 8*(2), 29–34.

Traoré, R. L., & Lukens, R. J. (2006). *This isn't the America I thought I'd find: African students in the urban U.S. high school.* University Press of America.

Tuck, E., & Yang, K. W. (2014). R-words: Refusing research. In D. Paris & M. T. Winn (Eds.), *Humanizing research: Decolonizing qualitative inquiry with youth and communities* (pp. 223–247). Sage.

UC Regents. (2023). Getting started. https://yparhub.berkeley.edu/getting-started

Ukpokodu, O. N. (1996). Africa in today's social studies curriculum. *The Social Studies, 87*(3), 125–132.

Ukpokodu, O. N. (2013). Fostering African immigrant students' social and civic integration: Unpacking their ethnic distinctiveness. In E. Brown & A. Krasteva (Eds.), *International advances in education: Global initiatives for equity and social justice* (pp. 215–236). Information Age.

Ukpokodu, O. N. (2016). *You can't teach us if you don't know us and care about us: Becoming an Ubuntu, responsive, and responsible urban teacher.* Peter Lang Publishing, Inc.

Ukpokodu, O. N. (2017). Perspectives of African immigrant parents on U.S. PK–12 school system. In O. N. Ukpokodu & P. O. Otiato Ojiambo (Eds.), *Erasing invisibility, inequity and social injustice of Africans in the diaspora and the continent* (pp. 1–29). Cambridge Scholars.

Ukpokodu, O. N. (2018). African immigrants, the "new model minority": Examining the reality in U.S. K–12 schools. *The Urban Review, 50*(1), 69–96.

Ukpokodu, O. N., & Otiato Ojiambo, P. O. (Eds.). (2017). *Erasing invisibility, inequity and social injustice of Africans in the diaspora and the continent.* Cambridge Scholars.

Ukpokodu, O. N., & Ukpokodu, P. (Eds.). (2012). *Contemporary voices from the margin: African educators on African and American education.* Information Age.

United Nations. (n.d.). Feature: Emerging from the black hole—the UN's fight against youth radicalization. https://news.un.org/en/story/2015/05/499342

United Nations (n.d.): Peace, dignity, and equality. Universal Declaration of Human rights. https://www.un.org/en/about-us/universal-declaration-of-human-rights

United Nations. (1989, November). *Convention on the rights of the child.* Author.

United Nations Population Fund. (2014). *The power of 1.8 billion: Adolescents, youth and the transformation of the future.* Author.

References

U.S. Census Bureau. (2012). The foreign-born population in the United States: 2010. https://www.census.gov/library/publications/2012/acs/acs-19.html#:~:text=The%202010%20ACS%20estimated%20the,total%20population%20(Table%201).&text=The%20foreign%2Dborn%20population%20from,foreign%20born%20(Table%202)

Usman, L. M. (2012). Communication disorders and the inclusion of newcomer African refugees in rural primary schools of British Columbia, Canada. *International Journal of Progressive Education, 8*, 102–121.

Valenzuela, A. (1999). *Subtractive schooling: Issues of caring in education of US-Mexican youth.* State University of New York Press.

Vasudevan, L., & Riina-Ferrie, J. (2019). Collaborative filmmaking and affective traces of belonging. *British Journal of Educational Technology, 50*(4), 1560–1572.

Vasudevan, L., Stageman, D., Rodriguez, K., Fernandez, E., & Dattatreyan, E. G. (2010). Authoring new narratives with youth at the intersection of the arts and justice. *Penn GSE Perspectives on Urban Education, 7*(1), 54–65.

Vejar, A. (2019). Meet African Stars FC, Utah's newest soccer franchise. *The Salt Lake Tribune.* https://www.sltrib.com/sports/2019/03/15/meet-african-stars-fc

Vickery, A. E. (2015). It was never meant for us: Towards a Black feminist construct of citizenship in social studies. *The Journal of Social Studies Research, 39*(3), 163–172.

Walls, J. (2021). Tangles and glimmers: How African immigrant students in an urban charter school describe congruences and disconnections in caring between home and school. *The Urban Review, 53*(5), 761–784.

Walsh, A., & Burnett, S. (2021). 'Seeing power', co-creation and intersectionality in film-making by Ilizwi Lenyaniso Lomhlaba. In F. Mkwananz & F. M. Cin (Eds.), *Post-conflict participatory arts* (pp. 33–53). Routledge.

Wandera, D. B. (2016). Teaching poetry through collaborative art: An analysis of multimodal ensembles for transformative learning. *Journal of Transformative Education, 14*(4), 305–326.

Wandera, D. B. (2019). Resisting epistemic blackout: Illustrating Afrocentric methodology in a Kenyan classroom. *Reading Research Quarterly, 55*(4), 643–662.

Wandera, D. B., & Farr, M. (2018). Interrupting ideologies of cultural deficiency: Illustrating curricular benefits of plurilingualism in a Kenyan classroom. *Journal of Language and Literacy Education, 14*(1).

Warrican, S. J. (2020). Toward caring language and literacy classrooms for Black immigrant youth: Combating raciolinguistic ideologies and moral licensing. *Teachers College Record, 122*(13), 1–22.

Wasser, J. D., & Bressler, L. (1996). Working in the interpretive zone: Conceptualizing collaboration in qualitative research. *Educational Researcher, 25*(5), 5–15.

Waters, M. C. (1994). Ethnic and racial identities of second generation Black immigrants in New York City. *International Migration Review, 28*(4), 795–820.

Waters, M. (1999). *Black identities: West Indian immigrant dreams and American realities.* Harvard University Press.

Watkins, J. (2021). List of female Africa presidents. https://afjn.org/list-of-female-africa-presidents-updated-july-2021

Watkinson, J. S., & Hersi, A. A. (2014). School counselors supporting African immigrant students' career development: A case study. *Career Development Quarterly, 62*, 44–55.

Watson, V.W.M. (2018). Envisioning the already-present literacy and learning of youth. *English Journal, 107*(5), 10–11.

Watson, V.W.M., & Beymer, A. (2019). Praisesongs of place: Youth envisioning space and place in a literacy-and-songwriting initiative. *Research in the Teaching of English, 53*(4), 297–319.

Watson, V.W.M., Johnson, L. E., Pena-Pincheira, R., Berends, J., & Chen, S. (2022). Locating a pedagogy of love: (Re)framing pedagogies of loss in popular-media narratives of African immigrant communities. *International Journal of Qualitative Studies in Education, 35*(6), 588–608.

Watson, V.W.M., & Knight-Manuel, M. G. (2017). Challenging popularized narratives of immigrant youth from West Africa: Examining social processes of navigating identities and engaging civically. *Review of Research in Education, 41*(1), 279–310.

Watson, V.W.M., & Knight-Manuel, M. G. (2020). Humanizing the Black immigrant body: Envisioning diaspora literacies of youth and young adults from West African countries. *Teachers College Record, 122*(13), 1–28.

Watson, V.W.M., Knight, M. G., & Jaffee, A. T. (2014). Beyond #talking and #texting: African immigrant youth's social–civic literacies and negotiations of citizenship across participatory new media technologies. *Citizenship Teaching & Learning, 10*(1), 43–62.

Watson, V.W.M., & Marciano, J. E. (2015). Examining a social-participatory youth co-researcher methodology: A cross-case analysis extending possibilities of literacy and research. *Literacy, 49*(1), 37–44.

Watson, V.W.M., Oviatt, R. L., Flennaugh, T., Byrd, C., Deloach, R., Jackson, S., & Pugh, J. (2020). "This research that we are doing is just the beginning of the conversation": Undergraduate researchers examining transition experiences. *The Journal of College Orientation, Transition, and Retention, 7*(2).

Watson, V.W.M., & Petrone, R. (2020). "On a day like this": How a youth epistemological approach can shape English education. *English Teaching: Practice and Critique, 19*(3), 245–251.

Whitelaw, J. (2019). *Arts-based teaching and learning in the literacy classroom: Cultivating a critical aesthetic practice*. Routledge.

Whitley, J., & Hollweck, T. (2020). Inclusion and equity in education: Current policy reform in Nova Scotia, Canada. *Prospects, 49*(3), 297–312.

Wiley, K. (2005). Napoleon leading the army over the Alps [Painting]. Brooklyn Museum, Brooklyn, NY, United States. https://www.brooklynmuseum.org/opencollection/objects/169803

Wilson, J., & Habecker, S. (2008). The lure of the capital city: An anthro-geographical analysis of recent African immigration to Washington, DC. *Population, Space and Place, 14*, 433–448.

Woods, J. C., Jr. (2021). Un(bundling) the Black experience at PWIs: Using assets-based frameworks to explore the lived experiences of black Sub-Sharan African-born graduate students in STEM. *Journal of Comparative & International Higher Education, 13*(5S).

References

227

Woodson, C. G. (1990). *The mis-education of the Negro*. Africa World Press. (Original work published 1933)

Woodson, C. G. (1933). *The mis-education of the Negro. Washington, DC: Associated Publishers.*

World Health Organization. (2019). Adolescent and Health and Development. World Health Organization. www.searo.who.int/entity/child_adolscent /topics/ adolescent_health/em/

Wynter, S. (2003). Unsettling the coloniality of being/power/truth/freedom: Towards the human, after man, its overrepresentation—An argument. *CR: The New Centennial Review*, *3*(3), 257–337.

Yeboah, N. (2016). *Performing "Afrika":* Sankofa *and the construction of post-colonial Black African identity in Ghana* (Publication No. 10043995) [Doctoral dissertation, Northwestern University]. ProQuest Dissertations.

Yosso, T. J. (2005). Whose culture has capital? A critical race theory discussion of community cultural wealth. *Race, Ethnicity and Education*, *8*(1), 69–91.

Young Center for Immigrant Children. (2020). *African immigrant children in America: Caught between hope and reality*. https://www.theyoungcenter.org/stories /2020/10/1/african-immigrant-children-in-america-caught-between-hope-and -reality

YouTube (nd). Ebola (La La) ~~ Parody of Fergie "LA Love" ~ Rucka Rucka Ali. https://www.youtube.com/watch?v=hiSsrEg3tks

Yusuf, E. (2020). *Experiences of institutional racism: Black graduate students navigating higher education* [Unpublished MEd thesis. University of Toronto].

Zong, J., & Batalova, J. (2014, October 30). Sub-Saharan African immigrants in the United States. Migration Information Source. https://www.migrationpolicy.org /article/sub-saharan-african-immigrants-united-states-2

Zong, J., & Batalova, J. (2016). The limited English proficient population in the United States. Migration Policy Institute. http://www.migrationpolicy.org/article /limited-english-proficient-population-united-states

Zong, J., & Batalova, J. (2017). *African immigrants in the United States*. Retrieved from http://www.migrationpolicy.org/article/sub-saharan-african-immigrants -united-states.

Index

Abdi, A. A., 46–47, 51, 154
Abdi, C. M., 141
Abu-Bader, S. H., 35
Abu El-Haj, T. R., 87–90, 93, 95, 97
Abu-Ras, W., 35
Achebe, Chinua, 40, 82
Achieng (STEM student), 18, 71–82, 193
Adama (film student), 110, 112, 117, 123–125
Addai-Mununkum, R., 11, 100, 108
Addams, Jane, 24
Adebisi, A., 150, 151
Adekanmbi, G., 100
Adenekan, O. K., 11
Adeniji-Neil, D., 150, 151
Adeola, O. A., 100
Adichie, C. N., 4, 17, 45, 165
Affect, of Congolese immigrant parents toward
    student learning, 100, 107–108
Afolalu, Lakeya, 13, 16, 100, 144, 161–172, 195
Afolayan, M. O., 6
African American Educational Achievement Plan
    (AAEAP), 164
African American History (AAH) class, 18–19,
    54–67; Black Lives Matter movement and,
    54, 57–58, 61–67; classroom and course
    descriptions, 55–56; Honors Academy, 18,
    54, 56–67; "Little Africa" neighborhood in
    Philadelphia and, 55; racial self-making and
    spacemaking and, 57, 58–67
African American students: adversarial
    relationship with Black African immigrant
    youth, 5–6, 37, 65; civic identities of,
    131–132; differences with Black African
    immigrant youth, 26–27, 34–36, 40, 63, 88,
    136, 140
African and Black Diaspora (journal), 10
African Club, 85–86, 129–142; civic identities
    of African American youth, 131–132;
    implications and conclusion, 141–142;
    methodology and findings, 133–141; nature
    of cultural/ethnic clubs, 132–133; theoretical
    framework, 130–131

African Family Health Organization (AFO),
    111, 113–114, 125
African Indigenous Knowledge systems, 18,
    40, 48–49, 50–52, 193. *See also* Indigenous
    (immigrant) ways of knowing
Africanness, history of legitimizing, 9–10
African Union Youth Charter, 26
Afrofuturism, 14; African Indigenous
    Knowledges and, 18, 40, 48–49, 50–52, 193;
    Binti (Okorafor), 18, 43, 45, 47–49, 51–53,
    193
After-school programs. *See* African Club;
    Participatory curriculum design/Lit Diaspora
Agar, M., 159
Agosto, V., 117
Agyepong, M., 4–6, 9, 11, 17, 30, 164
Ahola, A. N., 4
Akin-Sabuncu, Sibel, 13, 16, 85–86, 129–142,
    134, 194
Alaazi, D. A., 4, 108
Ali, A., 87–89
Alim, H. S., 130, 145, 162, 196
Allen, K. M., 7–8, 54, 131
Alter, Z., 179
Alvarez, P., 9
Alvarez, S., 100
Amaize, O., 184
Amanti, C., 159
American Civil Liberties Union, 22, 25
American Community Survey (ACS), 24, 27
American Educational Research Association, 184
American Psychological Association, 4
Amina of Kano, Queen, 33
Ammon, R., 150, 151
Amonyeze, C., 45
Anderson, M., 3, 148
Anderson, R., 193–195
Angolan immigrants/youth, migration through
    Mexico, 4
Aniya (history student), 59–63, 65
Annamma, S., 134
Annan, Kofi, 33

228

Index

Anti-Blackness. *See also* Curriculum violence; Deficit-based approaches; Racial violence; Racism: African immigrant communities and, 4; after-school African Club and, 85–86, 139–141; attitudes of Congolese immigrant parents toward student learning and, 100; Black African immigrant youth violence and, 31–41; contexts in the U.S. and globally, 10, 14, 194
Anucha, U., 7
Apple, M. W., 23
Arbery, Ahmaud, 22
Argenal, A., 88, 96, 97
Aroian, K. J., 35
Arthur, J. A., 2, 5
Asante, M. K., 9–10
Ashcroft, B., 165, 169, 171
Asian immigrants/youth, 131, 150, 153, 164
Àsìkò, 1, 192
Asim, J., 193
Asimeng-Boahene, L., 158
Asylees. *See* Refugees/asylees
Attewell, P., 46
Attiah, K., 185, 186–187
Australia, Black African immigrants/youth and, 7
Avoseh, Mejai Bola M., 2, 3, 51, 89, 95, 100, 177–178, 183, 185
Awokoya, J. T., 2, 6, 24, 27–29, 35, 88, 94, 129, 133, 163–164, 193
Ayalew, T., 108

Badaki, OreOluwa, 13, 16, 86, 110–128, 115, 194
Baffoe, M., 158
Bah, Mohamed, 25
Bajaj, M., 88, 96, 97
Bakar, A., 10
Baker-Bell, April, 28, 145, 149, 162, 165–168, 196
Ball, A. F., 10, 145, 162, 196
Ball, D. L., 66
Balogun, O. M., 6
Banda, Joyce Hilda, 34
Bangura, R., 7–8, 174
Banking model (Freire), 115
Banks, J. A., 3, 31, 38, 154
Bartlett, L., 88, 96
Baruch College, 129
Basch, L., 88, 90
Basford, L., 7
Bass, J., 182
Batalova, J., 1, 2, 4, 6, 9, 24, 35, 41, 148, 149
Bauer, E. B., 10, 163, 175
Bayeck, R. Y., 11
Beaman, J., 7
Bellepeau, Agnes Monique Ohsan, 34
Bennett, K., 192

Bennett, C. L., 29
Bentley, C. C., 158
Berends, Joel E., 9, 11, 13, 16, 33, 144, 173–190, 174, 184, 195–196
Bertrand, M., 173, 179, 180
Beymer, Alecia, 174
Bhattacharya, K., 45
Biden, Joe, 9
Bigelow, M., 6
Biklen, S. K., 134
Binte-Farid, I. A., 11
Binti (Okorafor), 18, 43, 45, 47–49, 51–53, 193
Birman, D., 10, 11, 147
Bitew, G., 7
Black, Indigenous, People of Color (BIPOC), 22–24
Black African immigrant youth (BAIY): academic exceptionalism myth, 4, 9, 24, 31–32, 36, 87; adversarial relationship with African American students, 5–6, 37, 65; anti-blackness and (*see* Anti-Blackness); in Canada (*see* Canada); challenges to misperceptions of Africa, 139–141; civic identities (*see* Civic engagement); context of contemporary migration and, 2–5; countries of origin, 27 (*see also names of specific groups from specific African countries*); critical literacies and (*see* Critical pedagogy/literacies); deficit approaches and (*see* Deficit-based approaches); differences with African American youth, 26–27, 34–36, 40, 63, 88, 136, 140; disciplinary problems and, 28; Ebola fears and, 4, 28, 29–30, 39, 111; in France (*see* France); heterogeneity of Black student experiences, 18–19, 35, 52–53, 54, 66–67; immigrant trends, 148–149; immigration statuses of, 26–27, 34–35, 43–45, 153; indigenous (immigrant) ways of knowing and (*see* African Indigenous Knowledge systems; Indigenous (immigrant) ways of knowing); institutional reckoning in U.S. schools and, 34–36; intersectional identities of, 2, 3, 11, 85, 113–114, 134, 140; invisibility of, 34–35, 37, 39, 40, 163–166, 169–171; lived realities in U.S. schools, 23–26, 27–41 (*see also* United States); marginalization and (*see* Marginalization (microaggressions)); Muslim youth (*see* Muslim youth); nature and characteristics of, 26–27; new African Diaspora and (*see* Diaspora studies); as a new model minority, 4, 9, 24, 31–32, 36, 87; population growth trends, 2–4, 41; racial violence and (*see* Racial violence); social cohesion and after-school club, 85–86, 129–142; Ubuntu-oriented education and, 37–38, 40–41; in the United Kingdom, 24

Black Alliance for Just Immigration, 25
Black immigrant literacies (P. Smith), 145, 196
Black language pedagogy (Baker-Bell), 145, 196
Black Lives Matter movement, 19, 22, 23, 54, 57–58, 61–67, 117–120, 193–194
Blackness: "Africanness" and new power dynamics in film course, 113–114; history of legitimizing, 9–10; invisibility of Black African immigrant youth, 34–35, 37, 39, 40, 163–166, 169–171; role in transforming educational experiences, 4; U.S.-centric vs. African-diasporic, 54; Whiteness vs., 195
Black Panther (2018 film), 1, 33, 161, 192
Blanc-Szanton, C., 88, 90
Blizzard, B., 9
Blommaert, J., 147
Blow, C., 141
Boal, Augusto, 110, 113, 115–117, 123–124, 126, 127
Boateng, Sandra, 15, 17–19
Bogdan, R. C., 134
Bokhari, E., 140
Bordonaro, A., 194
Born a Crime (Noah), 51
Boutte, G., 3, 11, 24, 50, 51
Boveda, M., 134
Boyte, H. C., 114
Braden, E. G., 10, 11, 100, 164
Braimoh, D., 100
Bredell, K. H., 54–56
Bressler, L., 134
Brion-Meisels, G., 179
Brobbey, G., 10, 132–133, 163, 164
Brooklyn Museum, 192
Brooks, M. D., 173, 179
Brooks, Rayshard, 22
Browdy, R., 11
Brown, Adrienne, 191–193
Brown, F., 163
Brown, Michael, 22
Brown, N., 29
Brunet, S., 78
Bryan, K., 10
Bryan, N., 24, 51
Bryce-Laporte, R. S., 164
Bucceri, J. M., 28
Bucholtz, M., 100, 108–109
Bukola, S., 4
Bullying, 27, 28–29, 35, 37, 110–111, 125, 166
Burger, B., 49, 51–52
Burkina Faso immigrants/youth, police brutality and, 25
Burnett, S., 118
Burundian immigrants/youth, 7

Busia, A. P., 143, 195
Byrd, C., 179, 182, 183

Caiah (history student), 60, 62–63, 65
Calabrese Barton, A. C., 175
Camangian, P., 173, 179
Cameroonian immigrants, police brutality and, 25
Cammarota, J., 134
Campano, G., 115
Campbell, D. D., 38
Canada: Black African immigrants/youth and, 5, 7, 24, 44, 46–47; Black female STEM education in Ontario, 18, 68–83; postsecondary education experiences of African immigrants in, 44, 46–47
Canady, A., 173, 179
Canlas, M., 88, 96, 97
Capodilupo, C. M., 28
Capps, R., 1, 2, 27
Caraballo, L., 179
Caring, 40–41
Carnegie Endowment for International Peace, 22
Carotenuto, M., 187
Carr, W., 116
Carroll, K. K., 9–10
Cascone, S., 192
Case, A. D., 140
Casillas, D. L., 100, 108–109
CBS, 32–34, 35
Césaire, A., 165, 169, 171
Chareka, O., 2, 7
Chen, S., 9, 11, 33, 174, 184
Chikkatur, A. P., 56
Chilisa, B., 9–10, 18, 100, 103, 108, 134
Chinese international students, 150
Citizen-centered politics (Boyte), 114
Civic engagement: after-school African Club, 85–86, 129–142; filmmaking in, 86, 110–128, 194–195; participatory civic learning and action-taking, 8, 9–10, 138; Sankofan approach and (*see* Sankofan approach); transnational approach to (*see* Transnational civic engagement)
Clandinin, D. J., 70
Clark, D., 192
Clark, M. K., 6
Clark, V. A., 3
Clarke, K. M., 57
Clay, K. L., 113
CNN Newsroom, 192
Coalition of Communities of Color, 29, 39
Cobb, C. E., 45
Cochran-Smith, M., 116
Coe, I., 68

Index

Cole, M., 114, 116
Coles, J. A., 54
Collaboration, in mathematics instruction, 49–52
Colletti, R., 28
Collins, S., 93
Colorism, in the U.S., 21–22
Community Cultural Wealth (CCW) framework, 14, 18, 69–82; aspirational capital, 69, 72–74, 79, 150; familial capital, 69, 72, 74, 80, 150; linguistic capital, 69; navigational capital, 69, 72–79, 81; resistance capital, 69; social capital, 69, 76–79, 81
Congolese immigrants/youth, 7; migration through Mexico, 4, 101; parent perspectives on student learning, 99–109, 194–195; participatory curriculum design/Lit Diaspora and, 173; police brutality and, 25
Cooper, H., 4
Corrêa, Priscila Dias, 13, 15, 18, 68–83, 69, 81, 193
Cosby, M. D., 11, 45–46
Council on American Islamic Relations, 35
Counterstorying, 15, 176, 178–179, 188–189
Countryman, M., 56
COVID-19 pandemic, 11, 73, 181–182; filmmaking with African immigrant girls during, 86, 110–128
Covington-Ward, Y., 27, 33
Critical pedagogy/literacies, vii–viii, 38–40; African American History (AAH) class and, 56, 65–67; critical mathematics education (CME), 18, 49–52; culturally responsive curriculum and, 38–40; defined, 38; film/theater-making and, 114–116, 117–126; importance for BAIY), 38–40; multilingualism, 36, 103, 148–150, 168–169
Critical Race Theory: Community Cultural Wealth (CCW) framework and, 14, 18, 69–82; diaspora narratives and, vii (see also Diaspora studies)
Croom, M., 175
Cultural ecology theory (Ogbu), 26
Culturally relevant education, 7–8, 14; after-school club, 85–86, 129–142
Culturally responsive education, 9, 10, 38–40, 112
Culturally sensitive education, 8
Culturally sustaining education, 85–86, 129–142
Curriculum design: curriculum violence and (see Curriculum violence); participatory (see Participatory curriculum design/Lit Diaspora)
Curriculum violence, 29–41; absence of curricular materials, 30–31; institutional reckoning and, 34–36; linguicism in, 30;

nature of, 29–31; recommendations to eliminate, 36–41; societal reckoning and, 32–34; worksheet curriculum and, 31
Curry-Stevens, A., 29, 39

Dabach, D. B., 165
Dallavis, C., 130
Damba Danjo, Nyimasata, 13, 15, 18, 43–53, 100, 193
Danielle, B., 1
Darling, J., 175, 177
Daro, Mr. (history teacher), 54, 56–67
Dattatreyan, E. G., 115, 116
Dávila, Liv T., 7, 10, 13, 16, 86, 88, 96, 99–109, 101–102, 165, 194
Davis, Jordan, 22
Dawn, Mrs. (teacher), 161, 164
Daza, S. L., 171
Decolonizing methodologies, 14–15, 154–160
De Costa, P., 180
Deficit-based approaches, 13, 21, 67, 68–70, 82, 85, 92, 99, 150, 159; applied vs. academic courses in STEM disciplines, 68–69; Black superheroes in reframing, 1, 33, 161, 192; Community Cultural Wealth (CCW) framework and, 14, 18, 69–82; countering with participatory curriculum design, 173–174, 177, 179; curriculum violence and, 29–41; Ebola virus and, 4, 28, 29–30, 39, 111; education of immigrant parents and, 102, 108; filmmaking in countering, 111–112, 125; misperception of Africa, 33–34, 36, 39, 139–141; Muslims and, 97 (see also Muslim youth); non-credit-bearing (NCBR) mathematics courses, 46, 47; rightful literary presence in disrupting, 173–174; stereotyping and stigmatizing of Black Africans, 32–34, 36, 45–47; Trump and "shithole" countries statement, 24, 39; Trump immigration restrictions and border security, 8–9, 94, 101; watchlist of "bad" countries, 32
De Haas, H., 149
De Haene, L., 72, 99, 108
Dei, G. J. S., 2, 9–10, 18, 87–89, 95, 130, 193
Deloach, R., 179, 182, 183
De los Ríos, C. V., 173, 175, 179
Delta Airlines, biased presentation of Ghana, 34
Democratic Republic of Congo (DRC). See Congolese immigrants/youth
Deng, Jonathan, 25
Dernikos, B. P., 103
Desai, K., 8
Diallo, Amadou, 24, 25
Diallo, R., 94
Diamond, K. K., 76

Diaspora studies, 14. *See also* Participatory curriculum design/Lit Diaspora; *African and Black Diaspora* (journal), 10; Black Lives Matter movement and, 19, 54, 57–58, 61–67; critical consciousness of home, 92–97; diaspora literacy (King), 145, 195, 196; diasporic Blacks and colorism on the U.S., 21–22; diasporic networks and, 90–91, 94–96; diversity of routes to the U.S., 88; interconnecting diasporic struggles of Black lives worldwide, 18–19, 65–67; new African Diaspora and, 2; ongoing violence in the African diaspora, 194; transnational civic engagement and, 87–97; understandings of Blackness and, 57; waves of existing scholarship on, 5–11

Diazgranados Ferráns, S., 138

Digital literacy, 141. *See also* Filmmaking with African immigrant girls

Dillard, C. B., 7, 9–10

Dinamic (Congolese student), 13, 16, 144, 173–190, 195–196

Dingfelder, S., 192

Dinishak, J., 70

Disadvantage, overlapping structures of, 76

Disciplinary problems, microaggressions and, 28

Discretionary spaces (D. L. Ball), 66

Divergent (Roth), 93

Dixon, I. R., 158

Dixon-Román, E. J., 46

Dlamini, S. N., 7

Domina, T., 46

Dominguez, A. D., 173, 179

Doucet, F., 132, 133, 137, 162–163, 166–167, 169

Doukmak, N., 10

Dozono, T., 97

Dreas-Shaikha Maryann J., 13, 16, 86, 110–128, 194

Dryden-Peterson, S., 7, 99

Du Bois, W. E. B., 9–10, 21–22, 191–193

Duchneskien, J., 55

Dumas, M. J., 4, 32, 129, 139

Duncan, G. A., 163, 167

Dundes, L., 9

Dyrness, A., 87, 88, 90, 93, 95

Ebola virus, 4, 28, 29–30, 39, 111

Echeverria-Estrada, C., 6

Edstrom, L., 8, 27

Ehret, C., 100

Ekeh, Harold, 4

Emerson, R. M., 134

Enin, Kwasi, 4

Enriquez, G., 115

Enumah, L., 66

Erasing Invisibility, Inequality and Social Injustice of Africans in the Diaspora and the Continent (Ukpokodu & OtiatoOjiambo), 7

Eritrian immigrants/youth, 27

Esquilin, M., 28

Essence magazine, 1

Esterline, C., 149

Esteve, F., 192

Ethiopian immigrants/youth, 7, 55. *See also* African American History (AAH) class

Ethnography, filmmaking and, 15, 116–126

Everson, H. T., 46

Falola, T., 2

Families. *See* Parents/families

Fanon, F., 88, 165, 169

Farr, M., 11

Fasheh, M., 48, 52

Fawcett, E., 180

Feinberg, R., 4

Felix, David, 25

Ferguson, D. E., 103

Ferguson, P., 7

Fernández, C., 111, 116–118, 120, 125, 127

Fernandez, E., 115

Fernandez, M., 4

Ferris, R., 3

Filmmaking with African immigrant girls, 86, 110–128, 194–195; African Family Health Organization (AFO) and, 111, 113–114, 125; "Africanness" and new power dynamics, 113–114; conceptual framework, 114–116; context of course, 111–113; methodology and findings, 116–126

Fine, M., 87–89, 134

Fix, M., 1, 2, 27

Flahaux, M., 149

Flennaugh, T., 179, 182, 183

Flores, Nelson, 145, 165, 166, 168, 196

Flowers, D., 8

Floyd, George, 22, 25

Fones, A., 165

Fragmentation, 39

Framework for Educating African Immigrant Youth, 11–14, 127; approach 1: emboldening, 12, 13, 14, 52, 82, 191; approach 2: navigating pasts, presents, and futures, 12, 13, 14, 111–112, 125, 191; approach 3: envisioning and enacting social civic literacies, 12, 13, 14, 191; approach 4: affirming and extending cultural heritage and embodied knowledge, 12, 13, 14, 52–53, 54, 85, 88, 96, 97, 137, 143, 147–160, 171–172, 191

France: Black African immigrants/youth in, 7, 25; Kadija (Muslim student) ties to, 85,

Index

90–94, 96; Paris terror attack (2015), 90–91, 93; police brutality against Black African youth, 25
Frankenstein, M., 45
Franklin, Benjamin, 24
Franklin, R., 148
Freeman, K., 78
Freire, Paulo, 38, 110, 114–115, 117, 120, 122, 127, 183
Frels, R. K., 184
French, Howard W., 32–34
Fretz, R. I., 134
Fülöp, M., 148
Funds of knowledge (González et al.), 159. *See also* Indigenous (immigrant) ways of knowing

Gadsden, V. L., 175
Galarneau, D., 78
Gallagher, K., 119, 125
Gambian immigrants/youth, Nyimasata Damba Danjo as example, 44–45
Garcia, A., 179
Garcia, P., 111, 116–118, 120, 125, 127
García-Cabrero, B., 138
Gay, G., 37
Gaze, of researchers, 18, 165, 169, 195
Gee, D. S., 17
Gee, J. P., 38, 166
Geertz, C., 167
Gender: *Binti* (Okorafor, Afrofuturist novella), 18, 43, 45, 47–49, 51–53, 193; filmmaking with African immigrant girls, 86, 110–128, 194–195; image theater (Boal) and female African bodies, 123–125; mathematics instruction and, 43–53, 193; moving away from women as victims, 125; notable female African leaders, 33–34; in STEM undergraduate disciplinary context, 17, 18, 44–45, 68–83, 193; stereotypes of Muslim bodies and, 89, 96–97; strong female characters in fiction, 93
Ghaffar-Kucher, A., 87–89
Ghanaian immigrants/youth, 7; acceptance by Ivy League colleges and universities, 4; biased presentations of Ghana and, 34; *Sankofa* and (*see* Sankofan approach)
Ghiso, M. P., 115
Gholson, M. L., 45
Ghong, M., 24, 27, 28, 38–39
Ghosh, S., 150, 158
Gibson, V., 11
Gigi (history student), 59–62, 65
Gilroy, Paul, 114
Girls Write Now, 93
Glaude, E. S., Jr., 22

Glick-Schiller, N., 88, 90
Global Migration Group, 26
Godreau, I. P., 65
González, N., 159
Goodwin, A. L., 23, 31
Gordon, A., 2
A Grain of Wheat (Ngugi Wa Thiong'o), 40
Grant, C. A., 129
Graves, Ms. (teacher), 161
Greene, G., 11, 50, 51
Griffiths, G., 165, 169, 171
Grinage, J., 100, 103
Grumet, M. R., 115
Guadalupe Pérez, M., 138
Guinean immigrants/youth. *See also* African American History (AAH) class: Kabeera (history student), 18, 54, 56, 57–66; police brutality and, 24, 25, 55, 58, 61–67
Gurib-Fakim, Ameenah, 34
Gustavo, S., 3
Gutstein, E., 49
Guy, T. C., 164

Haas-Dyson, Anne H., 162
Habecker, S., 6
Haddix, M., 115
Hailu, M. F., 2, 10, 74–75
Haitian immigrants/youth: cultural/ethnic clubs, 132–133; police brutality and, 25
Hansler, J., 9
Hartocollis, A., 180
Harushimana, I., 6, 24, 27–29, 129, 193
Hassan, Samia Suluhu, 34
Hatoss, A., 7
Hauslohner, A., 55
Hayes, A., 28
Heath, Shirley Brice, 114, 116, 162
Henry, A., 143, 195
Hera (STEM student), 18, 71–82, 193
Hersi, A. A., 7
Hip-hop culture, 5, 6, 157
Hirsi, I., 188
Holder, A. M. B., 28
Holloway, L., 182
Hollweck, T., 68
Holsey, B., 65
Hotchkins, B. K., 10
Hoye, S., 28
Hucks, D. C., 175
Hull, G. A., 166
Human Rights First, 25
Hunger Games (Collins), 93
Hunter, C. D., 140

Ibrahim, A. E. K. M., 5, 143, 163, 165, 195
Ibrahim, Awid, vii–viii, 6–7

234 Index

Identity formation, viii, 28–29, 44, 129; civic identities (*see* Civic engagement); filmmaking with African immigrant girls and, 86, 110–128, 194–195; intersectional identities and, 2, 3, 11, 85, 113–114, 134, 140; invisibility of Black African immigrant youth and, 34–35, 37, 39, 40, 163–166, 169–171
Ighodaro, E., 29
Ikhane, P. A., 100
Ikime, O., 168
Ikpeze, C., 6
Ima, K., 130n
Image theater (Boal), 123–125
Imasuen, Sarai (Nigerian student), 161–162, 164–167
Imoagene, O., 4, 7, 17, 54
Indigenous (immigrant) ways of knowing, 18, 109, 147–160; African Indigenous Knowledge systems and, 18, 40, 48–49, 50–52, 193; Akan (Ghana) concept of *Sankofa*, 151–152, 159 (*see also* Sankofan approach); Bengali *mem-bedesh* vs. *desi*, 150, 152, 159; cultural apparatuses for analyzing immigrant youth acculturation, 158–159; decolonizing methodologies, 14–15, 154–160; interepistemic synergy approach (Wandera) and, 148, 154–160; Kikuyu (Kenyan) concept of *harambee*-inspired collectivism, 155–159; literature review, 148–152; methodology and findings, 153–158; research questions, 152; understanding immigrant cultural assets, 159–160; Yoruban (Nigeria) concept of *Omoluabi*, 150–151, 152, 159
Interepistemic synergy approach (Wandera), 148, 154–160
Invisible Sojourners (Arthur), 2, 5
Ip, C., 32

Jackson, I., 7–8, 54, 131
Jackson, J., 11
Jackson, J. L, Jr., 116
Jackson, S., 179, 182, 183
Jackson, S. A., 57
Jacquet, M., 7
Jaffee, A. T., 8, 97, 130–132
Jaji, TsiTsi, 114
Jamaican immigrants/youth, Achieng (student), 18, 71–82, 193
Jensen, E., 3
Johnson, E., 115
Johnson, G. L., 3, 50
Johnson, Lauren Elizabeth Reine, 9, 11, 33, 174, 184
Johnson, L. J., 11
Johnson, Lyndon B., 24

Jones, Jasmine L. Blanks, 13, 16, 86, 110–128, 111, 112, 113, 114, 116, 194
Jones, N., 3
Jordan, S., 2, 10
Joseph, G. G., 52
Joseph, N., 140

Kabeera (history student), 18, 54, 56, 57–66, 193–194
Kadija (Muslim student), 85–97
Kah, H., 137
Kajee, L., 149
Kamya, H. A., 5
Kanno. Y., 7
Kanté, N'Golo, 176–178, 183, 184
Keatley, E., 72, 99, 108
Kebede, K., 10
Keegan, Patrick, 10, 13, 15, 17, 85, 87–98, 88, 89, 91, 97, 194
Kelland, Z., 34
Kelly, L. L., 180
Kemmis, S., 116
Kendi, I. X., 4
Kenyan immigrants/youth, 7, 11, 149; Kikuyu (Kenyan) concept of *harambee*-inspired collectivism, 155–159; parents/families and, 153–154
Kenyatta, J., 153
Keunang, Charley "Africa," 25
Khabeer, S. A. A., 57
Khala, Matt, 185
Khamala, Dorothy, 15–16, 85–86
Kim, J. H., 70
Kim, W. J., 175
King, J. E., 5–6, 129, 143, 145, 195, 196
Kingsley, M., 54
Kiningi, Slyvie, 33
Kiramba, L. K., 10–11, 17, 28, 70, 72, 74, 78, 80, 88, 100, 133, 149, 163–165
Kirkland, D. E., 132, 133, 137
Knight, Michelle G., 2, 7–8, 12, 27, 54, 71, 88–89, 96, 97, 130–132, 138, 158, 163, 174, 175
Knight-Manuel, Michelle G., 1–16, 2–10, 15–16, 17, 45, 52, 56, 85–89, 91, 93, 94, 100, 115, 118, 119, 125, 129–142, 130–132, 134, 139, 149–150, 158, 163–164, 177, 179, 191–196, 193, 194
Kontovourki, S., 115
Koyama, J. P., 129
Kress, G., 116
Kubengana, Dinamic, 13, 16, 144, 173–190, 195–196
Kumi-Yeboah, A., 2, 10–11, 24, 27–29, 72, 74, 80, 88, 100, 108, 131–133, 149, 163, 164

Index

Ladson-Billings, G., 3, 130, 159
Language and literacy: Black African literacies, 33, 162–166; Black American/Black English youth language practices, 162–166; Congolese immigrant parents and, 100, 105–106, 107, 108; English language proficiency, 36, 38, 46–47, 86, 149, 153, 163–165, 166, 168–169, 171; home language proficiency, 38, 104, 108, 153–154; of Kenyan immigrants/youth, 149; linguicism as curriculum violence, 30; linguistic bias, 39; linguistic capital, 69; moving beyond talk-centric forms of student participation, 167–172; multilingualism, 36, 103, 148–150, 168–169; multiliteracies, 161–162, 166–172; of Nigerian immigrant youth, 161–162, 164–167; visual arts in navigating linguistic discrimination, 163, 167–172
Larcher, A., 116
Larke, P. J., 24, 27, 28, 38–39
Larnell, G. V., 46, 47
Latinx immigrants/youth, 40, 68, 88, 93, 95, 131, 140, 141, 164
Lavin, D., 46
Leander, K. M., 100
Lee, C. C., 8, 11, 12, 147, 150
Lee, C. D., 3, 175
Lee, J. S., 100, 108–109, 182
Lee, S., 6
Lee, W., 4
Legislative theater (Boal), 126
Leonard, J., 45
Levey, T., 46
Levitt, P., 90
Lewis, C., 174
Liberian immigrants/youth, 7, 55. *See also* African American History (AAH) class; B4 Youth Theatre, 114
Literacy Futurisms Collective-in-the-Making, 8
Liu, K., 10
Lorenzi, J., 1, 24, 41
Lowenhaupt, R., 11
Lozenski, B. D., 3, 167, 179, 180
Luke, A., 115
Lukens, R. J., 5, 19, 24, 54, 164
Lukose, Ritty, 87, 88, 90
Luttrell, W., 91
Lyiscott, J. J., 179
Lyola, Patrick, 25
Lytle, S. L., 116

Maathai, Wangari, 33
Madagascaran immigrants/youth, 7
Madison, D. S., 163, 167
Maestripieri, L., 76
Mafeni, B. O. W., 168

Mahaba, Ally, 157
Mahiri, J., 166
Makoni, S. B., 154
Mallozzi, C. A., 115
Mandela, Nelson, 24, 33
Mann, Horace, 24
Manyoun, Deng, 25
Marciano, J. E., 179, 182
Marginalization (microaggressions). *See also* Deficit-based approaches: attitudes of Congolese immigrant parents toward student learning and, 100; bullying, 27, 28–29, 35, 37, 110, 125, 166; curriculum violence, 29–41; Ebola virus and, 4, 28, 29–30, 39, 111; misperception of Africa, 33–34, 36, 39, 139–141; Muslim youth and (*see* Muslim youth); nature of microaggressions, 27–28; "Other" and Othering, 30, 31, 47, 53, 129; persistence of, 27; racialized marginalization, 27–29; triple/quadruple marginality of Black African immigrant youth in the U.S., 22; types of, 28
Marrero-Guillamón, I., 116
Martin, D. B., 45
Martin, Trayvon, 22
Martina (film student), 112, 117, 118–121
Martinez, D. C., 173, 179
Masakure, O., 46–47
Mas Giralt, R., 149
Masinda, M. T., 7
Maswabi, K., 49
Mathematics, 43–53; asset-based lens/ community cultural wealth perspective and, 18; *Binti* (Okorafor, Afrofuturist novella), 18, 43, 45, 47–49, 51–53, 193; collaborative instruction in, 18, 49–52; critical African perspectives in, 18, 49–52; non-credit-bearing (NCBR) courses, 46, 47; stereotypes concerning Black African immigrant youth and, 45–47; tessallating triangle braids, 43, 48, 52; as "tool for liberation," 45–47
Matsepe-Cassaburi, Ivy, 33
Matza, M., 55
Mawuli-Sallar, A., 10, 11, 72, 74, 80, 88, 133, 149
Mazrui, Ali, 33
Mburu, W., 138
McArdle, J. J., 46
McCabe, K., 1, 2, 27
McClain, S., 149
McDade, Kendreck, 22
McDade, Tony, 22
McKenzie, L., 180
McLean, Cheryl A., 10, 162, 166
Medford, M., 153
Medina, C., 115
Medina, L., 3

236 Index

Mekawi, Y., 140
Mentor, M., 12
Merzouk, Nahel, 25
Michigan State University, 44
Microaggressions. *See* Marginalization (microaggressions)
Microinsults, 28
Microinvalidation, 28
Mignolo, W. D., 51, 154
Migration Policy Institute, 24
Migueliz Valcarlos, M., 117
Milner, H. R., 134
Milner, H. Richard, IV, 29
Milu, E., 11, 145, 196
Mims, G. A., 6, 7
Mims, M. J., 6, 7
Minnesota, Little Africa Festival (Minneapolis, 2014), 3
MinnPost, 188–189
Mirra, N., 179
Mkabela, Q., 103
Mohyuddin, Irteza Anwara, 13, 15, 18–19, 54–67, 193
Moje, E. B., 174
Molina, A., 175
Moll, L. C., 99, 159
Monea, B., 116
Moore, D., 7
Morrell, E., 179
Morton, T. R., 17
Moses, R., 45
Mthethwa-Sommers, S., 6
Muhammad, G., 175
Muki, A., 50
Multilingualism, 36, 103, 148–150, 168–169
Munasinghe, V., 57
Musa, Mansa, 33
Musambira, G. W., 7
Muslim youth, 8–9, 11, 28–29, 129, 194; African American History (AAH) class and, 54–67; conditional belonging and, 89; Council on American Islamic Relations, 35; Kadija (student) and transnational civic engagement, 85–97
Musser, A. D., 173, 179
Muwanguzi, S., 7
Mwangi, C. A. G., 99–100, 108, 129–130

Nabea, W., 149
Nabwire, N. S., 11
Nadal, K. L., 28
Nalubega-Booker, K., 10, 163
Narrative inquiry, 15. *See also* STEM disciplines
Narrative portraiture, 15
National Council for the Social Studies, 31
Ndemanu, M. T., 2, 10

Neal, A., 9–10
Nero, S., 149
New and Critical Literacy studies, 114–115
Newland, L. A., 6, 7
New London Group, 166, 174
New York Times, 22
Ngugi Wa Thiong'o, 40, 100
Nieto, S., 30
Nigerian immigrants/youth, 6, 7; acceptance by Ivy League colleges and universities, 4; language practices, 161–162, 164–167; Oyemolade (Molade) Osibodu as example, 44–46; visual arts in navigating linguistic discrimination, 163, 167–172; Yoruban concept of *Omoluabi,* 150–151, 152, 159
Njue, J., 7
Nkemka, A., 10–11
Nkrumah, T., 117
Nna, Augusta Uwamanzu, 4
Noah, Trevor, 51
Noel, F., 194
North African immigrants/youth, in France, 7
Norton, N. E., 158
Noy Neir, U. Y., 116
Nsaliwa, C., 108
Nsangou, A., 9
Ntseane, G., 9–10, 18
Nyamnjoh, E. B., 137

Obama, Barack, 192
Obiakor, F. E., 6
Ogbu, John, 26
Ogwal, Susan A., 13, 16, 86, 99–109, 101, 194
Ohuche, R. O., 51
Okeke-Ihejirika, P., 4, 108
Okokho (student), 163, 167–172
Okonkwo, H., 111, 116–118, 120, 125, 127
Okonofua, B. A., 101
Okorafor, Nnedi, 18, 43, 47, 48–52, 193
Okpalaoka, C. L., 7
Olongo, Alfred, 25
Oloo, James Alan, 10, 13, 15, 18, 68–83, 69, 70, 74, 78, 81, 100, 163–165, 193
Omi, M., 57, 163–164
Omogun, Lakeya, 10, 45, 158, 163, 177
Omolewa, M., 100
Onwong'a, J., 149
Onwuegbuzie, A. J., 184
Onyenekwu, I. U., 133
Onyewuenyi, A. C., 10–11, 28, 88
Oropeza, M. V., 7
Orozco, K., 3
Osei-Tutu, A. A., 179
Osibodu, Oyemolade (Molade), 11, 13, 15, 18, 43–53, 45–46, 49, 100, 193
Osunde, E. O., 29

"Other" and Othering, 30, 31, 47, 53, 129
Otiato Ojiambo, P. O., 5, 7, 17, 193
Oughton, H., 159
Oviatt, R. L., 179, 182, 183
Oyebade, A., 2

Pan-Africanism, Africa Club and sense of
  belonging, 130, 136–139, 142
Pangrazio, L., 119, 120
Parents/families: aspirations for students,
  99–100; Congolese parent perspectives
  on student learning, 99–109, 194–195;
  familial capital, 69, 72, 74, 80, 150; Kenyan
  immigrant/youth, 153–154
Paris, D., 130, 162
Park, J. Y., 7, 165
Parslow, K. A., 10
Participatory civic learning and action-taking, 8,
  9–10, 138
Participatory curriculum design/Lit Diaspora,
  173–190; next steps for teaching and
  research communities, 189; phases of,
  180–189; rightful literary presence and,
  173–190
Pechurina, A., 155
Pedagogy of the Oppressed (Freire), 110,
  114–115, 183
Pena-Pincheira, R., 9, 11, 33, 174, 184
Peralta, L. M., 182
Perry, K. H., 174
Persaud, F. J., 24–25
Peshkin, A., 12, 91–92
Petrie, B., 4
Petrone, R., 147, 173, 179, 180
Pew Research Center, 3, 22, 24–26, 41
Pierre, J., 57, 66
Ping, W., 150
Police brutality, 23–26; Black Lives Matter
  movement, 19, 22, 23, 54, 57–58, 61–67,
  117–120, 193–194
Positionality of authors: Lakeya Afolalu, 165,
  167; Sibel Akin-Sabuncu, 134; OreOluwa
  Badaki, 112, 113; Joel E. Berends, 174,
  175–176; Jasmine L. Blanks Jones, 111, 112,
  113; Priscila Dias Corrêa, 71; Nyimasata
  Dambu Danjo, 44–45, 46–47; Liv T. Dávila,
  103; Maryann J. Dreas-Shaikha, 112, 113;
  Patrick Keegan, 91–92; Michelle Knight-
  Manuel, 86, 134; Dinamic Kubengana, 173,
  175–176; Irteza Anwara Mohyuddin, 56–57;
  Susan Akello Ogwal, 103; James Alan Oloo,
  71; Oyemolade (Molade) Osibodu, 44–46,
  47; Natacha Robert, 134; Patriann Smith,
  145; Omiunota Nelly Ukpokodu, 22–23;
  Vaughn W. M. Watson, 174, 175–176
Postcolonial lenses, 14

Pratt, B., 3
Price-Dennis, D., 66, 115, 116, 120, 125, 174, 194
The Princess Steel (Du Bois), 191–193
Pugh, J., 179, 182, 183

Quijada, P. D., 173, 179

Rabe, M., 3
Racialization, 10, 88; as barrier for Congolese
  immigrant parents, 99, 100, 107; racialized
  marginalization, 27–29
Racial violence: Black Lives Matter movement
  and, 19, 22, 23, 54, 57–58, 61–67, 117–120,
  193–194; bullying, 27, 28–29, 35, 37,
  110–111, 125, 166; curriculum violence
  as, 29–41; lived realities of Black African
  immigrants/youth in the U.S., 23–26, 27–41;
  police brutality (see Police brutality)
Raciolinguistic hierarchies (Baker-Bell), 149
Racism. See also Anti-Blackness; Racial violence:
  as barrier for Congolese immigrant parents,
  107; colorism and, 21–22; status of "Other"
  and, 30, 31, 47, 53, 129; triple/quadruple
  marginality of Black African immigrant
  youth in the U.S., 22; in the U.S., 10, 21–22,
  129–130
Ramatulai (film student), 110–111, 112, 113,
  117, 123–125
Ramos-Zayas, A. Y., 57
Rana, J., 35, 57
Rasmussen, A., 72, 99, 108
Reem (history student), 59–63
Refugees/asylees: author positionality as, 103;
  Congolese, 101; invisibility in the U.S.
  education system, 2, 5, 17, 34–35, 37;
  limitations on U.S., 8–9; nature of, 26–27;
  Somali Bantu immigrants as, 7, 10, 11
ReiJay, L., 66
Reisman, A., 66
Retish, P., 7
Reuters Staff, 58
Rhoades, R., 119, 125
Rice, Tamara, 22
Rich, Adrienne, 38
Rickford, J. R., 145, 196
Rightful literary presence, 173–190; affirming
  approach to, 175–176, 179, 185–186;
  contextualizing approach to, 176–177,
  179, 186–187; evoking and historicizing
  approach to, 176, 177–178, 179, 187–188;
  nature and importance of, 173–174; phases
  of participatory curriculum design, 180–189;
  storyairing approach to, 176, 178–179, 188–
  189; theoretical framework for, 174–175
Riina-Ferrie, J., 113
Rink, N., 147

Ríos-Rojas, A., 6
Robert, Natacha, 16, 85–86, 129–142, 134, 194
Roberts, L., 117
Roberts, S., 4
Rodriguez, K., 115
Roegman, R., 8, 12, 27
Rogombe, Rose Francine, 33–34
Rong, X. L., 163
Rosa, Jonathan, 145, 165, 166, 168, 196
Rosemurgy, H., 182
ross, k. m., 4, 32, 129, 139
Rost-Banik, C., 76
Roth, V., 93
Roubeni, S., 72, 99, 108
Roxas, K., 7
Roy, L, 7
Rusert, Brett, 191–193
Rwandan immigrants/youth, 7

Saah, L., 24, 27, 28, 38–39
Salami, B., 108
Sallar, A. M., 10–11, 28, 88
Salt Lake (Utah) *Tribune*, 185
Samba, Catherine, 34
Sanchez, E., 34
Sánchez, L., 10, 163
Sánchez, P., 88, 96
Sanders, F. C., 54–56
Sandoval-Hernández, A., 138
Sankofan approach, 151–152, 159, 194; after-
    school African Club and, 130–131, 133,
    136, 137; civic engagement and, 89, 95–96;
    intentionality of a Sankofan lens, 8; nature of,
    8, 89, 95–96, 151; restrictive migration policies
    and, 8–9; Sankofa bird and, 95, 131, 151, 152
Sara (film student), 112, 117, 121–123, 125
Sarai (Nigerian student), 161–162, 164–167
Sawasawa, M., 187
Schmidley, A. D., 164
Schmidt, S. J., 11, 132, 133
Schön, D. A., 116
Schultz, K., 166
Schwartz, L., 99
Scribner, S., 114, 116
Sealey-Ruiz, Y., 12, 66, 174, 194
Sears, A., 2, 7
Sebestyén, N., 148
Senegalese immigrants/youth, 55. *See also*
    African American History (AAH) class;
    Kadija (Muslim student), 85–97
Shah, N., 72, 99, 108
Shaw, L. L., 134
Shirazi, R., 87–89
Shizha, E., 46–47
Shoro, K., 137

Sichra, I., 150, 158–159
Siegel, M., 103, 115
Sierra Leonean immigrants/youth, 7, 55. *See
    also* African American History (AAH) class;
    filmmaking with African immigrant girls,
    110–113, 117, 123–125
Silko, I. M., 82
Silverstein, J., 22
Simmons, M. C., 2, 10, 11, 74–75, 167, 184
Sims, D., 1
Sirleaf, Ellen Johnson, 33
60 Minutes (CBS), 32–33, 35
Skerrett, Allison, 10, 45, 145, 158, 163, 166,
    177, 196
Sky (film student), 112, 117, 118–121, 125
Slaten, C., 149
Smalls, Krystal A., 7, 165
Smith, C., 3, 167
Smith, D., 11
Smith, L., 154
Smith, Patriann, 1–16, 2, 4, 10, 16, 24, 27, 29,
    72, 74, 80, 115, 131–133, 143–145, 148,
    149, 162–164, 166–167, 177, 191–196, 193,
    195, 196
Smitherman, Geneva, 143, 145, 162, 166–167,
    195, 196
Smithsonian National Portrait Gallery, 192
Social science/education research on Black
    African immigrants/youth: 2000–2010 first
    wave, 5–6; 2010–2017 second wave, 6–8;
    2017–present third wave, 8–11; African
    Diaspora (*see* Diaspora studies); community
    cultural wealth and, 14, 18, 69–82; con-
    temporary contexts of migration in, 2–5;
    deficit narratives in (*see* Deficit-based
    approaches); framework for (*see* Framework
    for Educating African Immigrant Youth);
    hip-hop culture and, 5, 6, 157; language and
    literacy as social practice (*see* Language and
    literacy); migration trends of Black African
    youth, 6–8; participatory communal civic
    engagement and (*see* Civic engagement);
    Sankofan approach (*see* Sankofan approach);
    transformative and asset-based processes and
    practices, 14; transnational civic engagement
    and (*see* Transnational civic engagement)
Social studies/history: African American History
    (AAH) class, 18–19, 54–67; curriculum vio-
    lence and, 29–41
Solomon, D. B., 129
Somali immigrants/youth, Somali Bantu
    immigrants, 7, 10, 11
Soto-Santiago, S., 99
The Souls of Black Folk (Du Bois), 21–22
Soyinka, Wole, 33

Index

239

Sparks, D. M., 17
Spell, L., 3
Squire, V., 175, 177
Stageman, D., 115
Starkman, R., 119, 125
Statistics Canada, 69, 81
Stebleton, M. J., 6, 7, 76
STEM disciplines. *See also* Mathematics: applied vs. academic courses, 68–69; challenges of Black female undergraduate students, 73–76; decision to attend university, 71, 72–73; defined, 68; gender and, 17, 18, 44–45, 68–83, 193; methodology and findings, 70–82; motivation/resilience strategies, 78–80; pleasant and unpleasant university experiences, 76–78; theoretical framework of study, 69–70
Stereotypes: of African Americans, 99–100; of Black Africans, 32–34, 36, 45–47; European notions of Blackness and female beauty, 93–94; gender and STEM disciplines, 73–76; misperceptions of Africa, 33–34, 36, 39, 139–141; of Muslim bodies, 89, 96–97; nature of, 39
Stornaiuolo, A., 116
Storyairing, 176, 178–179, 188–189
Street, B., 114–116, 166
Strong, K., 64, 113
Stunner, Ms. (teacher), 170–171
Suárez-Orozco, C., 147, 159
Suárez-Orozco, M., 147, 159
Subedi, B., 171
Subramanian, M., 129
Sub-Saharan Africa (SSA) immigrants/youth: *Binti* (Okorafor, Afrofuturist novella), 18, 43, 45, 47–49, 51–53, 193; liberatory future for, 52–53; mathematics and, 43–53
Subtractive schooling (Valenzuela), 6, 24, 66
Sudanese immigrants/youth, 7; police brutality and, 25
Sue, D. W., 28
Sundiata, Keita, 33
Swartz, E. E., 6

Taarnby, M., 28
Tadesse, S., 100
Takougang, J., 5, 148–149
Takyi, B. K., 5
Tamir, C., 3, 164
Tan, E., 175
Taylor, A., 8, 12
Taylor, Breonna, 22
Teacher education: caring teachers and, 40–41; conscientious teachers and, 40–41; culturally responsive teaching and, 39–40; curriculum violence and, 30–31

Teachers College Record, 10
Temple, C. N., 8, 131
Tesfa, E., 11
Test of English as a Foreign Language (TOEFL), 47
Theatre of the Oppressed (Boal), 110, 115, 117, 123–124
Thelamour, B., 99–100, 108
Things Fall Apart (Achebe), 40
Thomas, D. A., 57
Thomas, E. E., 116
Thomas, K. J. A., 7
Tierney, R. J., 147–148, 154, 159
Tiffin, H., 165, 169, 171
Tlou, J., 29
Todorova, I., 147, 159
Togoan immigrants/youth, 7
Toliver, R., 56
Toliver, S. R., 193
Torino, G. C., 28
Trainin, G., 17
Tran, N., 10, 11
Transnational Black language pedagogy (Milu), 145, 196
Transnational civic engagement, 7–8; Africa Club and Pan-African sense of belonging, 130, 136–139, 142; critical consciousness of home in the African diaspora, 92–97; discussion and implications, 96–97; Dominican youth and, 95; funds of knowledge in, 88, 96, 97; Guatemalan youth and, 88, 93; Kadija (Muslim student) and, 85–86, 87–97; methods and data sources for studying, 91–92; Palestinian youth and, 88, 93, 95; Sankofan approach in, 8–9, 89, 95–96; transnationalism, defined, 90
Transnational feminist praxis, 7. *See also* Gender
Transnational literacy (Skerrett), 145, 196
Traore, H. M., 17
Traoré, R. L., 5, 19, 24, 29, 54, 164
Treviño-Villarreal, E., 138
Trinidadian immigrants/youth, language practices, 162–163
Trump, Donald, 8–9, 24, 39, 94, 101
Tsevi, L., 11, 100, 108
Tuck, E., 165
Turner, D. C., III, 113
Tutu, Desmond, 33

Ubuntu-oriented education, 37–38, 40–41
UC Regents, 179, 182
Ugandan immigrants/youth, 7; author positionality as, 103; police brutality and, 25
Ukpokodu, Omiunota Nelly, 4–7, 9, 13, 15, 17–18, 21–42, 24, 26, 27, 28, 29, 30, 31–33, 35, 36, 37, 38–39, 40–41, 54, 87, 193

240   Index

Ukpokolo, I. E., 100

Undocumented immigrants, 26–27, 35

United Kingdom, Black African immigrants/
youth and, 24

United Nations, 28; High Commissioner
for Refugees, 9; Population Division, 3;
Population Fund, 26; racial violence risks
for African immigrant children, 25–26;
Universal Declaration of Human Rights
(1948), 38

United States: Black African immigrant
youth in, 26–41; Black Lives Matter
movement, 19, 22, 23, 54, 57–58, 61–67,
117–120, 193–194; colorism in, 21–22;
diasporic Blacks in, 21–22; immigrants
vs. international student status of SSA
youth, 43–45; immigrant trends, 148–149;
institutional reckoning regarding Black
Africans, 34–36; lack of scholarship on
Africa and African immigrants, 21; lived
realities of Black African immigrants/youth
in, 23–26, 27–41; mathematics for the elite
and, 52; misperceptions about Africa in,
139–141; police brutality against Black
African immigrants/youth, 22, 23–26; racial
violence and, 19, 22, 23–26, 31–41; racism,
10, 21–22, 129–130; restrictive migration
policies, 8–9; societal reckoning regarding
Black Africans, 32–34; triple/quadruple
marginality of Black African immigrant
youth in the U.S., 22

U.S. Border Patrol, 4

U.S. Bureau of Population, Refugees, and
Migration, 9

U.S. Census Bureau, 3, 148, 164

University of Pennsylvania, 111–114

Usman, L. M., 7

Uyoata, U. E., 3

Valenzuela, A., 6, 24, 66

Vallianatos, H., 4, 108

Van Leeuwen, T., 116

Varghese, M. M., 7

Vasudevan, L., 113, 115

Vejar, A., 185

Vellanki, V., 179

Vickery, A. E., 17

Visual arts: Black superheroes in film, 1, 33,
161, 192; filmmaking (*see* Filmmaking
with African immigrant girls); in navigating
linguistic discrimination, 163, 167–172;
photography reenvisioning Black youth as
lead characters, 1, 192; portrait of Barack
Obama, 192

Wallace, Walter, 58–59, 61, 63–65

Walls, J., 4, 10

Walsh, A., 118

Wandera, David Bwire, 11, 13, 16, 100,
143–144, 147–160, 154, 159, 195

Wang, L., 150, 158

Wanjikũ/Ciku (student), 153–159

Warrican, S. J., 10

Warrior King (2023 film), 33

The Washington Post, 186–187

Wasser, J. D., 134

Waters, M. C., 35, 57

Watkins, J., 33

Watkinson, J. S., 7

Watson, Vaughn W. M., 1–16, 2–10, 7–8, 9, 11,
12, 13, 15, 16, 17–19, 33, 45, 52, 56, 71,
87–89, 91, 93, 94, 97, 100, 115, 118, 119,
125, 130–132, 138, 139, 144, 149–150,
158, 163–164, 173–190, 174, 175, 177,
179, 180, 182, 183, 184, 191–196, 193

Webb-Johnson, G., 24, 27, 28, 38–39

Welch, B. J., 115

West African immigrants/youth, 10–11, 46,
54–67, 87–97

West African Senior School Certificate
Examination (WASSCE), 46

Westing, Ms. (teacher), 55

Whitelaw, J., 115

Whitley, J., 68

Wiggan, G., 29

Wiley, Kehinde, 3, 192

Willis, A., 10, 163

Wilson, J., 6

Wilson-Forsberg, S., 46–47

Woman King (2022 film), 33

Woods, J. C., Jr., 17

Woodson, A. N., 17, 129

Woodson, Carter G., 24, 29

Worksheet curriculum, 31

World Health Organization, 26

Wynter, S., 51

Wynter-Hoyte, K., 3, 175

Yang, K. W., 165

Ybarra, A., 147

Yeboah, N., 151

Yohani, S., 4, 108

Yosso, T. J., 18, 69, 76, 82, 150

Young Center for Immigrant Children, 26

Youth Participatory Action Research (YPAR),
134–136, 141, 179–180, 182–183

YouTube, 29–30

Yusuf, E., 70

Zewde, Sahle-Work, 34

Zong, J., 2, 4, 35, 148

Zongo, Ousmane, 25

About the Editors and Contributors

Dr. Lakeya Afolalu is an assistant professor of Language, Literacy, and Culture in the University of Washington's College of Education. Her hybrid Nigerian and African American identity is reflected in her research that focuses on Black African immigrant youth. Specifically, she explores the role of language and literacy, including digital literacies, in Black African immigrant youth identity constructions and negotiations across school, community, and digital spaces. She pays particular attention to the intersection of racialization and socialization processes that influence their identities. Dr. Afolalu draws on her lived experiences, the wisdom of her former middle school students, and the arts to inform her creative approach to shifting static ideas about identity. A critical part of her work includes putting her research into practice through partnerships to support youth of color identities and overall well-being. Her academic scholarship has appeared in the *Journal of Literacy of Research*, *Teachers College Record*, and the *Journal of Research in Childhood Education*. Her public scholarship has been featured in *TEDx*, *ESSENCE Magazine*, *NPR Radio*, *ZORA*, and *SXSW*.

Sibel Akin-Sabuncu is an associate professor of Curriculum and Instruction in the Faculty of Education at TED University. She obtained her PhD in Curriculum and Instruction Program at Middle East Technical University. Dr. Akin-Sabuncu was a postdoctoral researcher and a visiting associate professor at Teachers College, Columbia University. Her research focuses on elementary teacher education; teaching and teacher education for social justice/ immigrant and refugee students/disadvantaged students; culturally relevant pedagogy; educational equity; and critical pedagogy. Dr. Akin-Sabuncu's recent research project, which aims to investigate teacher educators' perspectives across Turkey, the United States, and Hong Kong for preparing teachers for immigrant students, was granted a Global Education Research Award in 2021. Her recent work can be found in the *European Journal of Teacher Education*, *Urban Education*, and *Teachers College Record*.

Dr. OreOluwa Badaki is a postdoctoral fellow at Teachers College, Columbia University. Bridging research in critical literacy studies, multimodal scholarship, and environmental justice, Dr. Badaki examines how power moves through bodies and spaces within food and land systems. As a writer, movement practitioner, researcher, and educator, Dr. Badaki works with youth and communities of color to explore food and environmental justice through the creative and performing arts. She earned her PhD with distinction from the University of Pennsylvania's Graduate School of Education. Her dissertation work, which focused on the literacy practices of youth of color working in urban agriculture, received the Ralph C. Preston Award for Scholarship and Teaching Contributing to Social Justice. Prior to her doctoral work, Dr. Badaki was a middle school language arts teacher and a program specialist with the United Nations, working at the intersection of education for sustainable development and the cultural and creative industries.

Joel E. Berends is a doctoral candidate in the Curriculum, Instruction, and Teacher Education Department at Michigan State University. He works with secondary English interns and teaches courses on professional practice, social foundations of education, and critical literacies. His areas of interest are documentary poetics, public pedagogy, and critical literacies that engage with sports and history. Joel previously taught high school language arts and social studies, and he is an avid sports fan and former football (soccer) player and coach. Joel has written about antiracist discourse and pedagogy in the NBA and has published poetry about sports and coloniality as well as Dutch coloniality in Indonesia and his hometown of Grand Rapids, MI.

Sandra Boateng, a doctoral student at Michigan State University's College of Education, originally from Ghana, is an accomplished former English language teacher in her home country. Presently, she passionately engages in a tutoring program at Mt. Hope United Methodist Church in Lansing, MI, where she collaborates with a diverse group of Black African immigrant youth hailing from 14 African countries, including Central Africa and the Congo. Sandra's research interest focuses on exploring the language practices of African immigrant youth, with a particular emphasis on highlighting and centering African epistemologies and frameworks.

Priscila Dias Corrêa is an associate professor at the University of Windsor in Ontario, Canada. She is passionate about mathematics education and strives to offer her students high-quality and meaningful mathematics learning experiences. Priscila holds a PhD in Mathematics Education from the University of Alberta and a MSc in Electrical Engineering from the Federal University of Rio de Janeiro, Brazil. She has a BEd in Mathematics and a BEng in Electrical Engineering. Priscila has been involved in mathematics education research in Canada and Brazil. Her research areas of interest are mathematics curriculum, mathematics assessment, racialized mathematics learning experiences, mathematical proficiency, and computational thinking. Priscila brings her research into her undergraduate and graduate teaching, aiming to enhance

About the Editors and Contributors 243

and advance her students' teaching practices and mathematics knowledge for teaching.

Nyimasata Damba Danjo is a first-generation PhD student, a social entrepreneur, and a spirited health advocate. Nyima hails from a small rural village in The Gambia, where she got deeply inspired to pursue higher education at a world-class university. She would later become one of few Sub-Saharan African youth who were awarded the Mastercard Foundation Scholarship at Michigan State University (MSU). She graduated with Honors from MSU with a Bachelor of Science in Neuroscience and proceeded to pursue her ultimate goal of becoming an expert scientist. Nyimasata is now a third-year graduate student under the supervision of Professor Roger Cone in the University of Michigan Department of Molecular, Cellular and Developmental Biology. Her thesis research is particularly focused on understanding the role of a melanocortin receptor in the control of the hypothalamic-pituitary growth axis. Nyima's all-time favorite job is raising her baby boy and decoding baby gibberish.

Liv T. Dávila is an associate professor in the Department of Education Policy, Organization and Leadership at the University of Illinois at Urbana–Champaign. Her research focuses on languages, literacies, and communication writ large as they relate to learner identities, educational experiences, and broader social processes (e.g., of inclusion or exclusion). This research has focused primarily on adolescent immigrant and refugee learners in public K–12 institutions, as well as their families, and teachers; she also has explored questions around language access and interpretation in other community and institutional contexts, such as immigrant-serving community organizations, and in medical settings. She engages with applied linguistics, literacy studies, and educational anthropology to analyze how language learning and use in schools and communities are influenced by global phenomena, including migration, racism, and racialization.

Maryann J. Dreas-Shaikha is an international educator and manager for a Global Partnership for Education project at the UNESCO International Institute for Capacity Building in Africa. She oversees the project portfolios of 19 ministries of education in eastern, western, and southern Africa, and facilitates South-to-South learning and knowledge sharing between policy actors, education researchers, teacher educators, and practitioners. She is interested in the tension points between education policy and classroom realities, traditional education and student- and community-led learning, and international development and anthropology. Prior to her work with UNESCO, she taught literature, performing arts, writing, speech, and Model United Nations to middle school students in Pakistan, and served as the school assistant headmistress and head of English from 2015 to 2019.

Her other work includes ethnographic, documentary, and youth filmmaking in Philadelphia and Pakistan. Dreas-Shaikha holds a Master of Science in International Education Development from the University of Pennsylvania and a Bachelor of Arts in Political Science and Journalism from Dominican University.

Jasmine L. Blanks Jones is a dynamic theater nonprofit leader and award-winning educator, and holds a dual PhD in Education and Africana Studies from the University of Pennsylvania. She serves as executive director of the Center for Social Concern at Johns Hopkins University. Her research on theatrical performance as a civic engagement praxis illuminates global race-based inequities in education and health, lifting the potential of knowledge cocreation through the arts and digital cultural production. As founder of B4 Youth Theatre, a cultural performance company dedicated to community empowerment through the arts, she has more than 20 years of experience in youth development globally. She holds an MPP from the University of Minnesota and a BS in Music Education from Florida A&M University. She is a lecturer in the Program in Racism, Immigration and Citizenship at Johns Hopkins University, where she conducted research and public scholarship with Inheritance Baltimore.

Patrick Keegan is an assistant professor of education at Purdue Northwest. His areas of research are elementary social studies education, political emotion, and youth civic engagement. His most recent scholarship appears in *Theory and Research in Social Education, International Journal of Qualitative Studies in Education,* and *Democracy & Education.*

Dorothy Khamala is a PhD student in Curriculum and Instruction at the University of Denver and is originally from Nairobi, Kenya. She graduated with honors from Daystar University in Nairobi with a bachelor's degree in English and Literature and a master's degree in Library and Information Science from the University of Nairobi in Kenya. After teaching and working in libraries in Kenya, she embarked upon a career as a researcher. She is a Marbach, Weimar and Wolfenbuttel international intern recipient and has vast experience conducting research in school admission and retention among marginalized populations as well as strategies for women's economic empowerment in Kenya. She is also an alumnus of the Fulbright Foreign Language Teaching Assistant Program at Towson University in Maryland, where she taught her native language (Swahili) and acted as a cultural ambassador promoting Kenyan culture. She currently resides in Denver, CO, where she is a graduate assistant at the University of Denver's Office of Internationalization and works with the Dean of the Morgridge College of Education on the immigrant civic engagement process on a need-by-need basis.

About the Editors and Contributors

Michelle Knight-Manuel is dean of the Morgridge College of Education at the University of Denver. Previously, she served as associate dean and senior advisor to the provost/dean at Teachers College, Columbia University. Earlier in her career, she was a middle school ESL/French teacher and college advisor in Oakland, CA. Her scholarly work includes three distinct yet complementary strands of inquiry: college readiness and access, immigrant youth's civic strengths, and culturally relevant teacher preparation and professional development. She has published in such journals as the *American Educational Research Journal, Teachers College Record, Race, Ethnicity and Education, Review of Research in Education,* and *Journal of Educational Policy.* Her two books, coauthored with Joanne Marciano, are *Classroom Cultures: Equitable Schooling for Racially Diverse Youth* and *College Ready: Preparing Black and Latino Youth for Higher Education Through a Culturally Relevant Lens.*

Dinamic Kubengana attends Lansing Community College and plans to major in criminal justice and minor in business. Born in Democratic Republic of the Congo, and living in the United States since 2017, Dinamic enjoys playing sports, especially soccer.

Dr. Irteza Anwara Mohyuddin is a postdoctoral fellow in the Annenberg School of Communication. Irteza grew up Muslim in Virginia and moved to Philadelphia for her PhD. She wrote her dissertation about Black Muslim youth and considered the role of Islam, Blackness, and ethnic identity in the identity formation of these youth in a Philadelphia public school. Her greater interests include exploring how history shapes our present experiences and cultural memory. She is currently working on a project called "Archiving the Inner City: Race and the Politics of Urban Memory," which examines how Black histories and arts are produced, commemorated, and archived in Philadelphia.

Susan A. Ogwal originally from Uganda, holds a Doctorate in Education Policy, Organization & Leadership from the University of Illinois at Urbana–Champaign. Her academic pursuits revolve around the nexus of higher education and immigration, international education, and public policy. Dr. Ogwal's professional background encompasses over 15 years of experience in social services, teaching, training, and contributing to published research. Beyond her professional roles, she is a dedicated advocate for community programming, particularly with a strong social justice commitment, cofounding the C-U Black and African Arts Festival and actively volunteering as a community navigator and mentor. Currently, Dr. Ogwal serves as policy director at the Illinois Office of Lieutenant Governor Juliana Stratton, where she channels her dedication to community-centered public service. Her work at this position involves addressing various critical

246   About the Editors and Contributors

issues, including diversity in education, and tackling agricultural equity and food insecurity.

James Alan Oloo is an assistant professor in Educational Administration, Policy and Leadership at the University of Windsor, Canada. His research explores ways of improving learning experiences for all students. Oloo's research also seeks to better understand factors and conditions that enhance success among underrepresented students, including Indigenous students, Black students, and those from immigrant and refugee backgrounds. He previously worked as a schoolteacher in Kenya and in Canada.

Oyemolade (Molade) Osibodu is an assistant professor of Mathematics Education at York University located in Toronto, Ontario, Canada. Her research critically examines the experiences of Black youth in mathematics education. Dr. Osibodu is specifically interested in examining ways to decolonize mathematics education for liberatory futures, engaging with social justice issues, and exploring African Indigenous mathematics practices. Dr. Osibodu's work is supported theoretically by decolonial theory, critical theories of race, and Black geographies. Her research has been well-funded, including by the Social Sciences and Humanities Research Council in Canada. Outside of academia, Dr. Osibodu is a podcast listener, movie and TV watcher, a voracious reader of fiction and nonfiction books, and an avid traveler. You can often find her taking hours-long walks while listening to a podcast or an audiobook. Her most recent enjoyment is biking around the city of Toronto.

Natacha Robert is a doctoral student in the Department of Curriculum and Teaching at Teachers College, Columbia University. She is a former adolescent special education and social studies teacher. During her time directing and coordinating after-school programs, she worked with African American youth as well as immigrant youth from the Caribbean, Africa, and Asia. Her research interests focus on African-centered education, culturally relevant education, decolonial/decolonization, and ethnographic methodologies.

Patriann Smith serves as associate professor in the College of Education at the University of South Florida. As a distinguished scholar who works at the intersection of race, language, and immigration, she has proposed solutions such as "a transraciolinguistic approach" and the framework for "Black immigrant literacies" for transraciolinguistic justice in literacy classrooms. Her research is published in journals such as the *American Educational Research Journal, Reading Research Quarterly, Teaching and Teacher Education,* and *The Reading Teacher.* Patriann is a 2013 ILA Emerging Scholar Fellow, 2017 LRA STAR Fellow, and a recipient of the 2015 AERA

About the Editors and Contributors 247

Language and Social Processes SIG Emerging Scholar Award. A cofounder of the Caribbean Educational Research Center, she is the author of the book *Black Immigrant Literacies: Intersections of Race, Language, and Culture in the Classroom* (2023) and coauthor of the book *Affirming Black Students' Lives and Literacies* (2022) published by Teachers College Press.

Omiunota Nelly Ukpokodu is a full professor in the Department of Teacher Education and Curriculum Studies in the School of Education, Social Work and Psychological Services at the University of Missouri–Kansas City. She teaches courses in diversity education and social studies. Her research interests include transformative teacher education, critical multicultural education, transformative pedagogy, Ubuntu pedagogy, cultural competence, culturally responsive teaching, global/citizenship education, African immigrant education, and social justice pedagogy, among others. Dr. Ukpokodu has authored articles, books, and book chapters on multicultural education, African immigrant education and issues, global education, social justice, and citizenship development. Dr. Ukpokodu's works have appeared in national and international publications, such as *Social Education, The Journal of Interdisciplinary Education, International Journal of Curriculum and Instruction, The Social Studies, Multicultural Education, Multicultural Perspectives, Social Studies Research & Practice, International Journal of Critical Pedagogy*, and more. Dr. Ukpokodu has received several awards, including the International Assembly of the National Council for the Social Studies Distinguished Global Scholar Award, the International Assembly of the National Council for the Social Studies International Assembly Excellence in Service Award, the University of Missouri–Kansas City Chancellor's Award for Embracing and Promoting Diversity, AERA Multicultural/Multiethnic Education SIG Carlos J. Vallejo Memorial Award for Lifetime Scholarship, AERA Social Studies Research SIG Outstanding Contribution Award to the Field, National Association for Multicultural Education, National Association for Multicultural Education, and Equity & Social Justice Advocacy Award, among others. Dr. Ukpokodu is a Fulbright-Hayes Scholar, a visiting scholar, and has worked collaboratively with international institutions, including the University of Western Cape, South Africa.

Originally from Kenya, ***David Bwire Wandera*** is an associate professor in the Department of Special Education Language and Literacy in the School of Education at the College of New Jersey. His scholarship, which springboards from his dissertation project featuring a literacy-based exchange between middle schoolers in Aleknagik, Alaska, and Nairobi, Kenya, is located within the field of transcultural literacy studies. David is a linguistic anthropologist who studies the changing nature of language and identity practices among youth in globalizing localities. His scholarship is informed by his Sub-Saharan African premigration experiences and worldviews. His

248 About the Editors and Contributors

current project on decolonizing research traditions illustrates how the field of literacy studies can benefit from cross-cultural epistemic collaborations.

Vaughn W. M. Watson is associate professor in the College of Education at Michigan State University. Vaughn's research renders visible creative and artistic literacy and learning practices of Black youth and Black African immigrant youth across schools and communities in the global African diaspora. Vaughn has published findings of qualitative and participatory research at the interplay of creative, artistic literacy practices and youth's civic engagement in journals including *American Educational Research Journal, Teachers College Record, Review of Research in Education, Urban Education, International Journal of Qualitative Studies in Education, Research in the Teaching of English*, and *Journal of Literacy Research*. Vaughn is recipient of the National Academy of Education/Spencer Foundation Postdoctoral Fellowship; Cultivating New Voices Among Scholars of Color Fellowship (National Council of Teachers of English); and Outstanding Publication Award by the American Educational Research Association's Narrative Research Special Interest Group. He previously taught high school English in New York City and was pop music writer for *The Providence Journal*.